Oaxaca Resurgent

Oaxaca Resurgent
Indigeneity, Development, and Inequality in Twentieth-Century Mexico

A. S. Dillingham

Stanford University Press
Stanford, California

Stanford University Press
Stanford, California

©2021 by Alan Shane Dillingham. All rights reserved.

No part of this book may be reproduced or transmitted in any form or by any means, electronic or mechanical, including photocopying and recording, or in any information storage or retrieval system without the prior written permission of Stanford University Press.

Printed in the United States of America on acid-free, archival-quality paper

Library of Congress Cataloging-in-Publication Data

Names: Dillingham, Alan Shane, author.
Title: Oaxaca resurgent : indigeneity, development, and inequality
   in twentieth-century Mexico / Alan Shane Dillingham.
Description: Stanford, California : Stanford University Press, 2021. |
   Includes bibliographical references and index.
Identifiers: LCCN 2020052609 (print) | LCCN 2020052610 (ebook) |
   ISBN 9781503614949 (cloth) | ISBN 9781503627840 (paperback) |
   ISBN 9781503627857 (ebook)
Subjects: LCSH: Indians of Mexico—Mexico—Oaxaca (State)—Government
   relations—History—20th century. | Indians of Mexico—Education—
   Mexico—Oaxaca (State)—History—20th century. | Education and state—
   Mexico—Oaxaca (State)—History—20th century. | Rural
   development—Mexico—Oaxaca (State)—History—20th century. |
   Multiculturalism—Mexico—History—20th century.
Classification: LCC F1219.1.O11 D55 2021 (print) | LCC F1219.1.O11 (ebook) |
   DDC 305.800972/0904—dc23
LC record available at https://lccn.loc.gov/2020052609
LC ebook record available at https://lccn.loc.gov/2020052610

Cover art: *Helicopteros*, Sergio Hernández, 2007.
Cover design: Rob Ehle
Typeset by Newgen North America in 11/13.5 Adobe Garamond Pro

In memory of John H. and Carole J. Dillingham,
two children of Oklahoma who found each other and created a world

Table of Contents

Acknowledgments ix
Abbreviations xiii

Prologue 1

Introduction: The Double Bind of Indigenismo 6

1 Modernizing the Mixteca: Regional Approaches to Underdevelopment 22

2 "Was It God or the Devil?": Bilingual Radio Schools and Cold War Catholicism 47

3 Mixtec Land and Labor: Migration and State-Sponsored Resettlement on the Costa Chica 71

4 Indigenismo in the Age of Three Worlds: Oaxacan Youth and Mexico's Democratic Opening 93

5 Bilingual Teachers at the Front: The Rise of Dissident Trade Unionism and the Neoliberal Order 119

6 Anticolonialism in the Classroom: The Institutionalization of Multiculturalism 145

Conclusion: The Entangled Histories of Recognition and Resurgence 172

Notes 189
Bibliography 223
Index 243

Acknowledgments

In the summer of 2006, I enrolled in a Mexican history seminar held annually in Oaxaca City. That year the seminar intersected with what had previously been a relatively predictable public ritual: May 1 teacher strikes and negotiated settlements with government officials. But the 2006 strike became historic precisely for its unpredictability. The state governor, Ulises Ruiz Ortiz, rather than continue negotiations, ordered the police to remove striking teachers from the Zócalo, the historic town square teachers traditionally occupied. While police helicopters fired tear gas from above, riot police wielding batons violently removed the teachers from the square. The government's actions shocked not only union leadership but Oaxacans generally. Over the summer the conflict escalated, with teachers and their allies taking more dramatic action to oust the governor. Bypassing the existing union infrastructure, a movement headed by the Asamblea Popular de los Pueblos de Oaxaca (APPO) emerged to coordinate protests across the state. In late summer I returned to Washington, D.C., but I continued to follow events from a distance, as then-president Vicente Fox deployed federal police to put down what supporters began to call the "Oaxaca Commune." The movement was ultimately defeated through violent repression and political compromise. But the governor's political party, the Partido Revolucionario Institucional (PRI), was defeated in subsequent gubernatorial elections, a first in Oaxacan history. In subsequent years, the Oaxacan Truth Commission documented dozens of cases from 2006 in which government forces, often in plain clothes, engaged in acts of arbitrary detention, arrest, torture, and murder. This left many dissidents maimed, in jail, or in forced exile.

Oaxaca Resurgent began that summer, with the immediate questions of trying to understand what was happening around me. Why were the teachers striking? How did a dissident union movement emerge out of the historically PRI-aligned Sindicato Nacional de Trabajadores de la Educación (SNTE)? These questions led to larger ones—what specific role did Indigenous teachers play in the struggle? What was the history of education and development in the state? Oaxacan intellectuals and activists encouraged me to peruse these questions. This book would not have been possible without the 2006 social movement or their advice. *Mil gracias.*

A number of institutions and organizations provided material support for the research and writing of *Oaxaca Resurgent*. The San Diego State Mixtec Language Program and Federal Language and Area Studies grants supported my early work in Oaxaca. The Inter-American Foundation, the Smithsonian Institution, the Spencer Foundation, and the National Academy of Education all supported the project and provided spaces to share my evolving ideas with colleagues. The American Council of Learned Societies and the Andrew W. Mellon Foundation as well as the National Endowment for the Humanities provided crucial material support. The institutions where I have had the pleasure to teach along the way provided necessary assistance. They include the University of Maryland, Reed College, Spring Hill College, and Albright College. I am fortunate to have researched and written sections of the book at El Centro de Investigación y Estudios Superiores en Antropología Social, Pacifico Sur in Oaxaca City and at the Smithsonian's Natural History Museum in Washington, D.C. Both institutions fostered thoughtful research and community engagement.

I learned early on to value intellectual inquiry and the relationships it produces as their own rewards. I am deeply grateful for the experiences and friendships that I gained while researching and writing this book. The journey has taken me across the United States and back and allowed me to spend the greater part of a decade living off and on in Mexico. In Maryland, I learned a great deal from conversations with Ira Berlin, Barbara Weinstein, David Sartorius, Daryle Williams, Julie Greene, Karin Rosemblatt, Mary Kay Vaughan, Ted Cohen, and Jesse Zarley. Gabriela Pérez Báez helped me reflect on my research in Oaxaca during a fellowship at the Smithsonian. In Portland, Oregon, Elliott Young welcomed me into a group of Latin Americanists and kindhearted people. They include Enrique Cortez, Napoleon Landeata, Anoop Mirpuri, Radhika Natarajan, Paddy Reilly, David Garrett, Zirwat Chowdhury, Sameer ud Dowla Khan, and Victor I. Cares. From the Pacific Northwest I moved south to yet another rainy locale, Alabama's Gulf Coast. In Mobile I benefited from conversations and collaborations with Tom Ward, David Head, Kevin Funk, Claire Cage, Nicholas Wood, Timothy Lombardo, Alex Ruble, and Kelly Urban. As I completed the book, I began teaching at Albright College. I thank Karen Campbell, Guillaume de Syon, John Pankratz, and Patricia Turning for their support and encouragement.

I am fortunate to have been invited to share elements of the book at University of Illinois Chicago, Williams College, New York University, Abu Dhabi, Johns Hopkins University, Loyola University Chicago, the University of Notre Dame, and the Universidad Nacional Autónoma de México. Jaime Pensado encouraged me along the way and helped this book find a home at Stanford University Press. My editor, Margo Irvin, patiently guided me through the publication process, and I am grateful to the entire Stanford team that contributed to the final product, Cindy Lim, Emily Smith, and Elisabeth Magnus. As I developed a sense of the shape of the book, I benefited enormously from the comments of Tore Olsson, Dillon Vrana, Adam Goodman, Chris Boyers, Alec Dawson, Dixa Ramírez, Steve Lewis, Radhika Natarajan, Amy Benson, Brian Whitener, Tanalís Padilla, Pedro Monaville, Bertrand Metton, Andrew Cavin, Vanessa Freije, Julie Gibbings, Becky Tarlau, Gema Kloppe-Santamaría, Paula López Caballero, and Alexander Aviña.

Much of the book was written and conceived in Oaxaca and Mexico City. In Oaxaca, Víctor Raúl Martínez Vásquez and Alejandro de Ávila Blomberg first counseled me to pursue the story of bilingual teachers in the state. Salvador Sigüenza Orozco proved an early friend and constant supporter. Ronald Waterbury, Manuel Esparza, and María del Carmen Castillo all offered thoughtful suggestions on the project. My Mixtec instructors Juan Julián Caballero and Marcos Abraham Cruz Bautista patiently taught me their language and introduced me to a network of language activists and educators. Members of the Coalición de Maestros y Promotores Indígenas de Oaxaca generously shared their stories with me. Alverino López López deserves special mention for his generosity, intellectual rigor, and comradeship. Other scholars of Oaxaca nurtured the project along the way, including Daniela Trufano, Colby Ristow, Benjamin T. Smith, Berenice Ortega Bayona, Xicohténcatl Gerardo Luna Ruiz, and Xilonen Luna Ruiz. The Welte Institute in Oaxaca City is an invaluable resource for Oaxacan studies, and the staff at the Biblioteca Juan de

Córdova curated an excellent collection and offered an inspiring place to write. Toño Bolaños and Gabriela Rodríguez transcribed the majority of the oral histories. Portions of chapter 4 are drawn from material previously published in *The Americas*.

Friends supported the project over the years, providing me with perspective and much-needed distractions. In Oaxaca, Blanca Díaz Ordaz, Megan Martin, Omar Fernández, Richard Hanson, Sarahí Garcia, Karen Rasmussen, Whitney Duncan, Abbie Andrews, and Holly Worthen provided me with community. Daniel Robles, a talented photographer, became a fast friend and confidant and encouraged me to "*aplicarme*." Almost ten years later I figured out how. A writing retreat on Mexico's Pacific Coast with the *malaguas* collective—Devi Mays, Jennifer Boles, Dillon Vrana, and Chris Fraga—was everything it needed to be. In Mexico City, Stuart Easterling offered me a place to stay and proved to be a thoughtful coconspirator. The Tepoztlán Institute for the Transnational History of the Americas became an intellectual home over the years. The words and ideas we debate as scholars seemed more real there than in any other academic space. I thank the collective and the individuals who make the institute such a special place. I shared large portions of the book with participants there beneath Tepoztlán's striking cliffs, and the book is no doubt better as a result.

In my youth Tim Schwab dared me to question the way the world worked. Nihar Bhatt then asked me to help change that world. Later, Adam Goodman came along to remind me of the values that motivated this research. I am grateful for their friendship. My immediate family—Mom, Dave, Rachael and Rebekah, Blythe, Radu, Dad, and Sabine—are a constant source of strength and encouragement. My family has grown to include the Robles and Calderón clans. *A Silvia, Salvador, Tania, y Luis, les agradezco el apoyo, sentido de humor, y comida que me han compartido.* Over the course of my writing this book, my grandparents John and Carole passed away. My grandfather, an Oklahoma Choctaw, shaped me and by extension this book. I hope to replicate his quiet contemplation and ability to listen to others. Special recognition goes to my father, Alan Edward Dillingham. He introduced me to the world of books, nurtured my interest in Mexico, fielded calls from a distressed son at any hour of the day, and read an entire draft of this book. You're a good man, Charlie Brown. Finally, *Frida has sido mi compañera en una serie de aventuras. Gracias por ser mi equipo. Te prometo muchas más.*

List of Abbreviations

AAC	Acervo Alfonso Caso, Museo del ex Convento de Santo Domingo en Yanhuitlán
ACPO	Acción Cultural Popular
AGN IPS	Archivo General de la Nación, Dirección General de Investigaciones Políticas y Sociales
AGPEEO	Archivo General del Poder Ejecutivo del Estado de Oaxaca
AH-CCIMA	Archivo Histórico del Centro Coordinador Indigenista de la Mixteca Alta
APPO	Asamblea Popular de los Pueblos de Oaxaca
CCIMA	Centro Coordinador Indigenista de la Mixteca Alta
CMPIO	Coalición de Maestros y Promotores Indígenas de Oaxaca
CNTE	Coordinadora Nacional de Trabajadores de la Educación
COCEI	Coalición Obrera, Campesina, Estudiantil del Istmo
COCEO	Coalición Obrero Campesino Estudiantil de Oaxaca
DAAC	Departamento de Asuntos Agrarios y Colonización
DGEEMI	Dirección General de Educación Extraescolar en el Medio Indígena
DGEI	Dirección General de Educación Indígena
DGEI-CDEI	Dirección General de Educación Indígena, Centro de Información y Documentación de Educación Indígena, Mexico City

DGEI-SEP	Dirección General de Educación Indígena, Secretaria de Educación Publica
EMHR	Escuela de Mejoradoras del Hogar Rural
ENAH	Escuela Nacional de Antropología e Historia
EZLN	Ejército Zapatista de Liberación Nacional
FD-BJR	Fondo Documental, Biblioteca Juan Rulfo, Instituto Nacional de los Pueblos Indígenas, Mexico City
IEEPO	Instituto Estatal de Educación Publica de Oaxaca
IIISEO	Instituto de Investigación y Integración Social del Estado de Oaxaca
INI	Instituto Nacional Indigenista
NCPA	Nuevos Centros de Población Agrícola
PAN	Partido Acción Nacional
PPS	Partido Popular Socialista
PRD	Partido de la Revolución Democrática
PRI	Partido Revolucionario Institucional
SEP	Secretaría de Educación Pública
SEP DGEEMI	Secretaría de Educación Pública, Dirección General de Educación Extraescolar en el Medio Indígena
SIL	Summer Institute of Linguistics
SNTE	Sindicato Nacional de Trabajadores de la Educación
UABJO	Universidad Autónoma Benito Juárez de Oaxaca
UNAM	Universidad Nacional Autónoma de México
UNESCO	United Nations Educational, Scientific and Cultural Organization

Oaxaca Resurgent

Prologue

San Andrés Chicahuaxtla, 1899

THE WOMEN of San Andrés Chicahuaxtla refused to be measured. One day in the early winter months of 1899, they had gathered in the town plaza to barter their tortillas and eggs with traders from near and far. Located high in the Sierra Madre del Sur, San Andrés sits on the far western edge of the Mexican state of Oaxaca. A Triqui town, San Andrés is about twenty-five miles southwest of the district capital of Tlaxiaco. As the women bartered their wares, some with children in tow, they realized that a group of men had begun encircling them. The men acted on the orders of Frederick Starr, an American anthropologist on a journey through southern Mexico to document what he called "racial types" of the Indigenous population. He and his team aimed to measure, photograph, and create plaster busts of one hundred men and twenty-five women of each "tribe," including the people of San Andrés. As the men closed in, several women yelled out in alarm. A scene of chaos ensued. Some fled for the surrounding hills, screaming with terror. After multiple attempts, the men managed to round up a sufficient number for Starr, who recounted the moment as sport: "It was like nothing but the chase of deer by hounds." In total, he claimed to have measured 2,847 people on his trip.[1]

The women of San Andrés were not alone in their refusal. Despite traveling with an official letter from Oaxacan governor Martín González (1894–1902), Starr encountered resistance nearly everywhere he went. To combat this resistance, he cajoled, offered money, and even threatened to report the town authorities' noncompliance to the governor. In some instances, local authorities jailed uncooperative individuals. In addition to coaxing town authorities to assist him, Starr enlisted the help of local Catholic clergy.[2] In the ancient city of Mitla, located in Oaxaca's central valleys, a young man named José, described as "prideful" in a newspaper account, refused to be measured and was jailed in the town's municipal palace. The next day he escaped confinement, only to eventually be caught and measured by Starr. And on the Isthmus of Tehuantepec, where the state of Oaxaca narrows as it approaches Chiapas, the anthropologist's team allegedly required four policemen to subdue each of the town's legendary market women.[3]

The people of San Andrés were ultimately forced to be measured and photographed. Starr's photographer, Charles B. Lang, took group portraits of the men, women, and children of the town as well as "racial type" photographs, consisting of front and profile portraits. In his description of the group featured in figure 1, Starr, while commenting on the shape of the subjects' toes, noted a "nervousness" expressed in the positioning of their hands.[4] Taken as a whole, there is something discomforting in this

FIGURE 1. The people of San Andrés Chicahuaxtla, 1899.
Source: National Museum of the American Indian, Smithsonian Institution (N17575).

group portrait. One is left to wonder about the staging of the image. The women's and girls' disheveled hair and torn garments attest to how they were forcibly rounded up. Starr used these same characteristics to affirm his theory of racial hierarchy, which included ranked distinctions among Native peoples. He alleged the Triquis to be at the bottom. The women display varied reactions. One looks down at the ground. The girl on the right is visibly frightened. The two on the left both look straight into the camera. And the woman in the center stares defiantly ahead.

The girl on the far left, María Alejandra, was photographed twice by Lang. In the group portrait, her face partially covered by her hair, she holds an unidentified package, perhaps tortillas, wrapped in cloth, and an individual egg. María also appears in one of Lang's racial type photographs. In figure 2 she is seated on a chair in front of a backdrop, her hair pulled back in a braid, presumably at the request of Lang and Starr, who desired to chart facial phenotype. María sits slightly slouched and in the front-facing photograph furrows her brow at the camera. From the archival record, we know the circumstances in which María was forced to sit for the photographs. We know she was unwillingly rounded up with others

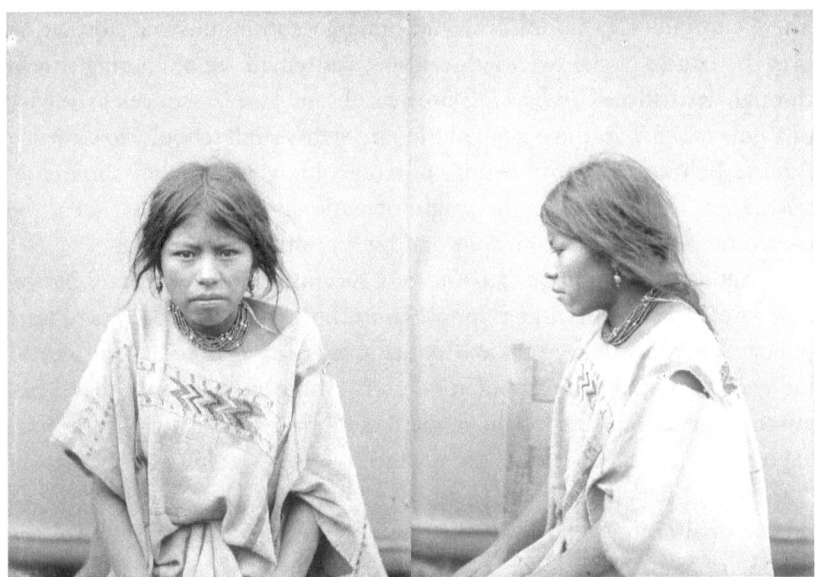

FIGURE 2. María Alejandra, 1899.
Source: National Museum of the American Indian, Smithsonian Institution (N16470; N16471).

while going about her daily routine. We know that some of the men of San Andrés assisted Starr and Lang in their efforts. We know María would have sat for an extended period of time given contemporary photographic technology. And it is likely Lang and María could not communicate in the same language.

The attempt to catalog different races was a central component of turn-of-the-century intellectual frameworks. The combination of photography and racial thinking proved a toxic blend. Starr, while subsequently dismissed by colleagues after the turn toward cultural anthropology, was no peripheral figure in 1899. He was central to the development of the anthropology program at the University of Chicago. The university went on to publish multiple studies from his trip.[5] Indeed, the president of Mexico at the time, Porfirio Díaz, a Oaxacan who had traveled extensively in the Mixteca Alta, applauded Starr's photographic album.[6]

Divergent claims regarding the relationship between modernization, development, and indigeneity have a long history in the Americas. As the anthropologist Deborah Poole noted, describing Starr's images and other turn-of-the-century photographic practices, "The Indian was marked simultaneously as both pure and degenerate, noble and servile, and, importantly, as at once incommensurably 'other' and sentimentally 'ours.'"[7] These contradictory impulses would undergo continuous transformation over the course of the twentieth century, yet remain an animating thread through virtually all *indigenista* projects. From José Vasconcelos's theory of a *raza cósmica*, to the postrevolutionary state's rural schools, to Gonzalo Aguirre Beltrán's theory of regions of refuge, indigenista policy simultaneously cast "the Indian" as the origin of national identity, a barrier to be overcome, and a source of inspiration for a multicultural future.

Yet as the people of San Andrés Chicahuaxtla demonstrate, *indigenismo* never went without a response from those marked as objects of state policy. Whereas intellectuals and policy makers have all too often framed indigeneity as the opposite of modernity, Indigenous peoples have creatively engaged and shaped the modern condition. The history of the Starr expedition reflects the long arc of anthropology's colonial engagement with Native peoples and the power dynamics inherent to anthropology's professionalization as an academic discipline. And the bold actions of the women of San Andrés form part of a broader history of refusals in Native communities.[8]

The subject of this book is the evolution of a politics of recognition over the course of the twentieth century. It tells the story of a particular state project of recognition, indigenismo, and the way it was contested through a series of engagements with Native peoples. It therefore privileges a state project and discourse while showing how those marked as the objects of indigenista policy navigated—and shaped—that project over time. The story of María Alejandra serves as a caution. While there were moments of negotiation and engagement with indigenista policy, whether in the guise of rural development, educational, or ethnographic projects, there were also moments of outright refusal: moments when those marked as Indigenous refused to be measured, refused to be seen.

Introduction

The Double Bind of Indigenismo

> The sigh of history rises over ruins.
> —Derek Walcott[1]

THE RUINS of the ancient city sit more than a mile above sea level. On a leveled mountain ridge, where the Sierra Madre del Sur and the Sierra Norte form the central valleys of the southern Mexican state of Oaxaca, lies Monte Albán. A Zapotec city once home to tens of thousands of people, Monte Albán was one of the largest metropolises of pre-Hispanic Mesoamerica. The ruins of the urban center, its expansive central plaza, raised platforms, and astronomical observatory, stand just above the contemporary state capital, Oaxaca de Juárez (Oaxaca City). During the rainy months, the stone structures stand out against the verdant green of the mountain ridge, a reminder of why the ancient Mixtecs referred to Monte Albán as Yucucui, "green mountain."

In recent years, urban sprawl has brought the ruins of Monte Albán and twenty-first-century Oaxaca City even closer. At roughly 1,200 feet above the valley floor, the ruins sit just above the western edge of the contemporary city. The ancient ball courts and elite housing that line the main plaza offer an impressive view of the capital of what is today one of Mexico's poorest states. Monte Albán, a city that endured as a center of pre-Hispanic civilization and empire for nearly a millennium, is feted as an international tourist destination. UNESCO declared the ruins and the colonial downtown a World Heritage site in 1987. In Oaxaca, as at other sites of pre-Conquest civilization, tourism has become one of the few profitable industries.

FIGURE 3. The ruins of Monte Albán.
Source: Roberto A. Turnbull, 1932. Courtesy National Geographic Society.

The dissonance between the boisterous city below and the now-silent series of blocks and boulevards of Monte Albán speaks to the broader dissonance within the indigenista project in the Americas. Indigenismo, which originated in the late nineteenth century as Latin American elites attempted to distinguish themselves from their former European colonial powers, has come to signal state discourses and practices that celebrate Indigenous aesthetics and a pre-Hispanic past while figuring contemporary Indigenous populations as a problem to overcome. The ruins, like other state celebrations of Indigenous aesthetics, cut both ways. On the one hand, they serve as a tourist attraction for national and international visitors alike, as well as a source of regional pride, with groups of local secondary students racing across the site almost daily. On the other hand, these very same state invocations of the Indigenous past have served as a cudgel against those marked as Indigenous today, as a glorious past is contrasted against an allegedly degraded Indigenous present. Monte Albán thus hangs over the city the way folkloric treatments hang over Indigenous people throughout the Americas. Indeed, the very act of memorializing and celebrating pre-Conquest sites casts Indigenous peoples as intrinsically part of the past.[2]

State invocations of indigeneity in the Americas have invariably framed Indigenous peoples as part of a colonial heritage, a subject of social reform, or a barrier to development and modernization—anything but a universal subject of history. The unique situation that Native peoples have faced in Mexico, and to varying degrees throughout the Americas, is to live in a context in which states invoke Native history and culture in projects of nationalism and state building. These national projects frequently have meant the loss of Indigenous land, language, and governing structures. Native peoples thus confront a situation in which their history and culture are wielded by others for divergent ends. Yet these same state invocations have proven useful to those marked as Indigenous to make claims for rights, resources, and autonomy. That dilemma, which I call the double bind of indigenismo, is the subject of this book.[3]

The relationship between the ruins of Monte Albán and the history of indigenismo is no mere metaphor. The person responsible for much of the site's modern excavation was Alfonso Caso. Beginning in 1931, Caso and his team initiated the large-scale excavation of the site's platforms, central plaza, and tombs. The Mexican and international press celebrated the team's discovery of the treasures of Tomb 7. While archaeological excavations had expanded during the final years of Porfirio Díaz's administration (1876–1911), Caso's excavation formed part of a broader postrevolutionary nationalism in Mexico. Following the 1910 Revolution, federal officials increasingly turned to the country's Indigenous past and regional aesthetics to form a new, national culture. Mexican art of the period, feted in New York and Paris, drew on similar aesthetic influences. Indeed, Mexico's entry into modernity was premised on its ability to invoke its Indigenous past in international arts and statecraft. Excavations of sites such as Monte Albán were part of this postrevolutionary state building. During the years of Caso's excavation, Oaxacan authorities inaugurated an annual folkloric dance festival, then called the Homenaje Racial and later renamed with the Zapotec term *guelaguetza*, in an effort to employ Indigenous music and dress as a unifying element in a politically fractious state.[4]

In this context, Caso excavated Monte Albán not out of an esoteric interest in the ancient past but rather as part of a vision of what constituted Mexico's present and future.[5] The archaeologist went directly

FIGURE 4. Alfonso Caso (center with glasses) and his Monte Albán excavation team. Also pictured are María Lombardo Toledano, Caso's wife, to his immediate right and Eulalia Guzmán, then an archaeology student, on Caso's left.
Source: Roberto A. Turnbull, 1932. Courtesy National Geographic Society.

from overseeing the excavation work and analyzing Mesoamerican codices to leading the Instituto Nacional Indigenista (INI), Mexico's Indigenous development agency. By midcentury, these earlier indigenista efforts fused with projects of modernization aimed at the transformation of both people and places marked as Indigenous. Midcentury indigenista policy reflected the broader assumptions of modernization theory, facilitating a transition from "tradition" to "modernity" and favoring industrial models of development. From the institute's founding in 1948 until his death in 1970, Caso directed the most ambitious Indigenous development agency in the Americas, overseeing an array of programs, including agricultural support services, public health campaigns, infrastructure construction, and education extension programs. Indeed, the man who excavated the ruins of Monte Albán, popularizing Mexico's Indigenous past for the world, became the top federal official in charge of transforming the contemporary Indigenous population for Mexico's modernist future.

As a project of applied social science, indigenismo required a discrete subject. For states, particularly those that emerged from Spanish rule, language practices often served as the primary marker of Indigenous difference. Throughout the twentieth century, the Mexican census used language ability to determine the percentage of the national population categorized as Indigenous. In the 1950s countryside, the decline of those who declared themselves speakers of Native languages was lauded by reformers such as the economist Moisés de la Peña, who declared that the Indigenous population had become "campesinos," a politically salient category that bore a nationalist character associated with the postrevolutionary regime. While slippage between the categories of "campesino" and "Indigenous" sometimes occurred, the policies of the Partido Revolucionario Institucional (PRI) generally privileged campesino political rhetoric up until the 1970s. The state's emphasis on language as the primary marker of indigeneity no doubt shaped subsequent Indigenous resurgence projects, which frequently focused on language revitalization as a primary struggle for Indigenous empowerment.[6]

While official constructions of Indigenous difference emphasized language, Oaxacans expressed indigeneity through a host of practices, including dress, foodways, and the celebration of hometown saints' day festivals.[7] Ultimately, indigeneity is a particular form of making the past speak to the present. These practices engage with a cleavage produced by colonialism, yet at the same time are unquestionably modern.[8] As the pages that follow show, those involved in Indigenous politics repeatedly debated the question of colonialism and colonial legacies over the course of the twentieth century. As they wrestled with Native peoples' relationship to contemporary states and persistent inequalities, they articulated varied theories of anticolonialism. Some viewed states as facilitating colonial exploitation of Indigenous peoples, while most indigenistas viewed statecraft as a tool to challenge said inequalities.

Indigenismo was an Americas-wide phenomenon. Indeed, the "Indian problem," articulated as such, was one of the defining intellectual constructions of modern Latin America.[9] Twentieth-century indigenismo went beyond aesthetics and was intertwined with development projects globally.[10] Popular and state invocations of the Indigenous past have distinct but parallel histories in the Anglo-Americas. Despite divergent colonial histories, one sees an analogous ideological operation at work in Canada and the United States as Native history and culture were employed to distinguish these national projects from former European colonial powers and to mark a vanishing frontier during westward expansion. In the twentieth century, oscillating projects of Indian removal, reservations, and assimilationist education policies found overlaps with their Latin American counterparts. Nonetheless, the unique form that Spanish colonialism took in the Americas differed sharply from its Anglo-American counterpart and produced distinct legacies of racialization.[11]

As a development practice indigenismo incentivized the self-representation of Indigenous people.[12] This spirit of self-representation directly counters the late nineteenth-century quest to measure and represent Indigenous peoples described in the Prologue. The ambivalent space of indigenista practice was far from monolithic or predetermined. Just as modernizing efforts threatened Indigenous particularism, indigenista agents also at times sought to empower Indigenous communities with tools to defend themselves. The goal of this book is to move beyond normative judgments of the indigenista project, beyond even the vocabulary of indigenistas themselves, to examine quotidian indigenista practice and the way in which understandings of indigeneity, both in state discourse and in individual self-identification, were shaped by the development process.[13]

Oaxaca Resurgent

This book focuses on the state of Oaxaca because it has been a prime site of thinking on indigeneity. Prior to Spanish arrival, the region's strategic position between the civilizations that inhabited the valley of Mexico to the north and Mayan societies to the southeast made it a key transit point and center of long-distance trade. Within its three mountain ranges lay the highland central valleys, which afforded an advantageous position vis-à-vis other regional powers. The Isthmus of Tehuantepec to the south, with its long-standing rivalry between the Zapotec towns of Juchitán and Tehuantepec, has been another key node of trade and commerce in the area from the pre-Hispanic period to the present. Within a relatively small geographic space, 58,279 square miles, one finds an astonishing diversity of climate, culture, and topography.

The Spanish arrived in the area in 1521 and named it Antequera. Colonial officials empowered the Dominican order to begin large-scale

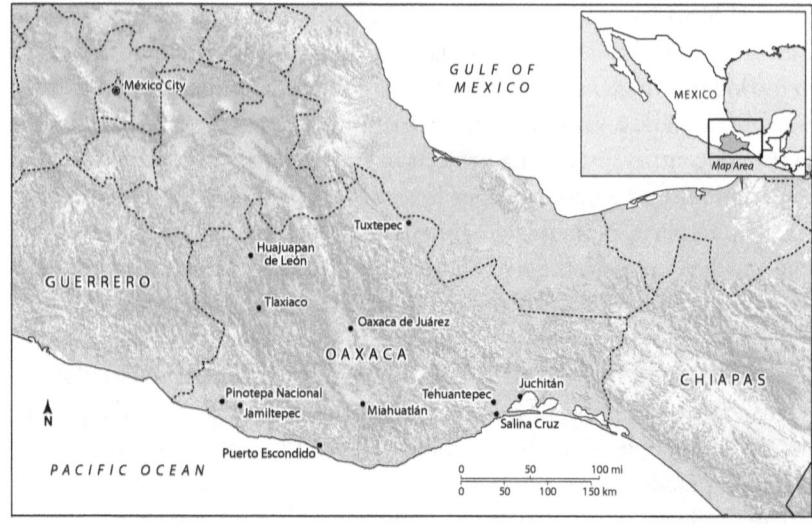

MAP 1. The State of Oaxaca

evangelization efforts, and Dominican priests and their Indigenous interlocutors created many of the early vocabularies of Native languages. A small Spanish merchant elite established itself in the central valleys and relied on Indigenous counterparts to facilitate trade and commerce. This model of colonial rule made Antequera a center of colonial wealth in New Spain, with silk and cochineal trades flourishing. Antequera was one of the wealthiest parts of the Spanish Empire, in part because of the relative strength of its Indigenous population and elites. This was reflected in colonial judicial proceedings, where the lingua franca was Nahuatl, the language of the Mexica Empire, along with other Native languages.[14]

With independence from Spain came the destruction of the *repúblicas de indios* system, a form of colonial rule that allowed a measure of autonomy for Indigenous communities through *usos y costumbres*, Indigenous customary law. Oaxaca was a center of liberal reform, producing one of Mexican liberalism's most important spokesmen and presidents, Benito Juárez.[15] Because of Indigenous retention of communal lands in much of the state, agrarianism did not take hold in the way it did in other areas of Mexico.[16] This has led some scholars to portray Oaxaca as a relative backwater during the 1910 Revolution. In 1915, Oaxacan governor José Inés Dávila organized a movement opposed to the centralization favored by President Venustiano Carranza and the Constitutionalists.[17] This effort, termed the sovereignty movement, drew on nineteenth-century traditions of Sierra *caudillos* mobilizing campesinos through kinship and clientelism, though anger over taxes also fueled campesino participation. In the Isthmus town of Juchitán, the cleavages produced by the Revolution nationally allowed for local insurgents to challenge long-standing forms of political power.[18]

In the twentieth century, Oaxaca became central to theorizations of Indigenous peoples' relationship to modernization and the site of multiple pilot projects of Indigenous education and development. The state's varied topography, its multiple mountain ranges, high central valleys, and coastal plains, had once supported pre-Hispanic civilizations and robust regional economies that persisted well into the nineteenth century. Yet that same topographical diversity increasingly became an obstacle to the models of development Mexico pursued in the twentieth century.[19] The microclimates and localized crops that had served to sustain regional production and consumption now emerged as barriers in a model of development that privileged monocultures and mechanized agriculture. Many in Oaxaca's central valleys fared well during this period, and *vallistas*, as the people of the central valleys are known, became prominent actors in the state's economy and politics. Nonetheless, by midcentury this development model favored northern rather than southern Mexico. Highland regions such as the Mixteca Alta and parts of the Sierra Juárez struggled at midcentury as development officials neither invested in large-scale agriculture in these regions nor reckoned with their unique characteristics. Indeed, many highland Oaxacans began migrating to northern Mexico and the United States to labor in growing industries and commercial agriculture. Development officials framed these dynamics as a problem of "underdevelopment" and claimed that regions such as the Mixteca Alta suffered from "overpopulation."

Oaxaca Resurgent explores the relationship between indigeneity, education and development policies, and anticolonial thinking. With over sixteen officially recognized languages, many with their own mutually unintelligible variants, Oaxaca is one of the most linguistically diverse regions in the world. Just within the Zapotec language family, one observes distinct forms of Zapotec spoken in the central valleys, the Sierras, and the Isthmus, with healthy rivalries over who speaks the correct form of Zapotec. Oaxaca's languages, from Zapotec to Mixtec, from Huave to Chinanteco, are unique in the Americas for both their diversity and their geographic proximity. While Oaxaca and in particular the Mixteca Alta serve as this book's primary case study, indigenismo was an Americas-wide project. I examine how that project was articulated in national and transnational networks. Throughout, I explore two related questions: First, how did ideas regarding the relationship between indigeneity and modernization change over the twentieth century? And second, what was the lived experience of indigenismo as a developmentalist and education practice in Oaxaca?

During the twentieth century, successive generations of indigenista intellectuals theorized and put into practice projects of Indigenous reform. Through institutions such as the Secretaría de Educación Publica (SEP) and the INI, Caso and other functionaries leveraged federal resources and political power in their efforts to transform Indigenous Mexico. In Oaxaca, state governors, municipal officials, and church authorities all held competing visions of modernization and sought to put them into practice. While modernization took place through a multiplicity of actors and forces, including the growth of national and international markets, private industry, the Catholic Church, and migration, the state played a disproportionate role in the history of formal efforts to transform Indigenous Mexico. Frequently Indigenous development brokers themselves, as teachers, public health campaigners, and agricultural extensionists, shaped the on-the-ground experience of modernization efforts in the state. These go-betweens, the central actors of this book, occupied a contradictory role, at times allying with top-down projects and at other times collaborating with and leading local struggles for progressive change.

While Oaxaca was a major target of indigenista efforts, material impoverishment remained a reality for most of the state's inhabitants throughout the century. In the 1950s and 1960s, federal and state officials transformed regions such as the Mixteca Alta through infrastructure initiatives, including roads and electrification, as well as public health and education campaigns. Large-scale development initiatives such as the Papaloapan Dam project in the northeast corner of the state, completed in 1954, were part of global high modernist trends that imagined regional development projects, such as hydroelectric projects, as transformative. The spread of the Green Revolution in agriculture did little to stimulate the economies of southern Mexico, where there were many small farmers. Rather, during the second half of the century, growing numbers of Oaxacans engaged in seasonal labor migration, traveling to the neighboring state of Veracruz, Mexico City, northern Mexico, and then increasingly areas in the western United States for work. Primary and secondary school teaching was one of the few consistently remunerated forms of employment in the state, and the education sector became a principal component of Oaxacan politics, both within the PRI and within oppositional politics. Given this context, development and education policies were a central site of contestation.

The PRI dominated Oaxacan electoral and mass politics. Indeed, Oaxaca was a net exporter of politicians, providing high-level federal functionaries to the PRI throughout the republic. These include Genaro Vicente Vásquez (1925–28), Victor Bravo Ahuja (1968–70), and Diódoro Carrasco Altamirano (1992–98), all of whom served as governors of the state before taking positions in the federal government. Mirroring national politics, a system centralized around the governor administered life in the state. The ruling party did not lose the governorship of Oaxaca until 2010, proving itself a bastion of uninterrupted PRI power. Compared to its eastern neighbor Chiapas, which witnessed an armed insurgency led by the Ejército Zapatista de Liberación Nacional (EZLN) in 1994, Oaxaca's political history might appear calm.

But formal PRI control masked the highly contingent forms of power holding in the state. Oaxaca's 570 municipalities frequently exchanged deference to outside authorities, voting for PRI candidates in state and federal elections, in exchange for local rule, often in the form of usos y costumbres. When governors appeared to not comply with local demands or understandings, they were overthrown. In 1947, a social movement in the state capital successfully ousted Governor Edmundo Sánchez Cano, in a dispute fueled by new taxes and state repression. Just five years later, a similar effort ousted Governor Manuel Mayoral Heredia. In the post-1968 era, students at the Universidad Autónoma Benito Juárez de Oaxaca (UABJO) sparked a movement that eventually overthrew Governor Manuel Zárate Aquino in 1977. In the town of Juchitán, on the Isthmus of Tehuantepec, a coalition successfully ousted the PRI from power in municipal elections in 1981. This is not to dismiss the staying power of PRI rule but rather to emphasize its unstable and negotiated nature.

As federal, cabinet-level agencies, the INI and the SEP were deeply entwined with the PRI's political project. Working within these agencies often required participation in the ruling party's internal politics or public events. In the pages that follow, I pay attention to the intersection of indigenista practice and PRI rule.[20] Anthropologists who occupied top positions in federal agencies had to navigate and participate in the ruling party by necessity. At the same time, federal security agents' surveillance of these individuals attests to the heterogeneity of political opinion among federal personnel. A central element of the party's power was its vertical control of trade unions and peasant federations. I examine a key moment in the unraveling of PRI rule, when the dissident Oaxacan teachers of Sección 22 of the Sindicato Nacional de Trabajadores de la Educación (SNTE) successfully broke from the party's control. I also explore Indigenous peoples' relationship to the PRI. Many Native individuals found a political home within party structures and participated in indigenista agencies as low-level staff members, anthropologists, and at times directors of INI regional coordinating centers. This reality undermines any facile Indigenous-versus-state dichotomies one might wish to employ. It also further demonstrates the heterogeneity that existed within the PRI project.

Perhaps because of the historical weight of the 1910 Revolution and the postrevolutionary state it produced, historians of Mexico have struggled to move their analytic frameworks beyond the nationalist politics that engulfed the country.[21] Scholars have often treated Mexico as a notable exception in twentieth-century Latin American history, with its relatively stable political system and close relationship to its northern neighbor standing in stark contrast to the civil wars, dictatorships, and US intervention that characterized much of the region.[22] Historians have recently challenged Mexican Cold War exceptionalism, demonstrating how hemispheric events as well as wellsprings of domestic opposition transformed the Mexican political landscape. I deepen this deprovincialization of Mexican history by demonstrating the ways the history of Oaxaca elucidates two related but distinct hemispheric trends: movements of Indigenous resurgence and official multiculturalism.

Struggles centering the experience of Native peoples' marginalization emerged throughout the Americas in the 1980s and 1990s. Scholars have often emphasized a rupture between previous models of politics focused on class and the rise of so-called identity politics. This scholarly emphasis on a political break has failed to reckon with crucial developments in the 1970s, specifically the cultural pluralism produced within New Left and Third-Worldist circles. As people throughout the globe articulated new theories of revolution, they reckoned anew with questions of culture and colonial legacies. A Oaxacan example of this global dynamic is the theory and practice of *comunalidad* (communality). Oaxacan intellectuals such as Floriberto Díaz and Juan José Rendón began to theorize a radical politics in dialogue with their own experiences of Indigenous communal life. Díaz and Rendón combined the academic studies and Left political practices they encountered in Mexico City with the traditions of communal work and obligation in their hometowns. As such, they articulated communality as a political practice based on the communal nature of many Oaxacan villages that could serve as a model for transformative politics. Communality was not a homogenous project, nor did it originate in just one individual. Liberation theology and Catholic base communities in Oaxaca shaped the development of these politics as well.[23]

Teachers working in the Indigenous education sector were also at the forefront of challenging PRI rule and rising economic austerity. The teacher trade union struggle unfolded in the late 1970s and early 1980s as the INI and the SEP simultaneously adopted policies of *etnodesarrollo*, ethnic development, and *indigenismo de participación*, participatory indigenismo. During this period, leaders within the PRI adopted neoliberal policies, which in turn created a crisis of legitimacy.[24] In the coming years, the government's inept response to the Mexico City earthquake of 1985, which killed upwards of ten thousand people, further eroded the legitimacy of the ruling party. Its leaders attempted to solve this problem, in part, through a multicultural reinvention of the party, embracing rhetoric and policies that celebrated Indigenous languages and cultural rights. And as formal policies of economic austerity and official multiculturalism emerged simultaneously, some scholars argued that neoliberal multiculturalism was nothing more than a tautology. I take a different view, underscoring how multicultural policies in Mexico emerged as a response to antiracist and anticolonial politics of the 1960s and 1970s.

Mexico was at the forefront of multicultural reform in the Americas. Beginning in the 1980s, state and federal governments enacted legislation and policies that officially recognized and embraced the cultural and linguistic diversity of the country. These included education reform as well as constitutional amendments officially recognizing Indigenous languages and customary law. Mexico's long history of indigenista policy placed it at the forefront of the multicultural turn, but there were significant differences from previous policies and rhetoric that celebrated *mestizaje*, or racial mixture, and the official celebration of the plurality of Mexico's

Indigenous peoples. Mexico was not alone in this multicultural turn; the International Labour Organization's Convention 169, organized in 1989, called for respect of Indigenous peoples' cultures, land, and access to natural resources. Many Latin American governments soon endorsed the international treaty.

This combination of economic austerity and the official celebration of Indigenous difference led critics to argue that as a model of governance, neoliberal multiculturalism articulated forms of social inclusion without reckoning with growing social inequalities. Within academic accounts, the multicultural turn has been treated with a healthy degree of skepticism. Scholars have rightly pointed out that talk of cultural rights appeared to emerge hand in glove with a conservative economic project that exacerbated existing social inequalities. As such, neoliberalism and multiculturalism have frequently been treated as one and the same.[25] In contrast, I offer a distinct periodization and historical explanation for the emergence of multiculturalism. I frame multiculturalism as a partial concession to antiracist demands. We fail to understand both neoliberalism and multiculturalism through facile narratives of neoliberal entrapment. In effect, scholarly cynicism has erased both the historical contingency of the 1970s and the demands of Indigenous activists.

The experiences described in this book reveal a different history, a history in which questions of cultural liberation and social transformation were intimately linked. Indeed, "cultural revolution" was a common analytical framework of anticolonial thinkers. The delinking of theories of cultural and social liberation during the neoliberal era should not distort our understanding of the past. Oaxaca today appears as the epitome of neoliberal multiculturalism, with its varied cultures and crafts commodified for an international tourist market. But even here, in a place that in recent years has embraced a model of development based on folkloric tourism, a radical history underlies the rise of state-sponsored multiculturalism. In sum, *Oaxaca Resurgent* traces the interaction of post–World War II development projects engaging Indigenous brokers, transnational discourses of anticolonialism, and education reform. In the 1970s these factors, along with the actions of Indigenous educators, produced two interrelated but distinct outcomes: an official multiculturalism that recognized and embraced Indigenous alterity, and a politics of Indigenous resurgence frequently marshaled against state authoritarianism. In this context multiculturalism emerges not merely as a clever hegemonic tool wielded by powerful interests but also as an antiracist achievement of grassroots activism and negotiation.[26]

Methods and Structure

Oaxaca Resurgent proceeds chronologically across the twentieth century. The first three chapters are a case study of post–World War II development policy in the Mixteca Alta. Midcentury modernizers imagined a totalizing transformation of "underdeveloped regions" directed by state agencies and savvy technocrats. This national policy included regional studies commissioned to assess the region's natural resources, demographic characteristics, and market potential. In chapter 1 I follow economists and anthropologists employed by federal authorities as they assessed the Mixteca Alta's levels of development and offered potential solutions. Among the proposed solutions were the extension of federal education efforts in the region and a voluntary resettlement of the highland population to Oaxaca's Pacific coast. In chapter 2 I analyze a pilot short-wave bilingual radio program initiated by the INI. In one of the first indigenista broadcasts in the country, INI personnel transmitted educational programing in Spanish and Mixtec to far-flung communities in the region. Their efforts sparked local opposition, which viewed federal education efforts through the lens of Catholic anticommunism. In chapter 3 I explore government authorities' efforts to relocate the highland population south along Oaxaca's coastal plains. Reflecting the high degree of confidence in state planning, technocrats believed the resettled migrants would find better material conditions there. But the small number of highlanders who chose to migrate south quickly found themselves in violent conflicts with already existing coastal communities and power brokers. All three of these chapters examine the unintended consequences of indigenista policy.

In chapter 4 I assess a distinct period of indigenista reform in which intellectuals, policy makers, and targeted communities called into question some of the fundamental assumptions of high modernist development. During this period theories of dependence, internal colonialism, and ethnocide took center stage. President Luis Echeverría (1970–76) strategically embraced some of these theories and attempted to revive the PRI political project through investment in rural development at home and advocacy of the New International Economic Order abroad. Chapter 4 follows the struggles of Indigenous youth for professionalization as teachers within the context of Echeverría's reformism. Chapter 5 follows these teachers as they struggled to democratize their local teachers' union, Sección 22. In this period of incipient neoliberalism, Indigenous teachers fought to obtain full rights and representation within the union and to rid it of a violent and authoritarian leadership. At the same time, federal authorities opened up space for alternative models within the Indigenous education sector. In chapter 6, I examine educators' and policy makers' efforts to institutionalize anticolonial pedagogies and bilingual methods in the classroom. *Oaxaca Resurgent* concludes by examining the contradictory nature of indigenista policies at the end of the twentieth century.

I have engaged a range of sources to uncover and examine the plurality of voices that constituted the indigenista experience in the Americas.[27] These include newspapers, photographs, oral interviews and personal papers of those involved in Indigenous education and development, academic publications from the period, and documents found in municipal, state, and federal archives. As a history that stretches from the beginning of the twentieth century to its end, this work necessarily relies on a wide variety of materials to tell the story, but two broad categories of sources deserve some explanation regarding the interpretative dilemmas they present. The first involves the declassified files of the Dirección Federal de Seguridad and Dirección General de Investigaciones Políticas y Sociales, two domestic intelligence services in Mexico, and the second involves archival documents and oral histories related to Indigenous subjects.

While I have drawn on materials from local, state, and federal archives, many collections have poor to no classification systems for the post-1940 period. This is no doubt partially a product of the long-standing interest in Mexico's revolutionary and postrevolutionary eras. Because of this, I, like other historians of midcentury Mexico, have relied disproportionately on the surveillance documents of Mexican intelligence services. Mexican spies kept detailed records on a wide range of individuals and groups, from dissident trade unions to top PRI politicians and their drinking habits. Spies gathered newspaper clippings on a variety of subjects, among them indigenista policy and Indigenous politics, and they monitored government anthropologists and their relationships with Indigenous communities. Declassified in 2002 during the *sexenio* of President Vicente Fox, these collections present their own interpretive challenges.[28] I have attempted to read against the grain of surveillance reports, taking a skeptical view of documents that appear to overstate the potential threat of government opponents or to inflate dissidents' propensity for violence. Where possible, I have cross-referenced information from surveillance reports with material gleaned from oral interviews. Sadly, authorities have since blocked access to both of these archival collections, limiting historians' and the broader public's ability to understand the past.

A history involving Indigenous subjects requires another kind of critical gaze toward one's sources and methods. As others before me have pointed out, those marked as Indigenous more often than not appear in government archives as a problem.[29] In official documents, Indigenous subjects are frequently figured as a uniform group, as an obstacle to modernization, as irrational, and as prone to violence. In the INI archives, they are explicitly objects of reform, something to be acted upon. How do I avoid replicating the violence and marginalization of archival representations of Indigenous people in my own research? I have attempted to critically interpret indigenista documents, lingering over the brief moments when Indigenous subjects' views and actions appear in state agents' reports. I also allow for the reality that silences in the archival record, traces of individuals who appeared in projects of reform or who were detained by state agents, and then disappeared as quickly as they appeared, tell us something meaningful about the subject at hand.

Finally, many actors in this history were eager to share their experiences. While conducting research for this book, I spent three years learning Mixtec, one of the dominant Native languages in southern Mexico. This training led to a series of interviews with those involved in Indigenous education and development. Those voices and histories serve not only to complement the gaps of information in the official archival record but also to underscore the inherently incomplete nature of projects of Indigenous incorporation. They are critical if we are to recuperate the plurality of Indigenous perspectives and agency in twentieth-century Mexico.

1

Modernizing the Mixteca
Regional Approaches to Underdevelopment

Today's Mixtecs—more than half a million—remain frozen in time, not necessarily in the ancient past but rather in the particular conditions created by the conquest.
 —Fernando Benítez, 1967[1]

Of all state simplifications, then, the imposition of a single, official language may be the most powerful, and it is the precondition of many other simplifications.
 —James Scott[2]

THE TOWN authorities of Santo Tomás Ocotepec heard they were coming. The INI delegation, which included the anthropologist Pablo Velásquez Gallardo, the medical doctor Rafael Torres, and two assistants, had gotten stuck nearby. The delegation's jeep could not cross a rising river, and they had sent for help. While Torres and his assistants went ahead toward Ocotepec on two of the INI's horses, town officials sent another horse and mules to transport the anthropologist and his supplies, including over 154 pounds of dichlorodiphenyltrichloroethane, popularly known as DDT. Once in Ocotepec, located in the Mixtec Alta, Torres explained to town authorities the delegation's mission to continue vaccinations begun by a state health delegation and to combat a lice infestation.[3] While waiting for Velásquez to arrive, Torres proceeded to identify and vaccinate those not yet treated by the previous delegation. These indigenista professionals understood development as a totalizing process, in which agricultural reform was intimately tied to education, personal health, and

FIGURE 5. Doctor Torres treating the children of Santo Tomás Ocotepec with DDT, August 6, 1954.
Source: Instituto Nacional de los Pueblos Indígenas, Fototeca Nacho López, Hermanos Mayo.

hygiene. Regional integration depended not only on the construction of infrastructure and improvements in communication to overcome the forbidding topography of the highland region but also on the physical and cultural transformation of the population. In this way indigenista development, with all of its attention to local conditions and culture, nonetheless equated the human geography of the region with other barriers to modernization, viewing it as another problem to be overcome.

By midafternoon, Velásquez arrived along with the mules carrying his equipment. As he dismounted, the town band welcomed him with a series of musical scores.[4] While the band played, the people of the town and surrounding rancherías were lined up, and health authorities sprayed DDT directly on individuals and their clothes, even in their homes, recording counts of those sprayed. This was one instance of a program to eliminate lice infestations, which officials estimated affected 90 percent of the population.[5]

Contemporary understandings of the carcinogenic effects of DDT certainly inform our reaction to the episode. Yet the public health campaign's significance also lies in the community's acceptance. The spraying of children with DDT was part and parcel of a global development practice.[6] In this case, Cold War public health campaigns that targeted so-called unintegrated regions of the global South intersected with legacies of Spanish colonial rule. The town authorities' welcoming of the federal delegation underlines the long history of colonial relations in the region, in which Indigenous self-government was achieved through deference to outside authority. The colonial *visita*, in which Indigenous authorities assembled their populations to perform loyalty to visiting peninsular officials, had a kind of parallel in the experience of twentieth-century social scientists and modernizing programs.[7] Indeed, as evidenced by the epigraph that begins this chapter, different articulations of "the colonial" were invoked by many involved in Indigenous development efforts at the time.

The health visit was also part of a new moment in the history of Mexican development. President Adolfo Ruiz Cortines (1952–58) oversaw an ambitious program of macroeconomic growth. Ruiz Cortines invested heavily in urban industry and provided support to large-scale commercial agriculture, particularly in northern Mexico. The postrevolutionary state's early emphasis on agrarian reform and land redistribution under President Lázaro Cárdenas (1934–40) had given way to more conservative economic policies. If Cárdenas represented the radical legacy of the 1910 Revolution, the presidents that followed, Manuel Ávila Camacho (1940–46) and Miguel Alemán (1946–52), focused on macroeconomic growth with less regard for the redistributive aspects of Cárdenismo. Ruiz Cortines doubled down on these policies, declaring an official position of austerity and initiating a campaign against corruption. Emphasizing what was termed *desarrollo estabilizador*, or "stabilizing development," the president devalued the peso in 1954 to improve Mexico's foreign trade and initiated a so-called *Marcha al Mar*, or March to the Sea, that aimed to stimulate a maritime economy and promote migration to Mexico's two coasts. The Mexican Miracle, as these broad trends came to be termed, linked Mexico to an increasingly integrated post–World War II global economy led by its neighbor to the north, the United States.

The economic impact of the Mexican Miracle was uneven. It disproportionately benefited urbanizing cities and northern agriculture. That unevenness was starkly reflected in areas of southern Mexico, such as Oaxaca, where regional economic production and consumption had once thrived. For areas such as the Mixteca Alta, the impressive economic statistics of the 1940s and 1950s were often experienced as decline. With the construction of national infrastructure, such as the Pan-American Highway, local light industries now competed on a national market, frequently to their detriment. The city of Tlaxiaco, the center of commerce and trade in the Mixteca Alta, had struggled to recover from the instability of the revolutionary era, and local elites faced declining fortunes during the Mexican Miracle. Contemporary development voices framed this experience as a lack of integration with "modern" sectors of the economy. In other words, the region's plight was due to internal rather than external problems.[8] The Mexican Miracle was consequently less than miraculous for much of Oaxaca.

Despite the nomenclature, the Mexican Miracle was neither unique nor particularly inexplicable. Disruptions in global trade in the 1930s meant that many countries in Latin America adopted a set of policies aimed at strengthening local economic production and consumption. These policies, termed import substitution industrialization (ISI), saw salutatory effects not only in Mexico but also in Brazil and Argentina. National policy makers and elites sought to strengthen domestic production and consumption through policies that sheltered domestic markets from the fluctuations of international trade. In the wake of World War II and decolonization, western Europe and the global South looked to either rebuild or jump-start their national economies, and thus "development" became a goal in and of itself. Regions of southern Mexico, such as Oaxaca, marked as "underdeveloped" and Indigenous therefore figured into a national development model as necessary, albeit subordinated, targets for developmentalist attention.

Driven by the anxieties of the Cold War, a diversity of post–World War II technocrats framed economic development as a political necessity. Regional development projects were a worldwide phenomenon and frequently paired science, technology, and engineering with public health and education initiatives. The midcentury witnessed a diversity of development models, inflected by divergent political contexts and social projects.

Regional development plans were adopted in British colonial territories, the US South, the Soviet Union, and nationalist Egypt as well as in postrevolutionary states such as Mexico.[9] These projects frequently shared the assumption that impediments to national development stemmed from regional "underdevelopment." In this schema, the inevitable march of national economic development was impeded by regions that were not integrated into modern systems of trade, commerce, and, less centrally, political participation.[10] The hubris of such plans earned the moniker "high modernism" for their bold, transformative visions.[11] While elements of indigenista development share some of these characteristics, the term itself obscures rather than clarifies events in the Mixteca.

This global post–World War II moment intersected with the singularities of postrevolutionary Mexico and its traditions of rural and agrarian reform. Postrevolutionary agrarianism combined with indigenista discourse that emphasized the centrality of Indigenous peoples to Mexican national identity. Mexican regional development diagnostics drew on these traditions, both projects of social uplift. These national traditions combined with international development frameworks that attributed poverty and inequality to regional barriers, such as lack of infrastructure or local monopolies and exploitative elites. Indigenista policies aimed to break down these barriers and transform populations who often lacked the ability to speak the national language, Spanish, and who were engaged in cultural practices that were believed to facilitate their exploitation by regional elites or were otherwise unfit for "modern" economic activity. Following this framework, the INI set up centers of regional development in the states of Chiapas, Chihuahua, and Oaxaca in the early 1950s.[12] While the Oaxacan experience confirms much of what critics argue were the limitations of state-led development, indigenista regional development efforts in the Mixteca Alta unleashed complex forces that had long-standing consequences.

In 1949, the economist Moisés de la Peña arrived in the Mixteca Alta to conduct one of the first regional studies, leading a team that collected information on demographics, existing industries, and natural resources, as well as agricultural practices. Four years later, the Salvadoran anthropologist Alejandro Marroquín conducted a study of the regional market in the city of Tlaxiaco. These respective studies shaped early indigenista efforts in the region. In 1954, the INI set up its offices in Tlaxiaco, dubbed a "coordinating center," to coordinate a range of development efforts. Pablo

Velásquez Gallardo served as the first director of the Tlaxiaco offices. As noted above, he began his work with an ethnographic survey and a public health campaign. These studies marshalled social scientific data to construct the Mixteca as a coherent "region," a concept that was increasingly salient for development thinkers. Despite the heterogeneity of these thinkers, language practices emerged as a prime marker of indigeneity. These efforts reflected the double bind inherent in indigenista policy, which simultaneously provided material assistance to Indigenous communities and linked poverty and exploitation with Indigenous culture and an alleged "colonial condition."

Not only was the construction of discrete "underdeveloped regions" key to midcentury development thinking, but such discourses linked indigeneity with material impoverishment.[13] Indigenista thinking, despite its attention to the specific forms of exploitation and inequality that Native people faced, risked naturalizing these inequalities. These dynamics occurred in Latin American countries with robust indigenista traditions as well as Anglo-American countries in projects such as detribalization and directed migration.[14] Before delving into the midcentury social scientific constructions of the Mixteca Alta and their particular diagnostics, let us turn to the historical forces and contexts that these intellectuals encountered upon their arrival.

Outsiders framed the Mixteca as a region well before the arrival of the Spanish. Prior to European conquest, Mexica emissaries labeled the diverse city-states to their southeast the "Mixteca," or the people of the clouds. The Mixteca Alta is part of the broader Mixteca region, which consists of much of present-day western Oaxaca, parts of eastern Guerrero, and sections of southern Puebla.[15] Historically divided into three main subregions, the Baja, the Alta, and the Costa, the Baja spans southern Puebla and the low-lying region of northern Oaxaca, while the high mountainous region in the western center of Oaxaca forms the Alta. Moving down from the mountains toward the Pacific Ocean is the Mixteca Costa, which overlaps with the Costa Chica, an area that boasts a tropical climate and coastal plains. While these subregions varied substantially in topography, economy, and culture and were isolated from one another by difficult terrain, they shared a common yet multivariant language, Mixtec, and a predominantly Mixtec Indigenous population along with relatively smaller Triqui and Amuzgo populations. After Spanish conquest, this diverse population was joined by African-descended peoples, brought as slaves to work on the

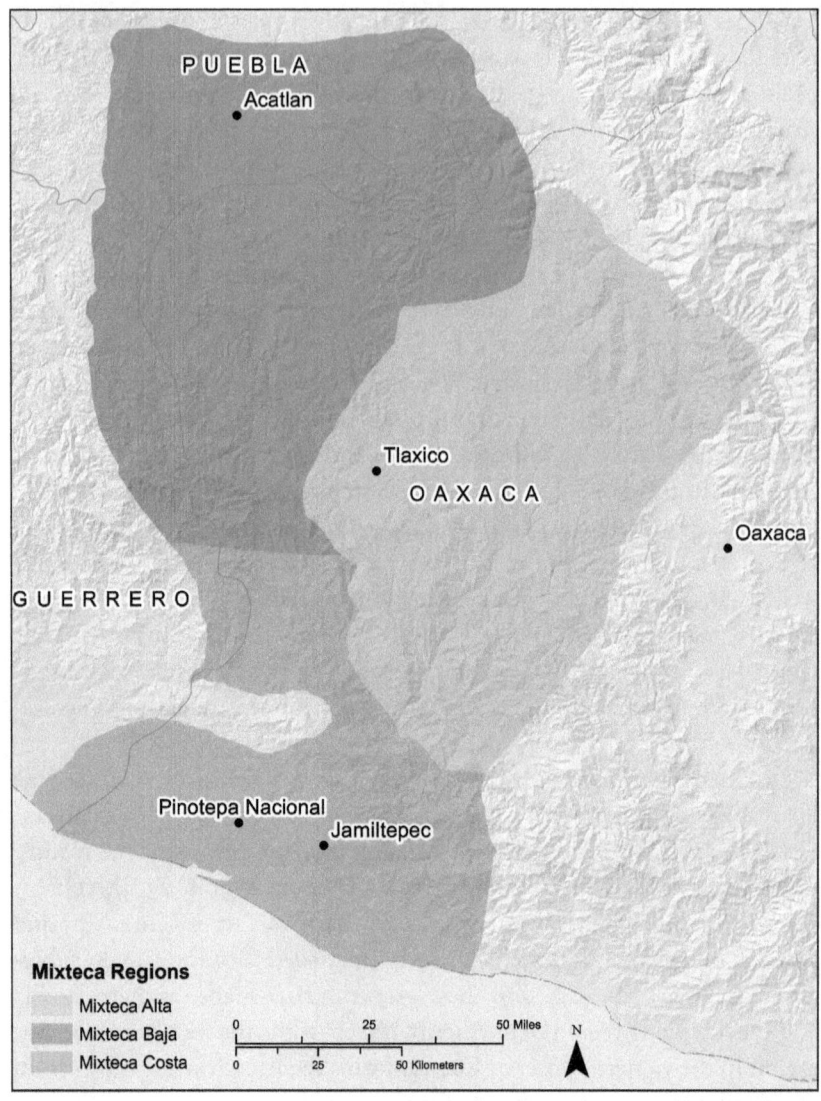

MAP 2. The three subregions of the Mixteca.

coast. Colonial rule in the Mixteca Alta left the Indigenous elite largely intact, with Spanish merchants relying on Indigenous systems of production of livestock and agriculture.[16] Oaxaca, then called Antequera, became one of the most prosperous provinces of New Spain because of the introduction of silk and most importantly cochineal, an insect used to make a crimson-colored dye.[17] Whereas other regions of colonial Spanish America experienced large-scale decline in Indigenous social organization from the intense labor demands placed on the populations, Antequera prospered because the sources of Spanish wealth were largely compatible with Indigenous social and economic organization.[18]

From París Chiquito to Postrevolutionary State Building

After independence from Spain, the municipalization of communities frequently left the internal structure of Native politics intact.[19] Nonetheless, over the course of the nineteenth century there was a transfer of power to elites in larger towns along with an increase in taxes on Indigenous communities.[20] One such town was Tlaxiaco. Located over 6,500 feet above sea level, Tlaxiaco became an increasingly powerful regional center of trade and commerce by midcentury, gaining *cabecera* or head town status in 1859.[21] At the end of the nineteenth century, in 1892, the Ferrocarril del Sur rail line was completed between Mexico City and Oaxaca City, its route connecting the eastern edge of the Mixteca at El Parían to national commerce. Tlaxiaco served as a hub of trade between the Pacific coast and the highlands, as well as areas north toward Mexico City. This position allowed for the growth of a mestizo, racially mixed, elite that represented itself as a cultured, European community, and the town came to be known as "París Chiquito," little Paris. These colonial and nineteenth-century experiences solidified a long history of local rule in the Mixteca, in which regional elites negotiated with outside authorities to maintain forms of local sovereignty. The region's social stratification was increasingly racialized, with smaller towns' Indigenous character equated with their relative poverty. Turn-of-the-century racialization in the Mixteca therefore contrasted dramatically with that which occurred in other areas of Oaxaca such as the Isthmus of Tehuantepec, where local elites frequently embraced and extolled Zapotec cultural forms as a point of regional pride. Later development thinkers implicitly drew on this history of racialization in the Mixteca in their assessments of its so-called underdevelopment.

By the beginning of the twentieth century, the Tlaxiaco merchant elite operated within a constellation of rural communities that retained their communal lands. While demands for the redistribution of privatized land fueled the 1910 Revolution nationally, the persistence of communal landholding in the Mixteca resulted in a relative absence of demands for agrarian reform. However, the political cleavages produced by the Revolution along with the intervention of multiple revolutionary armies shaped Oaxaca nonetheless. As President Venustiano Carranza (1915–20) and his Constitutionalist forces attempted to centralize power, their presence in the state sparked local opposition. This gave rise to the sovereignty movement, led by Governor José Inés Dávila, which declared its opposition to the Constitutionalist regime and asserted Oaxacan sovereignty. The movement engaged in multiple battles, including on the Isthmus of Tehuantepec and in the state capital. Governor Dávila eventually moved the state government into the mountains, where the movement enjoyed more support and could wage a guerrilla struggle against Carranza's forces. Dávila set up his provisional government in Tlaxiaco. This created large-scale instability in the region, as battles between the sovereignty movement and their opponents led to multiple sackings and occupations of the city.[22] In 1920, federal authorities and the movement leadership agreed to a negotiated settlement, but it was not until 1925, when Governor Genaro Vásquez consolidated his control over the state, that Tlaxiaco gained a semblance of stability.

During the postrevolutionary period, both state and national political authorities instituted a series of reforms in the Mixteca. State officials expanded primary education throughout the 1930s, including the creation of an *internado indígena*, an Indigenous boarding school, in Chalcatongo, due south of Tlaxiaco. State ministries' finances were precarious at best, and their inability to pay teachers on time resulted in a 1937 strike. This strike anticipated a move toward the federalization of education in the state, in which federal authorities contributed to teacher salaries.[23] President Lázaro Cárdenas's 1938 visit to the region in turn highlighted the increasing presence of federal authority in the Mixteca Alta. Cárdenas toured the entire republic proclaiming his apparent affection for the region and kept a vacation home in the area, leading some to refer to the region as "la Mixteca de Cárdenas."[24]

Not everyone in the Mixteca Alta was a fan of Cárdenas and postrevolutionary reform. For Tlaxiaco merchants, the violence of the Revolution and subsequent federal intervention coincided with their own declining position. Indeed, the provincial capital was one of the few towns in the country to build a monument to the former dictator Porfirio Díaz (1876–1911). This move reflected the provincial elite's nostalgia for a bygone era.

Into the 1940s, stark racial divides persisted, even as the Indigenous majority was the beneficiary of some federal and state reforms. Local Catholic officials synthesized a conservative critique of the Revolution and postrevolutionary reform. With deep roots in the Mixteca, the church skillfully adapted itself to local culture and language. The clergy opposed the expansion of primary education because of what they viewed as atheistic and socialist education models. Conflicts over the expansion of federal schools often revolved around questions of local governance and land tenure. This was the case during a violent conflict over control of the Tlaxiaco municipal government in which a Chalcatongo school director supported a particular *agrarista* faction.[25] While the Mixteca Alta did not witness the large-scale violence of the Cristero War (1926–29) in western Mexico, there was religious-fueled violence.[26] A seminary in Huajuapan de León, northeast of Tlaxiaco, trained local priests and fostered an insurgent Catholicism that persisted well beyond the postrevolutionary period. This conservative Catholic opposition in the Mixteca is addressed in chapter 2.

By the 1950s, the commercial role of Tlaxiaco, while not necessarily diminished, had undergone significant changes. With the growing nationalization of the economy through extension of roads and rail lines, local light industries such as soda and candle production suffered from national competition. A series of antimony mines near Tlaxiaco was one of the few profitable industries. Begun in 1935, production at the Tejocotes mine surged during World War II, as antimony was an important alloy in the production of munitions.[27] The mine attracted people from across the Mixteca Alta, employing a little over 1,500 workers. Miners' wages could be as high as eight to ten pesos a day, a stark contrast to the daily minimum of two or two and half pesos. Their spending power increased consumer demand in Tlaxiaco. However, with the end of the war came a collapse of regional commerce. In addition to fluctuating international demand, the other challenge for the mining industry was transportation. Any goods bound for export had to first be transported by mule train roughly sixty-two miles through the mountains to El Parían before being loaded on trains.

Despite the inroads of commercial products produced in Mexico City and Puebla and the boom-and-bust mining economy, Tlaxiaco's market continued to be the hub of the region's economy, with outlying communities coming in for the Saturday *tianguis* or market. The town center achieved limited electrification in 1951, which facilitated commercial activity into the early evening.[28] The outlying communities brought a host of products for trade and sale, ranging from flowers, fruits and vegetables, clay pottery, and furniture to firewood and charcoal. With the proceeds from their sales families bought corn, sugar, and liquor, among other products. Unfortunately, these rural families were sometimes exploited arbitrarily on their way to the market by local *delegados forestales*, forestry officials who might steal their goods or fine them. These officials were nominally charged with policing the incipient timber industry but frequently targeted small-scale producers whose products may or may not have violated local forestry norms.[29]

Much of the population continued to rely on small-scale agriculture for subsistence. Given the retention of communal lands, less than 10 percent of Mixteca Alta land was classified as *ejidal*, or agrarian reform land. Yet the continued existence of communal lands masked an increasing level of de facto privatization. In many cases, communal lands were managed privately. Where communal lands were shared or held by smallholders they were often of poor quality.[30] Infrequent rainfall and poor soil quality meant little land was agriculturally profitable. What resulted from communal landholding in the Mixteca Alta was thus a sharing of poverty, not collective empowerment. Among the more common forms of land tenure was *la aparecería* or *medianería*, as it was also called, a system in which landless campesinos rented others' land by paying the landowner half of the harvest.[31] In addition, violent conflicts and boundary disputes between neighboring communities were common features of regional politics.[32] The poor quality of land, its unequal distribution, and the conflicts these engendered were a key focus of subsequent regional development studies.

Despite the challenges of the land, Mixteca Alta communities produced a variety of crops for self-consumption, local trade, and sale. Corn was a regional staple, planted in the spring months, harvested in the early fall, and sold in *cajones*, a unit of roughly five liters. While there were areas of irrigated agriculture, most corn production was small scale and involved the stick-and-hole method for planting. Many Mixteca communities also engaged in palm production, using dried palm leaves to weave everything from floor mats to sombreros. These products garnered relatively low prices at the market despite the time-intensive labor involved. In many towns, men and women could be seen weaving palm while they went about other daily work. In contrast, coffee *fincas* (plantations), concentrated south of Tlaxiaco near the town of Putla Villa de Guerrero, were a lucrative industry.³³ The southwest-facing mountainsides received moisture from the Pacific Ocean and sat at a high elevation, making them an ideal setting for the crop. Men from surrounding towns traveled to the fincas seasonally to work the harvests. In the town of Santiago Nuyoó, INI anthropologists described how local coffee workers were kept in debt to the Compañía Exportadora e Importadora Mexicana, the state agency that facilitated coffee exportation.³⁴ Coffee workers protested and organized strikes against such conditions. *Rurales estatales*, the state police, repressed such labor organizing. These were just some of the conditions that indigenista intellectuals encountered when they arrived in the Mixteca Alta at midcentury.

Regional Approaches to Indigenous Inequality

The de la Peña and Marroquín reports were part of a longer tradition of regional studies of Indigenous Mexico. As early as 1922, Manuel Gamio combined a historical investigation of pre-Hispanic ruins, with an ethnographic approach to the contemporary Indigenous population of Teotihuacan, in the valley of Mexico. This study became a touchstone in indigenista thinking. As an applied anthropologist, Gamio developed a comprehensive analysis that would offer informed policy implications. Later studies led by Lucio Mendieta y Nuñez, one of the founders of Mexican sociology, similarly employed this kind of holistic approach. Mendieta y Nuñez oversaw research teams that developed extensive studies of the Purépecha people of Michoacán, then termed Tarascos, as well as the Zapotec population of the state of Oaxaca. In a 1938 speech in Mexico City, Mendieta y Nuñez declared that demographic heterogeneity—that is, Indigenous difference—was the "fundamental problem" of Mexico.³⁵

One of the most culturally and linguistically diverse states in the republic, as well as the site of major pre-Hispanic population centers, Oaxaca was of particular interest to indigenista intellectuals and the field of anthropology.³⁶ Bronislaw Malinowski, a key figure in the development of anthropology as a discipline, conducted a study of Oaxaca's regional market system in early 1940. Malinowski and his Mexican collaborator, the anthropologist Julio de la Fuente, who would go on to become a major figure in Indigenous development, examined the function of the state's major and minor markets in the local culture and economy. The Malinowski and de la Fuente study, published in 1957, emphasized the role of a dominating central market. For the authors, Oaxacan markets displayed the social ties

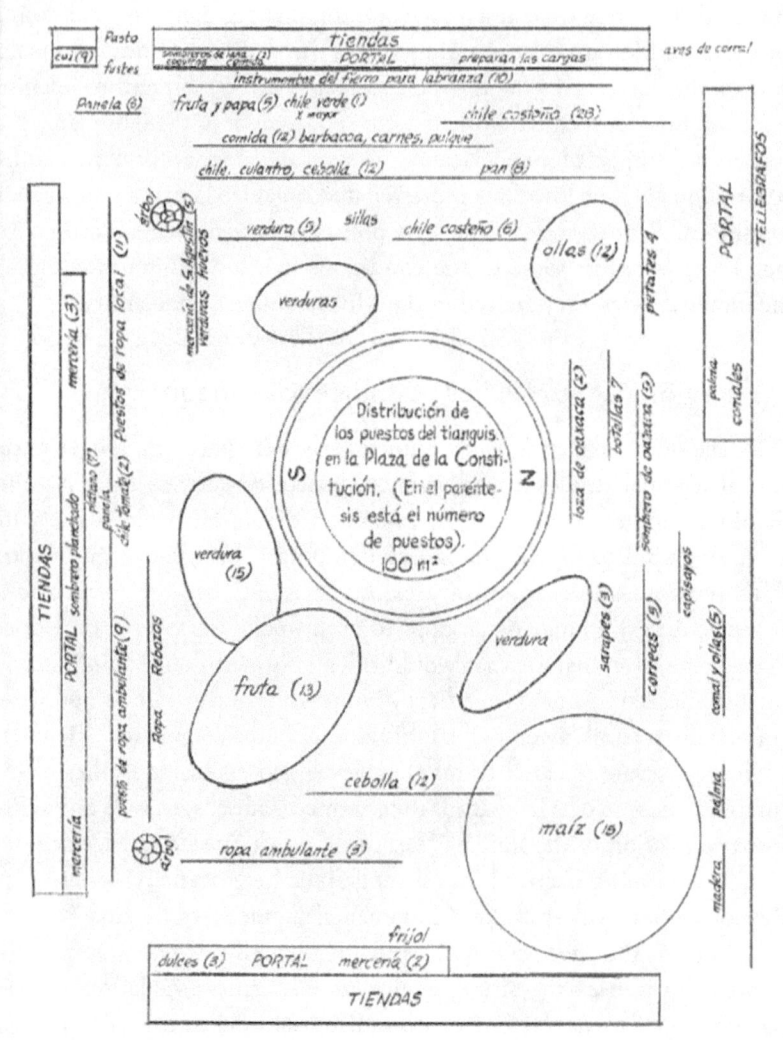

FIGURE 6. Diagram of the Tlaxiaco Saturday regional market. Alejandro Marroquín argued that it was here where elites and market vendors exploited the Indigenous population. *Source:* Alejandro Marroquín, *La ciudad mercado (Tlaxiaco)* (Mexico: UNAM, 1957).

of Indigenous Mexico—*trueque*, noncash trade, and interethnic relations.[37] Malinowski died in 1942, but his collaborative work in Oaxaca shaped the thinking of generations of anthropologists. Indeed, Marroquín's study of Tlaxiaco's regional market drew explicitly from the model Malinowski and de la Fuente had set out.

These midcentury studies sit at the nexus of two intellectual traditions: a Mexican tradition that emphasized rural and agrarian reform while centering Indigenous peoples and a post–World War II global trend that emphasized the modernization of "unintegrated" regions.[38] During this period, scholars and students working out of Mexico City's Escuela Nacional de Antropología e Historia (ENAH) developed regional diagnostics of Indigenous populations throughout the country. Prior to the establishment of the first-ever INI Coordinating Center in the state of Chiapas, researchers organized comprehensive studies of the areas surrounding San Juan Chamula and San Cristóbal de las Casas. In Oaxaca, federal authorities commissioned studies of the northeast area of the state, where two massive dam projects were planned that would involve the resettlement of the predominantly Mazatec population.[39] Anthropologists planned and led these projects with the goal of facilitating a modernization of Indigenous peoples while safeguarding elements of their culture and traditional practices deemed positive.

The regional studies and comprehensive development projects from this period were not exclusive to Mexico. Perhaps the most well-known example of Indigenous development efforts in Latin America was the Cornell Peru Project (1952–66). Begun during the same years as the INI's inauguration of its coordinating centers in Chiapas, Chihuahua, and Oaxaca, the Cornell initiative purchased a hacienda in the Peruvian highland community of Vicos to establish a pilot program for the modernization of the local population. Focused on the transformation of health, education, and agriculture, the experiment at Vicos illustrated well the intersection of indigenista thinking and modernization-theory development as Peruvian intellectuals and US anthropologists collaborated on the internationally financed project.[40] The INI's development work reflected similar tensions between nationalist, indigenista traditions and modernization paradigms, though both sought the transformation of populations deemed incompatible with modern lifeways.

Of the two major studies of the Mixteca, the first was led by Moisés de la Peña, at the time a respected Mexican economist and one of the first graduates of the Universidad Nacional Autónoma de México (UNAM) economics program. De la Peña fell squarely in the "Cardenista developmentalist wing of the revolution."[41] His research focused on questions of land distribution, and over the course of the 1940s de la Peña conducted regional studies in various states, including Chihuahua, Campeche, and Veracruz. His Mixteca study, published by the INI in 1950, was conducted by a team of six researchers that included economists, engineers, and one ethnologist. The Salvadoran anthropologist Alejandro Marroquín led the second study. Born in San Salvador in 1911, Marroquín was forced to flee his country in 1937 because of political persecution. A leftist radical, he found refuge in Cardenista Mexico and became a researcher at the ENAH in Mexico City. His study focused on the preponderant role of the Tlaxiaco weekly market in the regional economy.[42] The two lead authors had different intellectual and professional trajectories, but they agreed on the importance of progressive nationalism and agrarian reform. Their analyses focused on reframing a region often understood by outsiders as "hostile" and "inhospitable." In this regard, they were the archetypal high modernist intellectuals. But to paint them as merely high modernists would miss the long-standing Mexican traditions of agrarian reform and indigenista discourse that were an integral part of their work. Indeed, Gonzalo Aguirre Beltrán ascribed the INI's development work in the Mixteca as stemming from Alfonso Caso's archaeological excavations in the region during the 1930s.[43]

Citing the quality of the land, existing patterns of land tenure, and demographic growth, the de la Peña and the Marroquín studies both embraced the concept of "overpopulation" in diagnosing the region's problems. Each study also emphasized poor soil quality in the Mixteca Alta and underscored that while forms of communal property persisted, they did little to empower the local population. Where large landholding did exist, particularly on the coast, de la Peña listed the names and assets of property owners and wealthy families.[44] This inventory anticipated his emphasis on the need for further land redistribution. He framed the coast as rich in land, though that land was concentrated in the hands of a few. In contrast, he framed the highlands as too poor in land to sustain a growing population and thus as "overpopulated." The material conditions of the Alta consequently justified a federal policy of *colonización dirigida*, the voluntary resettlement of parts of the highland population to the coast. (That experiment is examined in chapter 3.) The authors' agreement on the overpopulated nature of the region reflected the reality of high birth rates in Mexico as well as global social scientific trends. Overpopulation as a concept had gained traction at midcentury, as state planners framed natural resources, industry, and populations as independent variables in their grand designs.

According to de la Peña and Marroquín, the material realities of the Alta facilitated the large-scale exploitation of the predominantly rural and Indigenous population by regional elites, especially intermediaries of various stripes who gained their profits from commerce and trade. In his ethnographic description of the weekly Saturday market, Marroquín labeled Tlaxiaco a "commercial emporium." His conclusions were straightforward: capital accumulation in Tlaxiaco was possible only through commerce; agricultural and industrial production were not profitable; and the Tlaxiaco economy was "parasitic" in nature, exploiting the Indigenous workforce.[45] Further, Marroquín insisted that the well-known *regateo* or bargaining at the market facilitated exploitation, providing examples of Indigenous consumers exploited through commercial transactions. De la Peña, for his part, identified the region's mining industry as an agent of exploitation, arguing that unless the industry was nationalized and placed under federal control, it would provide little benefit for the region's inhabitants and would continue to exhibit what he described as "starkly colonial characteristics."[46] Intermediaries also played an exploitative role in the region's coffee and timber industries. *Coyotes*, intermediaries in the coffee industry, kept coffee workers indebted through buying low and selling high, and timber companies and the aforementioned *delegados forestales* variously swindled or fined forest communities. With important exceptions, discussed at the end of this chapter, these studies emphasized the regional sources of "underdevelopment."

De la Peña and Marroquín understood inequality and exploitation in the Mixteca Alta as falling along racial lines. While neither employed explicit categories of race or racialization, they understood the majority of the population to be Indigenous and frequently identified intermediaries, the agents of Indigenous exploitation, as mestizo. They invoked the region's pre-Hispanic past both as a point of departure for indigenista development and as a factor shaping contemporary economic and social conditions. While they singled out certain persistent features of the pre-Hispanic past for praise—de la Peña highlighted the region's agricultural terracing as a practice worth preserving—they more often presented the legacy of the pre-Hispanic past as a degraded present. While other studies by de la Peña focused on entire states, his study of the Mixteca focused on an Indigenous region overlapping three neighboring states.[47] He was therefore compelled to define what exactly constituted "the Indian." As he put it, "The Indian is the transitional, the irredeemable, the culturally most backward and the most economically and culturally oppressed."[48] In this framing, Indigenous cultural practices were side effects of a colonial process, something to be overcome. Writing from Tlaxiaco, ten years after the arrival of the INI, Fernando Benítez, a prominent journalist, articulated a similar version of this idea. As he sympathetically characterized the INI's development work, Benítez wrote: "What today is the life of the descendants of those princes, priests, warriors, artists and *campesinos*, is not any less surprising. Today's Mixtecs—more than half a million—remain frozen in time, not necessarily in the ancient past but rather in the particular conditions created by the conquest."[49] In these constructions, rooted in midcentury modernization projects, indigeneity was colonial, a degraded cultural form whose roots lay in the conquest of the Americas. The colonial legacy was central to their definition of their Indigenous subjects.

The most significant of these characteristics, and the one that emerged as the primary marker to evaluate indigeneity, was language practice. De la Peña argued that the most distinctive quality of the Indigenous population was "the use of, if only in the home, their maternal tongue, even if one also speaks Spanish."[50] Along these simplistic lines of argument, de la Peña equated uplift of the Indian with ceasing to be Indian, choosing not to speak one's native language. This was an indigenista politics with little romanticizing of Indigenous language. For some, the assumption was as simple an equation as *language equals nation*. For example, if there was a decline in the number of Mixtec speakers, as de la Peña attempted to demonstrate through census data, then the region was more modern, with an increase in the number of "campesinos mexicanos," an admirable and politically salient category to be placed in.[51]

The de la Peña study collected a host of statistics related to language use and literacy rates. It mapped the region linguistically, finding monolingual communities in isolated and mountainous areas and increased levels of bilingualism in larger towns and municipalities. De la Peña emphasized that bilingualism and the process he termed *mexicanización* or *castellanización* (broadly, "Hispanicization" or "modernization") spread in response to commerce and migration rather than the formal education system, an implicit acknowledgment of the weakness of federal education efforts.[52] He insisted that the region's indigeneity was a transitory phase and an impediment to the social justice promised by agrarian reform. What he and Marroquín ultimately focused on, despite their positive invocations of pre-Hispanic terracing and artistry, was the need to overcome the indigeneity of the region. How was this to be accomplished? By teaching the Spanish language. They equated Indigenous language use with cultural backwardness, in keeping with the frequent comment among state planners that the people "do not know the language of Cervantes."[53] The statistics of language use, though probably inaccurate, thus could quantify the problem and, by demonstrating a declining population of monolingual Indigenous language speakers, could show that the state was making headway in solving it. While Gonzalo Aguirre Beltrán, who wrote the introduction to Marroquín's study, in subsequent years offered platitudes about the need to respect Indigenous languages, he oversaw a state project that identified language practices as one of the defining metrics for "national integration" and progress.[54] Thus these studies reflected the double bind of indigenista policy, casting Indigenous people as a problem while also serving as the social scientific justification for concrete development programs.

The Arrival of the Indigenistas

The Instituto Nacional Indigenista officially arrived in the Mixteca Alta in the spring of 1954. The Centro Coordinador Indigenista de la Mixteca Alta (CCIMA) opened its doors on May 4 of that year in a Porfirian mansion just off Tlaxiaco's main plaza. The building's previous tenant, one of the region's mining companies, had shuttered its offices after the postwar collapse of demand for its product.[55] Located across the street from the storied Hotel Colón, which had weathered the tumult of the 1910 Revolution, federal officials set up shop precisely where de la Peña and Marroquín identified the nexus of Indigenous exploitation in the area. The merchants and mestizo elite, along with the priests of Tlaxiaco, were the development agency's closest neighbors. Local authorities no doubt viewed the arrival of the indigenistas with ambivalence, for they represented an opportunity, in terms of access to federal resources and officials, but also a threat to their own authority in the region. For indigenista officials, their offices were a

FIGURE 7. INI director Alfonso Caso visiting the Centro Coordinador Indigenista de la Mixteca Alta in 1954.
Source: Instituto Nacional de los Pueblos Indígenas, Fototeca Nacho López, Julio de la Fuente, 1955.

convenience, as the location allowed them access to the broader region as well as communication networks to Mexico City.

The INI's strategy in the Mixteca relied on a two-pronged approach involving the creation of coordinating centers in the Mixteca Alta and on the Oaxacan coast. They set up the coastal center in Jamiltepec, roughly 125 miles due south of the Tlaxiaco offices.[56] This strategy was based on the premise of an overpopulated highlands and a materially abundant and underpopulated coastal region. Many of the federal staff who arrived in Tlaxiaco to establish the new center had visited and trained at the INI's Chiapas offices.[57] By sharing staff and training among the various regional centers, the federal agency formalized its development subject. Officials generalized from their varied experiences to hone effective national policy. The Tlaxiaco staff organized a series of administrative sections to systematize the INI's work in the region, including public health, education, agriculture, and economic planning. The local CCIMA director, at the time Pablo Velásquez Gallardo, coordinated the distinct sections. Velásquez launched the INI's work with a series of ethnographic trips, conducted with the Peruvian anthropologist Carlos Incháustegui. Their subsequent reports marked a departure from de la Peña's framing of indigeneity but confirmed his and Marroquín's analysis regarding the origins of Indigenous inequality in the region.

In February of 1954, Velásquez and Incháustegui journeyed south of Tlaxiaco on horseback, visiting the other major town in the district, Chalcatongo, or "Chalca," as locals call it. Along the way, the anthropologists met with local authorities and collected basic health, education, and demographic data. On the nineteen-day trip they visited Ocotepec, Nuyoó, Santa María Yucuhiti, and other nearby communities. Velásquez and Incháustegui's dress, equipment, and status as federal employees conferred upon them a certain respect upon their arrival in each town. No doubt Velásquez would have been referred to as "Don" or "licenciado" while visiting these communities. However, these encounters did not fit a simple dichotomy of state authorities versus Indigenous communities. Velásquez himself was from the state of Michoacán and was bilingual in his native Purépecha and Spanish. Born in 1920, he had served as a guide and translator for foreign researchers involved in the Proyecto Tarasco, created by the exiled US linguist Morris Swadesh.[58] With the help of those connections, Velásquez visited Berkeley in 1943 and took classes at the University of California.[59] He later enrolled in the ENAH in Mexico City, where he defended his thesis in 1950, just a few years before his assignment in the Mixteca Alta.[60]

Perhaps because of this training, Velásquez framed the Mixteca as part of a broader hemispheric constellation of Native practices and dilemmas. In their reports, he and Incháustegui compared the large houses of Chicahuaxtla with the communal houses common in the Brazilian Amazon. They associated the town church of Santa María Cuquila with the architecture of the Pueblo Indians of New Mexico.[61] In Las Huertas, a ranchería near San Juan Numi, the anthropologists described the woolen belts of the local women as being like those found in the Peruvian Andes.

And Velásquez speculated that the round domestic structures in the coffee-growing region of Nuyoó resembled African architecture.[62] The anthropologists sought to understand the specificity of the Mixteca Alta through these comparisons to other regions marked as Indigenous in the Americas.

Their invocation of African architecture was not incidental. As noted previously, African-descended peoples lived on the Pacific coast. In his introduction to the Marroquín study, Gonzalo Aguirre Beltrán, a pioneer of studies on Afro-Mexicans, noted that "their influence on the types of housing and other manifestations of material and psychic culture should not be overlooked when seeking adequate solutions to the vital problems of the Mixtecas."[63] Despite this injunction, the Marroquín study itself made no reference to the Afro-Mexican population or its attendant social needs. De la Peña, who spent more time assessing the coast, acknowledged the presence of an African-descended population and defended it against popular accusations of laziness.[64] But as in much indigenista discourse of the time, this issue was given no more than a passing mention. In the coming decades, the INI's lack of attention to coastal communities of African descent would contribute to violent racialized conflicts in the region.

In a report to INI director Alfonso Caso, Velásquez depicted the highlands as an agriculturally poor region whose inhabitants lived in unhealthy and unhygienic conditions. Noting the low productivity of the soil, he described local agriculture as a mere "cultural tradition," as opposed to a productive, self-sustaining activity, and he observed that many were therefore compelled to travel for seasonal work in the coffee-growing fincas near Putla. This *golondrina* or swallow migration followed the harvest cycle, with workers returning home to celebrate Día de los Muertos. Highland communities also traveled to the neighboring state of Veracruz to work the sugar harvests. To underscore their material impoverishment, the anthropologist noted the inverse relationship between the minimum wage and the rising cost of corn. In addition, large portions of the population suffered from yellow fever and lice infestation, whose remedy was the aforementioned DDT. Velásquez complained that people slept side by side with domestic animals and that in certain communities "public defecation is common."[65] He contrasted this sick and unhygienic population with Mixtec communities on the coast, who he said were cleaner and healthier because of access to better food and water.

According to Velásquez and Incháustegui, the highland population endured not only material privation but also social conflict and exploitation by local elites and authorities. In the town of Nuyoó, the anthropologists described how coffee workers were kept in debt, finishing their description with "As is well known, to date, there is no better beast of burden than man himself."[66] In their report, they suggested that the INI intervene to avoid a violent clash between coffee workers and the *rurales estatales*. They attributed such clashes and boundary disputes in the region to population growth's increased pressure on the land.[67] Velásquez commented that the *rurales estatales*, led by Isauro Zafra, often resolved such disputes with violent repression.[68] According to Velásquez, Zafra's *pistoleros* were the sole arbiter of conflict in Mixteca Alta, indiscriminately detaining Indigenous men and holding them without cause.

Velásquez also understood many of the conflicts in the Mixteca as racialized. During one of his early trips, the young anthropologist had a confrontation with a hotel owner in the town of Putla. Located southwest of Tlaxiaco, Putla served as an important hub of trade between the highlands and the coast. *Arrieros*, mule train drivers, used the town as the halfway point in their trips from one region to the other. The municipality even boasted an airstrip used by commercial interests and government agencies. Given its proximity to Triqui communities, Velásquez had traveled to Putla with a Triqui guide. When he attempted to reserve two rooms, the hotel owner refused service to his guide. Enraged, Velásquez wrote Caso directly, seeking his superior's support in making an official complaint. In the letter, he denounced what he described as "intense racial discrimination" in the major towns of the Mixteca.[69] He also confirmed Marroquín's depiction of discrimination by Tlaxiaco's merchant elite against the surrounding population.

Racialization in the Mixteca was frequently based on one's language abilities. Those who were monolingual in Indigenous languages or spoke Spanish with a strong accent were regularly marked as Indigenous. Velásquez was far more adept at noting the linguistic diversity of the region than other development officials. In addition to acknowledging the substantial Triqui-speaking population, he noted the presence of "Mexicano," Nahuatl-speaking communities, as well as speakers of Tacuate, a variant of Mixtec near the district of Jamiltepec. When Velásquez arrived in some towns, he was unable to locate anyone who admitted proficiency in Spanish. In other cases, town authorities claimed to be the only ones fluent in Spanish. Acknowledging one's bilingualism was frequently a strategic choice. Those who were bilingual might choose to represent themselves as monolingual if they desired to avoid communication with outsiders, in this case the government anthropologist. Velásquez's detailed and sympathetic treatment of the Mixteca's linguistic diversity perhaps reflected his own bilingualism in Spanish and Purépecha, though this goes unmentioned in any official reports.

Over the course of their three trips, Velásquez and Incháustegui depicted a stark contrast between the highlands and the coast. They underscored the distinct economic possibilities of each region and stressed the coast's economic potential through government investment. They viewed the coastal plains as ripe for commercial agriculture and livestock production. They contrasted divergent health and hygiene realities of the two subregions, depicting the highland population as sick and poorly fed. These economic and public health assessments were more than straightforward socioeconomic depictions. While seasonal migration testified to the material hardships of the highlands, these constructions drew on existing but contingent inequalities to naturalize an impoverished condition.[70] The Alta's apparent lack of economic potential conferred backwardness and ill health on the region, while conversely the coast's agricultural potential conferred health and progress. This is not to deny the stark differences that existed between the two regions but rather to underscore how development discourses risked naturalizing such differences. The very frameworks of these studies, which presupposed internal or more specifically regional barriers to development, attributed the poverty of the region to indigeneity, rather than to economic and structural dynamics that transcended region.

Conclusion

The midcentury regional studies and INI anthropological reports were far from a unified discourse. De la Peña treated indigeneity as a transitory phase, a colonial legacy that would fade with the modernization of the economy and agrarian reform. Velásquez, in contrast, openly described racialized exploitation in the Mixteca. Both aimed to combat exploitation and Indigenous inequality. The hotel incident, in which Velásquez's Triqui guide was denied admittance, speaks to the cultural understandings that undergird race and racialization in Mexico. Both Velásquez and his guide spoke an Indigenous language, Purépecha and Triqui respectively. Nonetheless it was the guide who was denied lodging. Here Velásquez's indigeneity, his community origin and fluency in Purépecha, was tempered by his educational background and federal affiliation. His Triqui guide, without such education or status, was subject to discrimination. Language practice was thus a key site of racialization.

The indigenista intellectuals profiled in this chapter sympathized with the plight of those living in the Mixteca Alta. They hoped to facilitate the material advancement of the region and the empowerment of its population. They used language practices as a marker for a host of social behaviors and thus were enthusiasts for Spanish language acquisition. For Marroquín, Spanish proficiency was a weapon that Indigenous producers could wield in their negotiations with mestizo merchants. While indigenistas might not have viewed the acquisition of Spanish as necessarily implying the destruction of Mixtec, their emphasis on Indigenous difference as a factor in the region's lack of development nonetheless linked indigeneity with material impoverishment.[71] If language was to be overcome, then a significant part of one's being was to be overcome.[72] Certain populations were asked to give up part of themselves and "become campesinos" in exchange for the benefits of a state project.

These constructions typify the double bind of indigenista development, which ostensibly valorized Indigenous cultures while simultaneously presenting them as a problem to be overcome. In the case of the development discourses directed toward the Mixteca Alta, they also risked naturalizing existing inequalities, whether between the highlands and the Pacific coast or between the highlands and other more industrialized regions of Mexico, by attributing these to the Indigenous character of the population. The more radical conclusions of the de la Peña and Marroquín studies, which highlighted not merely the role of regional intermediaries but broader forces shaping the region, disappeared in later development practice. De la Peña's framing of the mining industry as colonialist, indeed his call for it to be nationalized, never gained a serious hearing in subsequent development work. Nor was much institutional attention given to Marroquín's observation that the increasing integration of the region, not its marginalization or isolation, actually contributed to the decline of local industries. These examples pointed to national and international forces at work in shaping the "underdevelopment" of the region and did not fit with the establishment emphasis on regional barriers to national development. Rather than confront these broader forces, the INI focused on initiatives to transform the local population, through public health and educational reform. The INI's work in the neighboring state of Chiapas reflected similar compromises in the institute's ability to confront powerful interests that threatened Indigenous well-being.[73] Indigenista efforts were therefore not unlike other public policies that emphasized changing the behavior of the poor rather than confronting structural factors at the root of inequality. That the more radical conclusions of these studies were ignored in subsequent development policy confirms critiques that underscore the inherent limitations and depoliticizing nature of state-led development.[74]

Yet to emphasize only the way development discourses risked naturalizing existing inequalities would be to tell a partial history of indigenista policy. The establishment of a federal agency charged with Indigenous uplift in Tlaxiaco had material consequences for the region, as did indigenista efforts in other areas of Mexico and indeed the Americas.[75] The INI's establishment of an official presence in the Mixteca Alta empowered indigenista professionals, in this case a Purépecha anthropologist who became an authority in the region, commanded a small but significant budget, and had a direct line of communication with cabinet-level officials. The INI competed with and challenged local authorities, including church officials, merchants, state education officials, and rural police. The cleavages produced by the arrival of federal attention will be highlighted in the following chapter, which describes the INI's effort to expand and improve primary school education services in the Mixteca through a pilot project of bilingual radio broadcasts in Spanish and Mixtec.

2

"Was It God or the Devil?"
Bilingual Radio Schools and Cold War Catholicism

> The cultural radio station XEINI transmits its daily educational program to the Mixteca Alta radio education schools on the shortwave frequency 49 m/ 6145 kHz... To begin our work we offer a very good morning to all the teachers and students listening.
> —Centro Coordinador Indigenista de la Mixteca Alta[1]

IN 1958, in the Mixteca Alta town of Santiago Yosondúa, an INI auxiliary radio teacher, Isaías Sánchez López, gathered children and their parents for a Spanish literacy lesson. Sánchez was part of a pilot program that broadcast educational programming over shortwave radio to remote communities. The use of radio broadcasts was not new to educational efforts in the Americas. Governments throughout the hemisphere had pioneered educational broadcasting in the first decades of the century, and the pilot program was part of a renewed federal effort to expand education in rural regions.[2] But what set the program apart from its predecessors was its use of Mixtec on the radio. A "broadcasting teacher," transmitting from the district capital of Tlaxiaco, conducted literacy and arithmetic lessons in Spanish and Mixtec. During the first lesson, the children were astonished to hear their native language on the radio. And as Sánchez recounted, their parents, who had gathered to observe the lesson, were even more confounded. "They didn't understand what the radio was. Some said it was God, because the sound traveled over the air, and others that it was the devil . . . but what most caught their attention was that it was Mixtec. The people couldn't believe it. They knew the radio was associated with *gente de razón*, so why was it speaking Mixtec? It seemed strange to them. Why was the radio speaking Mixtec if it was not meant for poor people?"[3]

Why was the radio speaking "our poor language"? In rural Mexico, where colonial categories of *gente de razón* and *indios* continued to define daily life, the INI's use of radio technology and bilingual instruction challenged all those involved. Local education authorities, steeped in traditional Spanish literacy methods of rote repetition and prohibitions on Indigenous languages, confronted a new federal agency that advocated the use of bilingual instruction. Furthermore, many local parents viewed the acquisition of Spanish literacy as key to their children's advancement. Some were suspicious of the use of Mixtec in the classroom. As we have seen in the previous chapter, in Tlaxiaco the INI's arrival was controversial. The institute offered the benefit of federal attention and spending in the region, but the local merchant elite was weary of INI efforts to empower Indigenous communities. Local Catholic activists, with a long history of opposition to federal authority, viewed the agency's pilot radio school program through the lens of anticommunism.

The pilot program coincided with Adolfo López Mateos's presidential term (1958–64) and an intensification of Cold War politics. While Mexico has often been cast as an outlier in Cold War Latin America because of its relative political stability and close relationship to the United States, the political polarization and violence of the era nonetheless shaped the country profoundly. López Mateos's policies reflected the competing pressures of the moment, repressing several opposition movements while simultaneously initiating a host of progressive reforms. His government officially supported the 1959 Cuban Revolution.[4] Inspired by events on the island nation, the Mexican Left organized itself into a series of radical organizations, including the Movimiento de Liberación Nacional. In the south central state of Morelos, Ruben Jaramillo combined Mexican traditions of radical agrarianism with guerrilla warfare tactics similar to those of the Cuban Revolution. The president responded to these developments by conceding to popular pressure for change, distributing approximately eleven million hectares of land to small farmers across the republic, while using violent repression to put down more radical threats. Government forces killed Jaramillo in front of his family in 1962.[5] At midcentury, federal officials suppressed threats from the Left, putting down armed Jaramillistas and striking railroad workers and imprisoning the railroad workers' leader Demetrio Vallejo. As will become evident in this chapter, authorities also encountered pushback from a radicalized right-wing Catholic opposition.

The education sector was not immune to Cold War polarization. The president tapped the writer and politician Jaime Torres Bodet to lead the Secretaría de Educación Pública. This was Torres Bodet's second term as secretary of education; he had served previously from 1943 to 1946. Among his accomplishments during the López Mateos administration was the distribution of Mexico's first *textos gratuitos*, free textbooks, throughout the republic in 1960. While this period differed from the heady days of 1930s socialist education, reform still proved controversial.[6] The INI and increased federal presence in rural regions reignited conservative Catholic opposition. In 1962, the federal army put down an armed rebellion of Catholics in the Mixteca Baja, just north of Tlaxiaco.[7] This dynamic of the authorities successfully facing off threats from both the Left and the Right appears to confirm Peruvian writer Mario Vargas Llosa's famous description of the PRI as the "perfect dictatorship." The dynamics described below, however, suggest fissures within the ruling party as well as a profound inability of federal authorities to impose their will in rural regions.[8]

The INI's bilingual radio school program (1958–65) was a key component of its broader development efforts in the Mixteca Alta. It combined a technological solution for what INI authorities understood as regional "underdevelopment" with a linguistic one, pairing shortwave radio broadcasts with innovative bilingual instruction. That combination destabilized the assumptions held by many involved in the project regarding the relationship between indigeneity and modern technology. The pilot radio program was part of a longer tradition of experimentation with Indigenous language instruction in the Americas but also reflected a new enthusiasm for the possibilities radio technology offered as an instrument of modernization. The logistics of Indigenous language instruction in the Mixteca Alta were challenging. Foremost among them was the region's extreme linguistic diversity: the Mixtec language family contains numerous mutually unintelligible variants. Beyond Mixtec, the region's inhabitants speak variants of Triqui, Amuzgo, and Nahuatl, among others. Indeed, the station's call sign, XEINI, translates to "head" or "mountaintop" in Mixtec. And as a bilingual project, the program required bilingual personnel. Authorities contracted local youth on the basis of their indigeneity and bilingualism. This was a new phenomenon that would have unanticipated consequences. The program was discontinued in 1965, but its legacy endured throughout the professional trajectories of these youth, termed auxiliary teachers, who went on to be the earliest members of the Indigenous education sector.

Experimental Indigenous Education

Mexican experiments in Indigenous education began during the period of postrevolutionary reform. In 1926 the Casa del Estudiante Indígena, an Indigenous boarding school in Mexico City, was founded with the aim of transforming Indigenous students into fully assimilated, Spanish-speaking, modern citizens. In 1933, SEP officials inaugurated similar *internados indígenas*, Indigenous boarding schools, throughout the republic in an early institutional response to the depth of the country's linguistic and cultural diversity. In Oaxaca, federal officials set up two *internados*, one in Chalcatongo, south of Tlaxiaco, and the second in Ixtlán, in the Sierra Norte. Federal officials further expanded the boarding school system during the *sexenio* of President Lázaro Cárdenas.

The Casa del Estudiante Indígena employed the so-called direct method of Spanish language instruction and excluded the use of vernacular languages from the classroom, and so did most of the Indigenous boarding schools of the 1930s. But the seeming failure of the Casa del Estudiante Indígena (some 30 percent of its students ran away, were expelled, dropped out, or failed to complete their coursework) and its closure after seven years of operation led to consideration of more pluralist approaches to Indigenous difference.[9] Debates among education officials arose regarding how best to achieve a liberatory education for rural peoples and were informed by various currents of leftist politics and pedagogical theory. Notably, the US philosopher and pedagogue John Dewey visited Mexico during this period and shared and debated his theories with his Mexican counterparts.[10] A minority of officials, including Luis Chávez Orozco, influenced by Soviet theorizations of oppressed nationalities, favored instruction in Indigenous languages as a bridge to the acquisition of Spanish.[11] The SEP's educational radio station, XFX, which transmitted in Mexico City and the broader valley of Mexico, exemplifies the beginning of this shift. While XFX broadcast music deemed "civilizing," they did experiment with some Indigenous language broadcasts.[12]

Perhaps the most explicit call for linguistic pluralism came in 1939 at the Primera Asamblea de Filólogos y Lingüistas, where linguists and pedagogues argued for bilingual instruction not just as a bridge to Spanish but as an embrace of the inherent value and cultural knowledge embedded within those languages. The conference included notable figures in Mexican Indigenous policy, such as Othón de Mendizábal, Alfonso Caso, and

Rafael Ramírez.[13] The most prominent early bilingual pilot project was the Proyecto Tarasco. Implemented in the southwestern state of Michoacán from 1939 to 1941, this initiative involved collaboration between the SEP, US linguist Morris Swadesh, and the Summer Institute of Linguistics (SIL), a US Protestant missionary organization. The project broke with the direct method and instead promoted literacy in the native language, Purépecha, first, prior to Spanish instruction. The SIL helped design didactic materials in Purépecha. Discontinued in 1941, this early attempt at bilingual instruction demonstrates the deep internal divisions within indigenista policy.[14]

Governments throughout the Americas experimented with alternative models of Indigenous education. Another pilot project that addressed indigeneity was the Warisata School in Bolivia, created in the 1930s by educators and community members in the town of Warisata, northwest of La Paz. Involving the participation of the entire community of mainly Aymara speakers, "the *ayllu*-school" combined literacy instruction with agricultural education and communal labor, *minkas*. Its brief existence, for just two decades, underscores the insurgent nature of projects aimed at upending hierarchies of class and race. The Bolivian Revolution of 1952, which expanded educational services, displaced these more experimental projects with a focus on policies of *castellanización*, now narrowly defined as Spanish language instruction.[15]

Formal policies of Indigenous language instruction remained a minority current within indigenista and education circles in the first half of the century. But as the SEP expanded its rural school programs, it did recognize the country's diversity by incorporating particular local practices and traditions into its nationalist curriculum. At the same time, it emphasized the importance of Spanish language proficiency. Rafael Ramírez (1885–1959), the education official most associated with this trend, stressed the progressive quality of Spanish language acquisition for peasant justice and warned rural teachers to avoid the use of Indigenous languages in the classroom.[16] With the advent of the INI in 1948, experimental programs in bilingual instruction received a second wind.

The institute hired and trained members of the local population as education and development brokers, or *promotores bilingües*. This was a shift from the SEP practice of recruiting normal school–trained teachers from elsewhere to serve in remote areas. The institute justified its policy by emphasizing the need for personnel with Native language skills. These promoters employed their bilingualism to facilitate the institute's mission of "integrated" development. The experiments with bilingual development efforts had mixed outcomes. A generation of bilingual Tzetzil and Tzotzil Mayan promoters facilitated the agency's work in the neighboring state of Chiapas. And it was the INI bilingual hand puppet troupe, Teatro Petul, that succeeded in winning over the cooperation of local communities. Designed to entertain as well as educate, at times involving the participation of literary luminaries such as Rosario Castellanos, the Teatro Petul thrived as a bilingual vehicle for indigenista efforts. In contrast, the INI's bilingual instruction among the Mazatec-speaking population near the Papaloapan Dam project appears to have been short-lived, shut down by internal divisions among the staff.[17] In the Mixteca Alta, officials developed the pilot bilingual radio project in an effort to overcome a lack of fully trained teachers and to communicate with largely monolingual communities in far-off locales.

The INI relied on normal school–trained teachers from rural regions to head up their initial education reform efforts. In the Mixteca Alta, the institute tapped Ramón Hernández López (1923–2015), from the town of San Agustín Tlacotepec, to lead their work. As a child, Hernández had attended the nearby Chalcatongo boarding school. Having studied music, he obtained a scholarship to continue his education in Mexico City, completing secondary school at the Secundaria Técnica Industrial, "Rafael Dondé." There in the nation's capital in 1946 he and other youth formed the Confederación Nacional de Jóvenes Indígenas (CNJI), a national organization of Indigenous youth who advocated for their representation within the ruling party. Many of the confederation's members were teachers (Hernández completed his normal school training in Oaxaca in 1948), and they were involved in a variety of leftist political organizing activities.[18] Members frequently defended the use of Indigenous languages in the classroom, and Hernández's graduating normal school thesis advocated the utility of bilingual instruction. Small in stature but large in personality, Hernández was a natural leader with deep ties to the Mixteca.

Prior to assuming responsibility for INI education efforts in the region, national leaders sent Hernández to observe the pilot coordinating center in San Cristóbal de las Casas, Chiapas. Upon his return to the Mixteca, he toured the region's schools and wrote an evaluation of the situation. Hernández noted that many communities had physical schools

FIGURE 8. Children in a rural classroom in the Mixtec Alta, ca. 1965.
Source: Instituto Nacional de los Pueblos Indígenas, Fototeca Nacho López.

but an insufficient number of qualified teachers. In addition, these schools rarely offered all six grades. Local Catholic activists, for their part, had often opposed federal schooling efforts and at times opposed the federal model of coeducation. During his tour, Hernández detailed the condition of the schools, numbers of children attending, gender ratios, and the students' language practices. He observed that schools had weak attendance during harvest season and that many families from rancherías sent their children to school for the week without formal sleeping arrangements and with little more than tortillas, salt, and chile for food.

Established in the late 1920s and 1930s, federal rural schools in the Mixteca formed part of the postrevolutionary government's crusading drive to bring literacy and social justice to the Mexican countryside. Rural schools in towns such as Chalcatongo and Yosondúa engaged in creative strategies of community theater, hygiene education, and agricultural education, in addition to antialcohol campaigns. Teachers also encouraged dispersed populations to move closer together in order to facilitate educational and modernizing reforms. Federal school inspector reports emphasized the alleged racial characteristics of students, describing monolingual communities as *mixtecos puros*, *raza mixteca*, or even *inditos*, little Indians.[19] Conflicts between communities and rural teachers involved issues of alcohol abuse, financial disagreements with municipal authorities, and, often, religion.

More far-flung communities still struggled to access the few federal schools in the area. To make up for a lack of normal school–trained teachers, communities informally employed literate locals in these schools, often referred to as municipal teachers. Those who had finished primary school were still very much a minority in the Mixteca Alta, and the completion of secondary school was a major achievement.[20] Hernández confirmed this dynamic in his reports and noted that while smaller rancherías and *agencias* lacked sufficient schools or teachers, certain communities had much stronger schools. For example, in the town of Cuanana, an *agencia* of Santiago Yosondúa, six teachers served the relatively small community. This was partly because the town had a tradition of migration to Mexico City, where relatives financially supported educational efforts in their hometown, but also Hernández speculated that educational authorities favored the area because a town local was serving as a federal deputy.[21]

Another reality of primary school education at the time was corporal punishment. Local teachers often meted out harsh penalties to students who spoke Mixtec in the classroom. While corporal punishment was a common practice in schooling at midcentury, it was harsher in rural, Indigenous regions. In San Juan Mixtepec, northwest of Tlaxiaco, one former student recounted how if a child was caught speaking Mixtec in the classroom, the teacher forced the entire class to participate in spanking the offending student. Another technique involved a kind of stress position, in which students were forced to kneel on sand at the front of the classroom, facing their classmates, while holding rocks in their outstretched hands.[22] This sanction had clear religious overtones, invoking crucifixion. These punishments perpetuated a colonial logic that forbade Indigenous languages in the school, which was meant to be a modern, Spanish-speaking space.

For Hernández, the INI's educational mission faced three competing authorities in the region: the existing SEP schools, Oaxacan state education officials, and the Catholic Church. Questions of education reform were frequently tied to conflicts over land, the role of the church, and state authority. Thus Hernández aimed to position the institute as a force for social change generally. INI officials frequently attempted to reform existing SEP schools to win over locals to the institute's authority more broadly. In the case of one misbehaving teacher in the town of Santiago Nuyoó, accused of alcoholism and absenteeism, INI anthropologist Carlos Incháustegui traveled to Oaxaca City with the town authorities to request that the teacher be replaced. As Hernández argued, "I believe that if we obtain the new teachers we will be able to direct the education system according to the interests of our institute."[23]

Perhaps the more difficult challenge was confronting competition from the Catholic Church and Catholic activists. In the town of Santa Cruz Itundujia, the local priest combined educational services with catechism delivered to both young boys and girls. While this example contradicted Hernández's view that Catholics uniformly opposed coeducation, the priest's efforts were nonetheless viewed as competition by INI officials, who attributed the church's influence to the lack of state-led efforts in the region. This view failed to reckon with a long-standing conflict dating back to the educational and agrarian reforms of the 1930s, which imbued discussions of education reform with competing notions of Catholic identity and anticlericalism.

The hostility the INI faced from Catholic authorities was part of a broader politicized conservative oppositional culture centered in the Mixteca Baja, just north of Tlaxiaco. At the beginning of the century, the church hierarchy struggled to assert its power in the state and competed with more popular syncretic Catholic traditions. By the 1930s, however, the Oaxacan clergy had successfully reasserted themselves, bolstering the number of priests in service in the state and strengthening religious education and Catholic social organization.[24] The limited federal reforms of the 1930s, which introduced rural schools and agrarian reform, were frequently met by Catholic-led opposition.[25] Indeed, many conflicts surrounding federal schools were connected to broader fights over land between the federally backed *ejidatorios* and the *socios* of Catholic land organizations. This politicized Catholicism, forged in the 1930s, was a rejection of socialist education that combined antisecularism with pride in the local culture and language.[26] Much of this militantly conservative Catholic vision originated in a seminary in Huajuapan de León, located in the Mixteca Baja. Clergy in the Mixteca Alta most likely trained with figures from Huajuapan, and the main church in Tlaxiaco continues to display images of Cristero martyrs. Celestino Fernández y Fernández served as bishop of the area from 1952 to 1967. While Fernández had adopted a more conciliatory approach to federal power, negotiating agreements between himself and federal authorities, popular religious organizations continued to voice hostility toward federal education. These traditions of local Catholicism combined with renewed fears of communism during the Cold War to further radicalize conservative Catholic activists.

The church's sustained engagement with Mixtec culture and language should not be overlooked. Not only in the colonial period, when Dominicans first developed Mixtec vocabularies with their native counterparts, but even into the nineteenth century, church officials created Mixtec catechism materials and trained priests in the language.[27] These efforts predated those of the radical indigenistas who proclaimed the desirability of the use and preservation of Native languages. Despite the INI's and the church's hostile rhetoric toward each other, both shared a commitment to engage with highland Indigenous communities, and both had to reckon with local power and customs in order to survive. At midcentury the church and the state exhibited their own forms of paternalism toward the Indigenous subject of their efforts. Most priests were still drawn from mestizo and elite families, and the INI continued to rely on outside experts, in this case social scientists, to bring enlightened change to the region. The two institutions, church and state, also shared a similar trajectory over the course of the century, shifting from more paternalist postures in the 1950s to an emphasis on Indigenous self-determination and agency in the 1970s.

Radio as a Solution

The idea of a system of radio schools as a solution to the Mixteca's lack of primary school coverage combined two experimental policies: a bilingual method of instruction in Spanish literacy and math, and the use of radio in education. While instruction in Indigenous languages was not new in the 1950s, it did go against the dominant model and practice of primary schooling that, as described above, employed the direct method of language instruction and prohibited the use of vernacular languages in the classroom. The INI spearheaded the use of bilingual instructors through their recruitment of promotores bilingües at their first coordinating center in Chiapas.

There were precedents for educational radio programming in Mexico, and international organizations such as UNESCO touted its effectiveness.[28] INI officials drew on the experience of Catholic literacy efforts

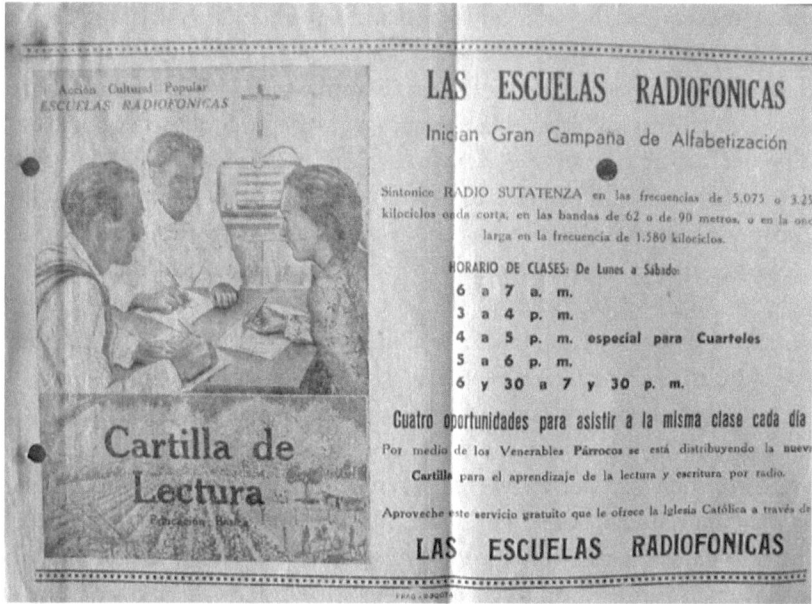

FIGURE 9. Poster for a Colombian literacy campaign using shortwave radio signals, sponsored by the Catholic organization Acción Cultural Popular.
Source: Archivo Histórico del Centro Coordinador Indigenista de la Mixteca Alta, Tlaxiaco, Oaxaca.

employing shortwave broadcasts in Colombia.[29] A priest, José Joaquin Salcedo Guarin, pioneered Radio Sutatenza, located in the valle de Tenza, northwest of Bogotá. Begun in 1947, and then expanded under the auspices of Acción Cultural Popular (ACPO), the program distributed shortwave radio receivers to peasant communities and relied on local priests to distribute the *cartillas* (primers) that facilitated the lesson plans. The program eventually garnered support from Catholic organizations, Colombian authorities, UNESCO, and Phillips and RCA radio companies. Radio Sutatenza expanded over the course of the 1960s and into the 1970s, achieving fame throughout Latin America.[30] Radio technology appeared to solve the geographic problem of uneven development.

The INI sought to build on the success of Radio Sutatenza but added the bilingual component of broadcasts in Spanish and Native languages, in this case Mixtec and Triqui. Ramón Hernández López was a vocal advocate of bilingual instruction for monolingual Indigenous students. According to Hernández, he had witnessed firsthand the inefficacy of the direct method at the Chalcatongo boarding school in the 1930s. There students learned to repeat but not to understand the content of the words they parroted. Hernández's subsequent normal school thesis emphasized the need to employ vernacular languages in the classroom. Nonetheless, bilingual instruction proved controversial in the Mixteca. When Hernández explained the INI's plans to his hometown's community assembly, he encountered opposition. During the assembly an elderly man seated in the back requested a turn to speak. When the town authorities called on the man he said: "*Pinche* Ramón! We sent you to Mexico [City] to learn *la castilla* [Spanish] so you could return and teach it to us. Now it turns out you want to teach us in our own language?"[31] Popular support for bilingual instruction varied by community, but for many, schools were one of the few spaces where children could learn the practical ability to speak Spanish. They therefore viewed Mixtec in the classroom as a barrier to learning to speak and understand Spanish well. Indeed, the word most often used in the region was the formal, *castellano* (*castilla* in the above quotation is a shortened form) as opposed to *español*. The use of the term *castellano* reflected the still-pervasive colonial understanding of Spanish as a language of power and prestige, unlike the "poor languages" or mere "dialects" of local towns.

To test the bilingual method, Hernández set up two experimental programs, one in his hometown of San Agustín Tlacotepec and the other in San Pedro Molinos in May 1957. Julio de la Fuente, an anthropologist at the time working out of the INI's national office, collaborated in this effort, visiting the schools and observing classroom instruction. Hernández reported that the children in these programs, who ranged in age from six to eight years, learned to count in both Spanish and Mixtec and that instruction in Mixtec was more effective in achieving Spanish language proficiency.[32] The radio schools relied on support and collaboration between the INI, the SEP, and the Comité Nacional de Comunicaciones Vecinales.[33] While the program was to begin with just ten schools, the number quickly increased to fifty, and Hernández began recruiting youth from the region to be trained as auxiliary radio teachers. The onus was on INI officials to prove the utility of Mixtec language instruction, both to the communities and to educational authorities.

The INI and Hernández were not alone in their efforts to put Indigenous language on the radio. Inspired by Radio Sutatenza in Colombia, Catholic officials and lay people throughout the hemisphere combined radio technology with broadcasts in Native languages. In Guatemala, Maryknoll missionaries experimented with Maya language broadcasts in their adult literacy and catechism work in the country's highlands. In Bolivia, mineworkers developed their own radio stations in the aftermath of the 1952 Revolution. Miners, a politically powerful group in Bolivia, broadcast trade union news, politics, and cultural programming in both Quechua and Aymara. In the United States, the chief of the Sac and Fox Tribe of Oklahoma broadcast a weekly program, *The Indians for Indians Hour*, out of the University of Oklahoma's radio station, WNAD. *The Indians for Indians Hour* united the diverse "international Indian Country" in the state through news, a community board service, and live musical performances.[34] While Indigenous languages on the radio were a novelty at midcentury, across the hemisphere one heard Native voices explaining national literacy campaigns, expressing religious beliefs, and analyzing history and politics for their audiences.[35]

For Native speakers, the experience of hearing one's language on the radio could be jarring, as the opening anecdote to this chapter demonstrates. Many Indigenous languages of the Americas, such as Mixtec, were primarily expressed orally and most often experienced in interpersonal contexts. What did it mean to take such a language and broadcast it over an entirely depersonified medium like shortwave radio? For some, it was a disconcerting experience. For others, hearing their Native language on the radio, which colonial logics had diminished as belonging to the uncivilized poor, was an empowering experience. While national homogenizing projects often dismissed Indigenous languages as mere dialects, not proper languages such as those found in Europe, the sound of Indigenous languages on the radio demonstrated their validity, value, and cosmopolitanism.

To inaugurate the system, INI director Alfonso Caso traveled to Tlaxiaco on March 29, 1958, for the opening ceremony. Also invited to attend were the Oaxacan governor, Alfonso Pérez Gasca (1956–62) and Mario Aguilera Dorantes, a top official in the Secretaría de Educación Pública. Hernández had already assembled the first fifty auxiliary radio teachers, traveling throughout the region and recruiting youths who had completed primary school, some of whom were assisting teachers in their home communities. Replicating long-standing patriarchal trends in Mexican rural education, out of the first fifty radio teachers just nine were women. In this regard, INI educational reform remained consistent with SEP practices. Fernando Benítez, a prominent journalist, later visited the center and interviewed the radio teachers. He described them, with his characteristic flair, as "the new Mixtec princes, the only hope for the thousands of sombrero weavers, campesinos and shepherds that live in the Mixteca Alta. For now, there is no other hope in this desolate landscape."[36] In indigenista thinking of the era, of which Benítez was a prolific popularizer, the radio teachers served as a bridge between a glorious pre-Hispanic past and a tragic Indigenous present. They were a vehicle for modernization and social uplift.

Hernández trained the youth in a month-long program in Tlaxiaco, but he assumed that most of their training would take place while they were in service. Once in the field, the teachers were paid a small sum, initially 60 pesos and eventually 240 pesos a month. They were to work with groups of first- and second-grade children in the mornings. The mechanics of the program involved a *maestro locator*, or broadcasting teacher, who conducted the lesson from the pilot radio station in Tlaxiaco, and an auxiliary teacher directing the students in the community. Radio teachers were assigned battery-powered receivers.[37] In some communities, antennas were installed to improve signal reception. According to official thinking at the time, "The radio schoolteachers, by acting in part as robots, but doing it daily, will obtain in a year a pedagogic capacity faster and better than the common teacher."[38] Hernández, as the broadcasting teacher, conducted the lessons in Spanish and Mixtec. The lessons included Spanish language instruction, literacy, and arithmetic, along with musical programming.[39] The radio schoolteachers' charge was to mimic Hernández and further explain his instructions.

A typical broadcast lasted two hours for each grade and combined formal lessons, student-teacher interaction, and music. Just as in federal rural schools, students began the week with a military-style salute to the flag and patriotic songs. The broadcasting teacher often began the day's lesson by saying, "I want to help you learn to speak Spanish, to read and write, and also do basic arithmetic."[40] He alternated between specifically directing the students in their assignments and instructing the auxiliary teachers in the lesson plan, allotting time for the teachers to work with the students on particular assignments. Hernández's personality was said to fit the medium well, and he attempted to create rapport with the students despite his physical absence. As Antolín Osorio, an auxiliary teacher, described Hernández's approach to the educational transmissions: "He [would say], 'Okay, children, pay attention,' guiding the group. 'Okay, Manuel, you go to the blackboard, and tell me what is there.' And then, 'Look, you are

FIGURE 10. Instruction manual for one of the Phillips radio receivers under consideration in the INI's radio school program.
Source: Archivo Histórico del Centro Coordinador Indigenista de la Mixteca Alta, Tlaxiaco, Oaxaca.

not doing what I say, Manuel; teacher, tell Manuel to do what I say.' And then the radio teacher would take it from there: 'The teacher says that you, you raise your hand or show us the drawing or the poster.' That is how the radio teacher would take over."[41] The radio receivers had a red or blue light when turned on, and the auxiliary teachers at times used this to discipline students, insinuating that the broadcasting teacher could see them through the light, that it was a "little eye." While Mixtec was used in the broadcasts, the language's multiple variants created challenges for the teachers. Despite the hoped-for mutual intelligibility of Mixtec within the former district of Tlaxiaco, there were still difficulties in translation. It fell to the auxiliary teachers to use their own variants in the classroom.

In radio transcripts, the Mixtec elements of the broadcast are denoted only by the word *mixteco* or the phrase *auxilio en mixteco*. Hernández most likely performed this element of the broadcast extemporaneously. He spoke in his Tlacotepec variant, which would have been intelligible to many but not all of the communities in the broadcast radius. The challenge of navigating the region's linguistic diversity was compounded by the fact that the auxiliary teachers were not always sent to their home communities.[42] Officials acknowledged this dilemma early on, in an internal document that noted, "If this incapacity [the multiple variants of Mixtec] is more significant than it appears, it will become necessary to use less Mixtec in communicating with the children and to teach more in Spanish."[43] This was one of the major challenges and barriers to bilingual instruction in regions with linguistic diversity. Nevertheless by 1963, forty-nine INI schools operated with thirty-five auxiliary teachers and twenty-three federal teachers (teachers with federal accreditation). The two groups of teachers served an official enrollment of 2,314 students. It was an impressive achievement just seven years after the institute's arrival to the Mixteca Alta.

A sign of the program's initial success was its expansion to a second, Triqui language broadcasting system. The Triquis are an Indigenous group culturally and linguistically distinct from Mixtecs, but they share parts of the Mixteca Alta and Baja as their homeland. For decades, Triqui towns had a combative relationship with neighboring communities as well as state authorities. Popular lore portrayed Triquis as *gente brava*, inherently violent people. These stereotypes had a long history. Frederick Starr, the anthropologist profiled in the Prologue, placed the Triquis at the bottom of his racial hierarchy of Native peoples. Contrary to these negative depictions, the Triquis' plight had a concrete and quite modern origin. In the postrevolutionary period, government redistricting split Triqui lands into distinct political jurisdictions. This externally imposed division of Triqui land contributed to violent internal conflicts and long-standing land disputes.[44] Wary of the divisive role of government authorities, by the 1960s multiple Triqui communities had expelled state and SEP-sponsored

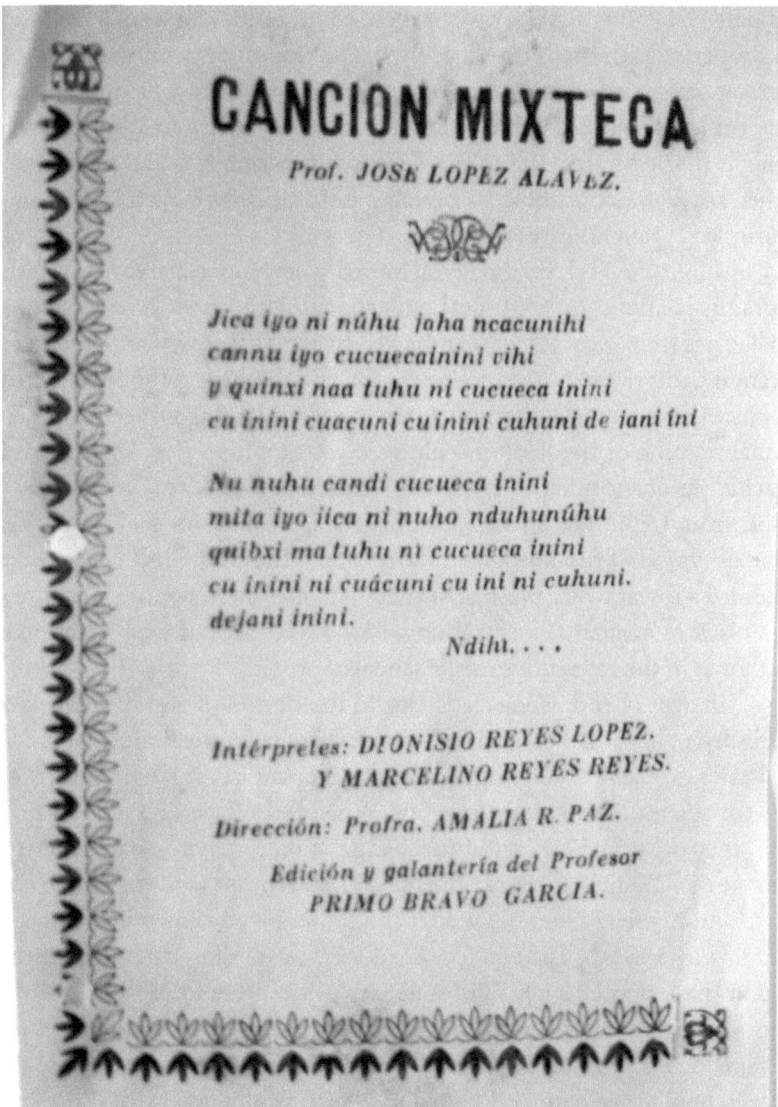

FIGURE 11. "Canción Mixteca," by José López Alvez (1912), translated into Mixtec.
Source: Archivo Histórico del Centro Coordinador Indigenista de la Mixteca Alta, Tlaxiaco, Oaxaca.

schools. When Hernández visited these communities, he convinced them to cooperate with the INI. Allegedly, Triqui leaders responded to Hernández's appeal to collaborate, saying, "With the INI yes, but not with the government."[45] The INI then assumed authority over a handful of Triqui schools in the Mixtec Alta.[46] The Triquis' distinction between the INI and other government authorities reveals the institute's singular appeal as it expanded throughout rural Mexico.

While the INI eventually achieved a level of collaboration and a working relationship with local educational authorities, it faced serious challenges from local teachers employed by the SEP as well as the state education authorities. At the local level, the SEP teachers in the Mixteca Alta dismissed the young radio teachers as upstarts, lacking either the professional training or the level of "culture" necessary for a true Mexican rural teacher. As one former radio teacher recounted, federal teachers dismissed those from the INI as *huarachudos*, or sandal-wearers, for the cheap, thick sandals typical of rural people in the region.[47] The young INI teachers represented a threat to the prestige of rural schoolteachers, not only because of their lack of normal school training, but also because of their indigeneity, as shown in the reference to their sandals.

The use of Indigenous language in the classroom also threatened established educational authorities. State-level bureaucrats drafted an official objection to the INI's bilingual method, complaining to the president that it went against conventional practice. When INI officials became aware of this, they organized, as part of the inauguration ceremonies, a demonstration of the bilingual method. The radio class went off without a hitch, and Caso and Aguilera Dorantes used it as a power play against state-level education authorities.[48] The two federal officials asked those assembled if they found the lesson effective, and state authorities were forced to agree that the bilingual method worked and to accept the presence of the INI. While it remained a tenuous relationship, the institute inserted itself into the local schooling system, and Hernández successfully obtained SEP *plazas*, full-time positions, for some of the radio teachers, gaining them access to professional development and significantly higher pay. By 1964, the INI's presence in the region was such that José Sánchez García, a SEP teacher from El Imperio, a ranchería of Yosondúa, who had been unable to obtain a teaching SEP assignment in his hometown, petitioned to be transferred to the INI in order to serve his community.[49] Teachers used the cleavages in educational authority produced by the INI's arrival to improve their own positions.

Catholic Opposition to Indigenista Education

In 1955, Mexican composer Vicente Garrido Calderón penned the lyrics, "Muere el sol en los montes, con la luz que agoniza, pues la vida en su prisa, nos conduce a morir" (The sun dies in the mountains, with its light fading, because life in its haste, leads us to death). Garrido penned the stoic lines to accompany Oaxaca's de facto state anthem, the nineteenth-century waltz "Dios nunca muere."[50] And as the INI sought to extend its influence in the highlands, its experience there appeared to confirm the song's claim that "God never dies." While the institute faced an uphill battle in promoting the bilingual method and often lacked resources to fully train its radio teachers, its primary problem was hostile Catholic figures. Priests and lay activists painted the INI as secular, communist, and a threat to Catholic values. While the center continued to struggle with this religious opposition, Ramón Hernández López's reputation grew. Just three years after the inaugurating the radio program, Hernández rose from head of the CCIMA's Education Section to subdirector of the center itself, presaging a storied career in indigenista education efforts. In the fall of 1961, Héctor Villaverde Hernández, Tlaxiaco's municipal president, invited Hernández to speak at the town's annual Independence Day celebrations. As per tradition, the Independence Day festivities were held in the center of town on the evening of September 16.[51] This was a high-profile event, and the municipal president's invitation spoke to Hernández's growing influence in Tlaxiaco and regional politics.

On the night of September 16, Hernández spoke from a podium in front of the municipal palace. After ofering some prefunctory patriotic remarks, he lamented that "the fruits of Independence, the Reform, and the Revolution remain an aspiration for many regions across the country." He went on, criticizing employers and Tlaxiaco merchants who, he argued, exploited the Indigenous population through poor wages and price manipulation. Not holding back, he denounced priests for confusing locals "with the specter of communism" and for "attempt[ing] to infringe upon the freedoms of the people."[52] Before he could finish his remarks, which

Hernández knew would be controversial, a local priest, speaking through the church's loudspeakers directly across from the municipal palace, denounced Hernández. Rallying the townspeople via the loudspeakers, the priest called on the town to punish the offending teacher. Hernández himself escaped any personal violence. But a nearby army detachment was deployed to protect the INI's Tlaxiaco offices. The following day, a priest, seminary director, and vicar organized a march through the town center. They denounced the INI's alleged communism and posted "Viva Cristo Rey!" (Long live Christ the King!) graffiti on town walls.[53] Hernández was confident enough to publicly challenge regional elites and Catholic leaders in 1961, but they too were willing to take to the streets and respond to the provocation. The conflict reached the state level when Oaxacan governor Alfonso Pérez Gasca intervened and scolded Hernández for his speech. Ultimately, Alfonso Caso counseled Hernández to avoid such confrontations with church officials.

Catholic activists framed the conflict between themselves and federal authorities as one between "good" and "evil" and "God" and "the devil." They frequently labeled federal schools as "evil" and encouraged local families to send their children to private parochial schools. This antipathy drew on long-standing opposition to federal authority and Catholic activists' effective fusing of regional and religious identities. Activists had successfully framed the church as the "region's natural guardian."[54] This conservative Catholic culture drew on traditions formed during the 1930s in the wake of the first and second Cristiadas but also on an increasingly polarized contemporary context. Secretary of Education Torres Bodet's issuing of free, and importantly, obligatory, textbooks in 1960 was understood within such frameworks. The chapter's opening anecdote is all the more intriguing in this context. When parents, upon hearing Mixtec on the radio, asked, "Was it God or the devil?" their religious language was not incidental. Those who thought it was the devil could surely have been drawing on the Catholic oppositional culture. Those who thought it was God perhaps thought Mixtec on the radio was a reflection of God's power, inverting the colonial hierarchies that contemporary observers and development discourses invoked. Or were federal education authorities who broadcast Mixtec on the radio doing the work of the devil by mixing Indigenous languages with modern technology? Did this constitute an inversion of Catholic narratives that emphasized an Indigenous past tied to religion and the land?

Whatever the case, conservative Catholic opposition to federal authority was a generalized trend in the Mixteca into the early 1960s. A little over a year later, on November 17, 1962, Catholic and Partido Acción Nacional (PAN) activists launched an attack on an army barracks in Huajuapan de León, just north in the Mixteca Baja. The armed attackers killed a soldier and stole weapons before retreating into the countryside. They too invoked God and accused the federal government of moving toward communism. The armed rebellion, while quickly put down and repressed, was connected to a loose plot of conservative activists throughout the republic aimed at attacking federal authority.[55] If in 1961 and 1962 conservative activists challenged, at times violently, the PRI and federal agencies throughout the Mixteca, the most iconic example of conservative violence, the 1968 lynching of five university workers in San Miguel Canoa, Puebla, north of Oaxaca, offers an interesting counterpoint. The infamous events in Canoa involved a conservative priest rallying his community members to commit violence against people they viewed as communist outsiders. In this case the priest, Enrique Perez Meza, was an ally of the PRI, and the violence was directed not just at the university workers but also at locals who had supported the Central Campesina Independiente, an independent peasant federation hostile to PRI rule.[56] Anticommunism remained a powerful political discourse, and in 1968 Puebla the town priest and the PRI were allied against real and perceived leftist opposition. In 1961 in the Mixteca Alta, Catholic activists viewed the INI as a communist force to be opposed.

There was an irony in Catholic opposition to the INI radio school program. It was of course Catholic individuals who had pioneered the use of educational radio broadcasts at midcentury elsewhere in the Americas. Indeed, the INI drew direct inspiration for their pilot program from Catholic radio broadcasts in Colombia. That program, begun by a parish priest, grew into ACPO and received funding from Catholic organizations internationally, including groups in the United States, and combined evangelization with literacy and community development projects. ACPO's efforts were explicitly anticommunist, meant to serve as an antidote to leftist calls to revolution in the hemisphere. Parallel radio education efforts in neighboring Guatemala also became enmeshed in that country's civil war, with the military dictatorship supporting such radio initiatives. Catholic opposition to the INI's deployment of similar methods speaks to the longer history of Catholic organizing in Mexico as well the polarization of politics during the Cold War.[57]

Nonetheless Catholic anticommunism in the Mixteca was also a reaction to the growth of Marxist and revolutionary nationalist politics in the region. Particularly among educators, Marxism was a salient ideology that offered an explanation of the impoverished present as well as a vision for a more just future. Isaías Sánchez López, the auxiliary teacher who later served as a Mixtec broadcaster, came into contact with Marxist politics while attending SEP training courses in Oaxaca City. After a professional development course for teachers in the state capital, many gathered in the patio of an Oaxaca City home. Under the shade of a grapefruit tree, they listened to Marxist speeches about inequality and wealth.[58] They in turn brought those ideas back to the highlands. Ramón Hernández López's fiery Independence Day speech as well as his participation in the Confederación Nacional de Jóvenes Indígenas is another example of the increasing presence of left-wing ideas in the education sector. A number of federal teachers in the Mixteca also participated in Vicente Lombardo Toledano's Partido Popular Socialista (PPS).[59] For many Oaxacan teachers, their professional development, access to education, and political formation were intrinsically intertwined. Mixteca Alta anticommunism thus responded to the reality of radicalizing teachers, as well as an imagined notion that the federal government was on the edge of a communist takeover. The ruling party could then reference such hostile Catholic opposition to justify its own authoritarian rule.

In addition to the political, religious, and educational conflicts faced by the INI, the radio program was beset by a host of technical problems. One was that the center had a limited window in which to transmit because of signal interference. Another station based in Guatemala, Radio Quetzaltenango, frequently interrupted XENI broadcasts. Radio Quetzaltenango's signal interfered with the INI broadcast after 1:00 p.m., so the station was forced to schedule all of its programming in the morning. INI officials were also hemmed in on the morning side of the schedule. Many students walked long distances to their local radio school and struggled to arrive on time.[60] Nor was the maintenance and upkeep of radio receivers in communities with little electronics experience an easy task. When receivers suffered damage, they were sent to Tlaxiaco and often then on to Mexico City for repair, taking months to be returned. In the town of San Juan Bautisa Coixtlahuaca, rats ate through the electrical wiring of a radio school's installation.[61] Radio schoolteachers' attempts at repair could also be dangerous. One afternoon in 1963, while fixing the antenna of his radio receiver, a teacher working near Magdalena Peñasco was hit by lightning and died.[62] In addition to the problems radio teachers faced in the field, the Tlaxiaco station itself struggled with technical difficulties. In 1964 the quality of the studio's microphones deteriorated to such an extent that new ones had to be ordered. While replacements were ultimately obtained, the substitutes never matched the potency of the original equipment.[63]

Conclusion

These technical problems coincided with changes in the INI's educational mission nationally. By 1964, the SEP created the Servicio Nacional de Promotores Culturales y Maestros Bilingües, a national service of bilingual promoters. The budget for training bilingual youth as educational extensionists in turn grew substantially. INI and SEP authorities now prioritized the training and deployment of larger numbers of promotores bilingües throughout the republic. This policy undercut one of the central justifications for the radio schools: the lack of trained personnel in remote communities. This shift, along with Ramón Hernández López's departure from the Tlaxiaco INI center in 1965, contributed to the decline of the pilot radio initiative. Increasingly, more attention went to training the promoters as educators without the pilot radio model. The program was suspended later that year. Despite the end of the bilingual broadcasts, the initiative served an important precedent for later community-based Indigenous radio. In 1979 the INI created a national system of Indigenous, bilingual radios stations.[64] Increasingly, communities employed bilingual broadcasts to exchange messages within Indigenous regions of Mexico and later between those communities and Indigenous migrants living in the United States.

Bilingual radio schools were just one piece of federal authorities' "integral development" plan for the Mixteca Alta. A technological and linguistic solution to the region's perceived underdevelopment, the radio schools, along with the public health campaigns described in chapter 1, formed part of a robust regional development initiative. While indigenista development did not achieve the coherence and totalizing effects it imagined, it did transform the Mixteca Alta in several regards. Ramón Hernández López and the INI contracted a generation of promotores who were bilingual and who came from the communities they served. Many of them went on to play pioneering roles in the emergent Indigenous education sector. In later years they would struggle for and achieve professionalization as federal teachers. While beset by a host of challenges, the pilot radio program was a crucial moment of experimentation in Indigenous language instruction. Throughout the hemisphere, these projects were often fleeting, involving the participation of foreign experts and the commitment of a handful of individuals motivated by alternative theories of education. The projects struggled to maintain themselves during the expansion of education at midcentury. The radio schools were eclipsed by the growth and institutionalization of the Indigenous education sector in subsequent decades. Nonetheless they were a precedent for the larger-scale Indigenous radio programming that the INI launched in the late 1970s and that served as hubs of linguistic revival and communication networks for Indigenous migrants in Mexico and beyond.

These efforts were part of a second wave of federal expansion in Mexico. While the Cardenista reforms of the 1930s are often extolled as transformative, indigenista development in the Oaxacan highlands demonstrates that in many areas of rural Mexico the extension and consolidation of federal power had a different periodization. In the Mixteca Alta and other parts of southern Mexico, local elites' stranglehold on power was not significantly challenged until midcentury.[65] While INI officials sought to transform the people and the place, their diagnosis of "overpopulation" meant the above efforts would ultimately be insufficient in addressing the problems of the Mixteca Alta. The voluntary resettlement of the highland population to the Pacific Coast was key to the INI's regional development plan. As with these other reforms, the subjects of development frequently rejected state designs and articulated their own strategies for navigating a modernizing world.

3

Mixtec Land and Labor
Migration and State-Sponsored Resettlement on the Costa Chica

We were from the Mixteca Alta and screwed, screwed, screwed . . .
 —Nicolás Morales Hernández[1]

Twentieth-century economics also has a colonial genealogy.
 —Timothy Mitchell[2]

THE COSTA Chica stretches along Mexico's extensive Pacific coast, from Acapulco, Guerrero, southeast toward Puerto Escondido, Oaxaca. In the early 1960s Puerto Escondido was a small fishing village. In subsequent decades the town's profile and population grew as fishermen, beatniks, political exiles, surfers, and Italian bohemians popularized the place.[3] Highway 200, which today connects the coastal plains northwest to the state of Nayarit and southeast to Mexico's border with Guatemala, was only completed in 1978. Prior to that, a weekly flight between Pinotepa Nacional and Mexico City was one of the few connections between Oaxaca's Costa Chica and the outside world.[4] Bordered to the north by the Sierra Madre del Sur, the Costa Chica's relative isolation appeared to confirm midcentury development officials' emphasis on the necessity of regional integration in Mexico.

Federal planners identified the coast as an area ripe for development. As described in chapter 1, indigenista intellectuals contrasted the impoverished highlands of the Mixteca Alta, where land quality was poor and population growth high, with the fertile and relatively sparsely populated coastal plains. Rich in tropical flora and fauna, the coastal lagoons supported various species of migratory birds, crocodiles, and fish, and its plains were suited to cattle ranching. In the 1940s, federal planners developed Acapulco as an international tourist destination. INI officials, however, arrived on the Oaxacan side of the Costa Chica in 1954 and emphasized agricultural development. They set up a coordinating center in Santiago Jamiltepec, a municipality in the center of the Costa Chica, in January of that year. The anthropologists who arrived dutifully mapped out the region's social topography, with a mestizo elite, often referred to as *gente de razón*, dominating a population of Mixtec, Amuzgo, and African-descended peoples. The anthropologists struggled to make sense of this heterogenous population but emphasized stark racial cleavages and a local proclivity toward violence.[5]

One town federal officials presumed was typical of the region was La Tuza. Roughly twenty-five miles due south of Jamiltepec, La Tuza sat on the northern edge of Laguna Monroy within walking distance from the Pacific shoreline. Great egrets and little blue herons nested in the dense vegetation and one could see manta rays jumping offshore. Crabs filled La Tuza's streets, particularly during mating season. The sparse population survived through fishing and small-scale agriculture. The area was alleged to be uninhabited as late as the early twentieth century, and development officials claimed that the first settlers had arrived in 1945 from nearby Pinotepa Nacional. INI officials described these first settlers as *morenos*, people of African descent.[6]

In 1963, twenty-five families from the highland Mixtec town of Santa María Teposlantongo, located roughly one hundred miles north, settled in La Tuza. Over the next few years, what had once been a sleepy, semi-desolate hamlet was consumed by violence arising from racialized tensions brought on by this migration.

By May 1968, the families from Teposlantongo were living in fear. Some had resorted to sleeping on the surrounding mountainsides. Over the past five years, they had been assaulted, threatened, and shot at by the *pistoleros* of a powerful local *cacica*, Francisca Meza viuda de Iglesias, popularly known as Doña Pancha. In the spring of 1967, two highlanders had been shot dead in La Tuza. Doña Pancha, along with migrants from the state of Guerrero, coveted the land where the families had settled. The parcels offered wide open plains and plenty of water, ideal conditions for agriculture and cattle grazing. The conflict was also racialized. Federal officials claimed that many of the *morenos* worked at the behest of the

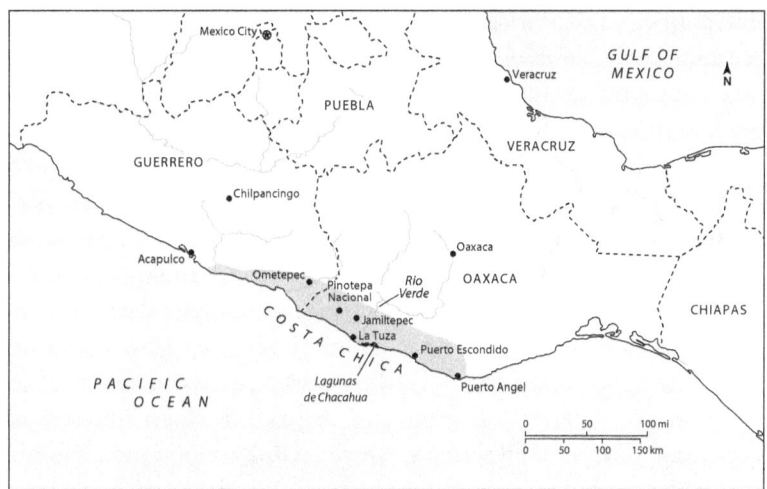

MAP 3. Mexico's Costa Chica.

powerful Iglesias Meza family. According to officials, it was these *morenos* that menaced the relocated highland communities. In one incident, Modesta Paz, a monolingual Mixtec speaker from Teposlantongo, was told to "go back to your damn Indian land" and was threatened with a machete as she planted corn.[7] Hostility toward the resettled highlanders was not exclusive to African-descended communities. Some coastal Mixtecs also opposed their presence. The intensity of the conflict provoked state and federal intervention. State judicial police arrived to patrol La Tuza. INI officials wrote their superiors in Mexico City seeking assistance. While Oaxaca had a long history of land and boundary conflicts, this one was different. This dispute centered on a group of highland Mixtec families who had been officially encouraged to resettle on the coast through a federal program. By the fall of 1968 the program was in disarray. INI officials in Jamiltepec assured the resettled highland families that they were working for justice for Emiliano Ramos Chávez, one of those killed in the previous spring. They also offered financial assistance to the highlanders, some of whom planned to return to the Mixteca Alta.[8]

The violence in La Tuza was one of the last moments of a botched effort by federal officials to promote *colonización dirigida*, the voluntary resettlement of the highland population to the Costa Chica and the Isthmus of Tehuantepec. Sponsored by the INI and the Departamento de Asuntos Agrarios y Colonización (DAAC), the project encountered similar problems in other coastal areas where federal authorities sought to establish agricultural settlements. A component of the INI's regional development efforts, the project also formed part of Mexico's *Marcha al Mar*, or March to the Sea. Initiated by President Adolfo Ruiz Cortines (1952–58) and continued under President Adolfo López Mateos (1958–64), the March to the Sea aimed to populate and stimulate economic growth on Mexico's two coastlines through investment, highway construction, and the modernization of ports. Mexican policy makers identified the tropical lowlands of the country's southeast as particularly ripe for agricultural development.

Rural-to-urban migration was on the rise in the 1950s. Throughout the Americas, the rural poor flocked to urban centers in search of jobs and opportunity. National governments engaged in major infrastructure projects, highways and rail systems, which facilitated migration and often unwittingly undermined regional economies. In reaction to the economic tumult of the 1930s, many governments encouraged the growth of domestic manufacturing and industrial production, which further concentrated employment opportunities in urban centers. Mexico was no exception to this trend. Presidents Ávila Camacho and Alemán deemphasized prior governmental attention to rural regions as they prioritized urban growth. Along with rail lines, Mexico expanded its highway system. The Oaxacan segment of the Pan-American Highway was completed in 1942.[9] The combination of the pull of wage labor, the increasing precariousness of subsistence agriculture, new infrastructure, and the expansion of rural education efforts all facilitated this wave of people toward urban centers. The influx of rural peoples into cities created anxieties among the urban public and state planners. How would rural people adapt to modern city living? A range of theories were offered on the process. Would urban migration modernize "traditional" peoples? Would these new city dwellers damage democratic politics by being easily swayed into supporting populist leaders?[10] Either way, migration was far more than a mere economic process and raised anxieties regarding race, social place, and religion.

National governments intervened in the migration process. From South America, where countries sought to populate their Amazonian frontiers, to the United States, where the Bureau of Indian Affairs encouraged Native American migration to urban centers, state planners saw migration as a culturally transformative process for would-be migrants and nation-states. Even indigenista thinkers who sought to preserve "positive aspects" of Indigenous culture saw migration as an opportunity to turn migrants into modern citizens. While most state efforts reinforced broader trends of urbanization, others defied such trends and promoted migration to unsettled, sparsely populated regions. The INI's voluntary resettlement initiative for the Mixteca Alta constituted one such project. Drawing on a then-popular social scientific concept, planners diagnosed the highlands as suffering from "overpopulation" and identified the Costa Chica as a potential solution to this problem. The intellectual origins of the project were in the 1950s, but it was not until 1961 that the initiative got under way.

From 1961 to 1968, state and federal officials attempted to relocate and settle hundreds of Mixtec families to what they considered an underpopulated coast. Their goal was to "solve" the overpopulation of the highlands by turning Mixtec campesinos into profitable agricultural producers on the coastal plains. The project failed to achieve large-scale resettlement. Many highlanders outright refused to leave for the coast. The program also suffered from a lack of funding and coordination in its implementation. Moreover, those who did resettle on the coast frequently faced opposition from local actors. Many who journeyed south ultimately chose to return to the highlands.[11] This initiative stands in stark contrast to the dramatic rise of unsponsored migration, particularly seasonal migration, from the Mixteca Alta during the same period. In the second half of the century, highlanders migrated north in increasing numbers, effectively establishing a Mixtec diaspora in northern Mexico and the western United States.[12]

In this chapter, I use these two realities, a failed state-sponsored resettlement project and the simultaneous acceleration of seasonal migration, to answer a series of questions. In a context of immiserating poverty, what survival strategies have Oaxacan Indigenous communities employed? Relatedly, how have Native peoples navigated the rise of systems of wage labor? In addition, how did Afro-Mexican populations figure in indigenista planners' designs for the region?[13] And finally, a question that hangs over this chapter but also the broader history of indigenismo is whether INI officials effectively challenged colonial hierarchies or reproduced such hierarchies in new forms. In considering these questions, I describe the project's origins and implementation, tracing INI recruitment efforts in the highlands, community responses, and the experiences of some of those who left for the coast. In the process, I explore the evolving relationship between INI officials, resettled highlanders, and coastal elites.

This history is more than just another example of a failed development initiative. It demonstrates that indigenista thinkers, despite their attention to language, culture, and land tenure, failed to appreciate the significance of community identity and territoriality in the Mixteca Alta. Mixtec communities engaged in seasonal wage labor migration as a survival strategy, and development efforts that were aimed at regional integration or resettlement more often than not facilitated labor migration. At the same time, federal resettlement plans appeared to ignore the African-descended population of the Costa Chica. This long-standing blindness and hostility to Blackness was central to indigenista thinking and contributed to racialized violence and conflict on the Oaxacan coast at the end of the 1960s.[14]

To Populate the Coast: "Overpopulation," Indigenous Migration, and State Planning

Where did this project originate? It is easy for historians, with the benefit of hindsight, to look back at unsuccessful development projects and scoff at the hubris of those involved. How did they not anticipate this? Why did they not consider that? Such accounts have limited analytical yield and fail to reckon with the substantive political commitments and visions of many of those involved in such projects. A confluence of global development thinking and long-standing Mexican agrarian reform traditions provided the intellectual basis for the voluntary resettlement program. As described in chapter 1, Moisés de la Peña's 1949 study contrasted the highlands and the coastal plains and proposed that migration from the former to the latter would solve the development problems of each. De la Peña and others emphasized the dire poverty facing the Mixteca Alta.[15] They argued that poor agricultural yields and rapid population growth were the principal causes of such poverty. Through this line of analysis, the project drew on a popular idea at the time, that of "overpopulation." Conceptually, overpopulation presumed that a fixed set of natural resources of a particular region was inadequate to support the population. As others have pointed out, this theorization presumed that resources were limited by space and failed to reckon with questions of power and the distribution of resources.[16] By framing development within "regional" studies, the concept of overpopulation naturalized scarcities and other social problems that were political in nature. While de la Peña identified and critiqued the unequal distribution of land in the Mixteca Alta, he and subsequent federal policy nonetheless embraced a concept that avoided confronting existing inequalities in the highlands.

After the presidencies of Miguel Alemán and Adolfo Ruiz Cortines, President López Mateos (1958–64) famously declared himself at "the extreme left within the limits set by the constitution."[17] His leftist legacy is more ambiguous than the quotation suggests. For example, López Mateos suppressed striking railroad workers and jailed dissidents. On the other hand, he did revive agrarian reform and land distribution in the countryside. In 1962, a new law of *colonización* (colonization) allowed for the creation of Nuevos Centros de Población Agrícolas (NCPAs), New Centers of Agricultural Populations. The voluntary resettlement project was part of this NCPA program. It asked would-be participants to formally propose an NCPA in designated regions of the coast. While some settlers were directed to newly nationalized land on the Isthmus, others settled on existing ejidal lands. This put them at the mercy of frequently hostile local authorities. The NCPAs received technical and institutional support from the DAAC and the INI. Policy makers therefore wedded the theory of the Mixteca Alta's overpopulation to a policy of agrarian resettlement. This version of agrarian reform did not challenge the highlands' patterns of unequal land tenure but instead resettled highland families in coastal regions.

FIGURE 12. INI tractor in Jamiltepec, 1965.
Source: Instituto Nacional de los Pueblos Indígenas, Fototeca Nacho López, Hermanos Mayo.

The archetypical high modernist act, state-led population transfers to planned agricultural communities presumed an ability to move people and resources across space as one moves pieces on a chessboard. The Soviet Union's decades-long program of rural agricultural collectivization is perhaps the most notorious example, but the history of state-directed reorganization of rural societies and agriculture is long and diverse. These projects took different forms, whether in postindependence East Africa or Mao's China, and were inflected with different political ideologies. Yet despite their diversity, they shared a similar fate: failure.[18] Soviet collectivization is perhaps most clearly associated with failure, but globally, state-directed relocations of rural peoples have rarely achieved the desired outcome. While some have focused on modernizing so-called traditional agriculture, others aimed to facilitate large-scale infrastructure efforts.

In Mexico, the closest antecedent to the INI's efforts in the Mixteca, in terms of geography as well as chronology, was federal authorities' construction of a hydroelectric dam in the Papaloapan region, located in the northeast corner of Oaxaca and parts of the state of Veracruz. That project involved the forced removal of the river basin's predominantly Mazatec population. State planners sought to remove roughly eight thousand residents from the floodwaters' path. INI anthropologists ran the relocation efforts and attempted to protect specific aspects of Mazatec culture in the process.[19] Some residents resisted removal. INI planners attributed this opposition to an attachment to native lands. Despite their efforts to conduct a culturally informed project, officials sought minimal input from the target population.[20]

In contrast, the United States' Federal Urban Relocation Program expressly sought the assimilation and "detribalization" of Native peoples. Begun by the Bureau of Indian Affairs in 1948, the Urban Relocation Program aimed to relocate Native Americans from their tribal lands to urban centers. The voluntary program provided travel costs, job training, and housing support for participants. Much like other projects of Indigenous resettlement, the Urban Relocation Program acknowledged the existing reality of Native migration and attempted to intervene in and spur the process on. Officially framed as "Americanization" of Native Americans, the bureau's project was assimilationist, in contrast to the INI anthropologists' efforts of managed cultural preservation. Some participants had already migrated to cities such as Los Angeles but signed up for the program retroactively in order to receive its benefits. These participants shrewdly navigated federal policy for their own ends.²¹ Similar to other initiatives, the Urban Relocation Program sought a cultural transformation of its participants. Nonetheless, at the end of the 1960s, a growing urban Indian movement rejected the program's assimilationist policy and advocated Native cultural revival.

Perhaps the closest parallel experience to the INI's voluntary resettlement of the Mixteca Alta was the Puno Tambopata project in Peru. Directed by the International Labour Organization and Peruvian authorities in the late 1950s, the Puno Tambopata project drew on a similar diagnosis of "overpopulation" of the highland region of Puno, near the border with Bolivia. The project likewise promoted the resettlement of the predominantly Aymara population of Puno down to the tropical Tambopata region, part of the Peruvian Amazon. Officials viewed the Amazon region as not yet fully integrated into the nation and its settlement as a nation-building project. International Labour Organization planners had noted that the highland population was already engaged in migration, albeit to the urban centers of Cuzco and Arequipa. They thus aimed to redirect existing migration trends for the presumed benefit of the people and the state.²² Regardless of the specifics of each resettlement project, development planners sought to intervene in already existing migration patterns and direct them along state designs. This was the hemispheric context for the project in the Mixteca.

The resettlement project relied on coordination between the INI's Tlaxiaco center in the highlands and the Jamiltepec center on the coast. The institute established both in 1954, but each confronted a distinct local context. Rafael Mijangos Ross served as the Jamiltepec center's first director until 1960. Jamiltepec, like Tlaxiaco, was a hub of economic activity and racialized political power. An often-cited example of Jamiltepec's racialized divisions was its cemetery, which boasted separate Indigenous and *gente de razón* sections. Early on, the institute commissioned ethnographic studies of the region's diverse constellation of communities and peoples—Mixtecs, Amuzgos, Chatinos, Afro-Mexicans, and mestizos—but frequently simplified these into binaries intelligible to a national audience.²³ From the outset, Director Mijangos had a collaborative relationship with prominent members of Jamiltepec society, including the Iglesias family. Perhaps out of necessity, INI officials on the Costa Chica sought a close relationship with local elites, going so far as to sponsor a young member of the Iglesias family in the town's carnival queen competition. This period of INI efforts involved a delicate balance of ingratiating themselves with powerful families while attempting to establish their legitimacy as a defender of Indigenous interests. INI officials appeared to succeed in this balancing act. However, over the next decade that relationship was tested as the coastal highway, *la costera*, opened the region to demographic and commercial interests from neighboring states.

On June 14, 1962, representatives of the communal land committees of over a dozen Mixteca Alta towns gathered in Chalcatongo de Hidalgo to hear of a new government program. There, in front of the municipal palace, the Oaxacan state *procurador* (deputy) of the DAAC, Sebastián Bautista Mariscal, described the details of the initiative, which he said had been approved by President López Mateos. Citing tracts of land on the Isthmus of Tehuantepec recently expropriated by the federal government, he told the assembled representatives that federal authorities would guarantee ten hectares to every willing and eligible head of household from the region. His agency, the DAAC, along with the INI, would also provide material assistance to the volunteers, including travel costs, food allowances, housing materials, health and educational support, seeds, and agricultural credits. But, he underscored, none of this was free. Rather, these costs were to be paid back by the participants after their first and subsequent harvests on the new lands.[24] This scene was repeated multiple times throughout the month of June in the highlands as INI and DAAC officials toured the region to promote the program. The representatives of communal land committees were to share the news with their hometowns. The eligibility requirements were straightforward: participants were to be between the ages of eighteen and thirty-five, completely landless (hence the focus on land committees), and literate in Spanish.[25] The targeted communities willing to migrate would submit to INI officials a census form of those interested and eligible, along with other documentation.

The response to the government's initiative was mixed. A handful of communities and individuals expressed enthusiasm for the offer. Santiago Nuyoó, a town southwest of Chalcatongo, was one such community. They responded quickly and positively to the call for volunteer relocation. Nuyoó authorities wrote Ramón Hernández López, by then director of the Tlaxiaco center, multiple times. In their letters, they described their lack of access to arable land and calculated that each head of household had just over one hectare to farm. In addition, they underscored the poor quality of their soil and high levels of erosion that made corn production nearly impossible. Even local banana and coffee cultivation had failed to resolve their dilemma. They noted that many community members traveled seasonally to Veracruz as agricultural laborers. None of this, they argued, had improved the "anguished panorama" of their rural life.[26] A handful of other solicitations to participate in the program, such as those from San Miguel el Grande, invoked patriotism in their requests.[27] They hoped their fealty to the president, party, and nation would grant them access to federal support.

However, many, if not most, communities rejected the program outright. Given the predominance of usos y costumbres, towns held assemblies regarding the proposed resettlement initiative. These meetings often produced little to no interest in the program.[28] Those from the Santiago Amoltepec thanked Hernández politely but said their people did not like the idea of moving to such a hot climate. In October 1962, the municipal president of Santiago Teotongo reported that those who had previously expressed interest had now become disinclined to go. Others cited the age restrictions of the program as a barrier. By capping participation at thirty-five years of age, the program effectively broke up extended families. Even in Hernández's hometown, San Agustín Tlacotepec, local authorities said there was *poco ánimo*, little interest, in leaving for the coast. Finally, Magdalena Peñasco, one of the Mixteca Alta towns that had drawn indigenista attention because it suffered most from high levels of soil erosion and poverty, opposed participation in the program, confounding INI officials.

Twentieth-Century Oaxacan Migration

¡Pinche Oaxaco! (damn Oaxacan!) is a common slur one might hear deployed in Mexico City or points north in the twenty-first century. It could be directed at a domestic worker, a street cleaner, or some other low-paid laborer. Highly racialized, the term implicitly equates Oaxaca's indigeneity with poverty and ignorance. While *Oaxaco* converts the noun *oaxaqueño/a* into a hard-edged, derogatory sound, reminiscent of *indio*, a plethora of other slurs exist, such as *pueblerino*, *negro*, or *huarachudo*, and even *indio* by itself can serve as an insult. Regardless of whether the victim is from Oaxaca, the epithet draws on the history of large-scale seasonal and out-migration from the state to other parts of the republic. The terms further reflect a broader racialized division of labor and inequality, in which Indigenous Oaxacans often find themselves in the most marginal forms of

employment. These inequalities are highly spatialized, with Oaxaca cast as part of a poor, backward, Indigenous South and much of northern Mexico conversely cast as modern, mestizo, and white. Over the course of the 1950s, Oaxaca, like much of the republic, experienced waves of rural-to-urban migration. This took the form of migration to Oaxaca City as well as the nation's capital, particularly outlying municipalities such as Ciudad Nezahualcóyotl.[29] By the early 1960s Oaxaca also witnessed a substantial rise in seasonal migration to northern Mexico. This pattern of migration only increased in the following decades and became a defining feature of many rural Oaxacan towns. The state's migration dynamics varied by region, with highland and central valley communities engaged in seasonal migration at much higher rates than those on the Isthmus. Government officials frequently termed seasonal migration *golondrina*, "swallow migration," invoking the bird's annual travel cycle. This *golondrina* migration became central to the state's economy and culture by the end of the century.

If Oaxaca became known nationally for migration, the Mixteca Alta was even more closely associated with large-scale seasonal migration. As described above, the pull of urbanization and jobs drew many from the highlands into migratory labor, as did increased levels of Spanish literacy and education through the expansion of rural schools in the 1930s and 1940s. The development of new highways and other infrastructure further facilitated migrant labor. Problems of land tenure, land quality, and debt were typical push factors in the region. Despite the persistence of formal communal landholding, many Mixtecos had insufficient access to arable land and were forced into sharecropping arrangements.[30] Journalistic accounts of the Mixteca from the 1960s emphasize the region's poverty and hunger.[31] While some depictions may involve traditional journalistic sensationalism, poverty, in the form of an inability to meet one's basic needs, was on the rise in the Mixteca in the 1950s and 1960s. This no doubt fueled people's decisions to migrate.

One such town was Magdalena Peñasco. Situated about ten miles due east of the district capital, Tlaxiaco, Magdalena Peñasco was a municipality of roughly 1,500 people in the mid-1960s. It sat in the shadow of a dramatic eight-thousand-foot mountain that locals referred to as El Gachupín. In 1968, a majority of the population were monolingual Mixtec speakers, and the municipality had just one, shared phone line.[32] The people of Magdalena survived on subsistence agriculture as well as palm production, an industry of woven goods that provided its residents with

FIGURE 13. Primary school in Santo Tomás Ocotepec, ca. 1965.
Source: Instituto Nacional de los Pueblos Indígenas, Fototeca Nacho López.

some cash revenue. They sold their palm hats, baskets, and rugs to visiting intermediaries or at Tlaxiaco's weekly, Saturday market. Weavers spent their days in cave-like structures built to keep the material moist and pliable for weaving. The town's arable lands suffered from extreme erosion, with some tracts reminiscent of moonscapes. Carlos Incháustegui, the Peruvian anthropologist who had worked with the INI in the Mixteca since its arrival, described local health conditions in 1968 as "deplorable" and government services as nonexistent. According to Incháustegui, local agriculture was, in effect, "ceremonial" given its low yield.[33] Because of these conditions, significant numbers of community members began to migrate in search of support for themselves and their families. At the time, just under a third of the population were engaged in seasonal labor elsewhere. Most had traveled northeast to the border region between Oaxaca and Veracruz. There, on the tropical plains between the two states, people from Magdalena Peñasco worked harvesting pineapples and sugarcane. They made sure to return home in May for the annual corn planting.

Magdalena Peñasco was not atypical of Mixtec towns during the 1960s. Other highlanders also engaged in seasonal migration, not only to Veracruz but also southwest toward the coffee-producing regions surrounding Putla. These practices created precedents for what would become a wave of migration, this time further north to the emerging commercial agricultural fields of Sinaloa, Sonora, and Baja California.[34] Indeed, by the late 1960s one could witness up to one thousand men gathered in Tlaxiaco on a given day ready to depart for these northern states.[35] *Enganchadores*, labor recruiters, targeted locals to work in the booming agricultural fields, which required large amounts of seasonal labor for tomato and other fruit and vegetable harvests. Federal authorities devoted significant development aid to these regions, which became synonymous with the Mexican Green Revolution. They were targeted for investment in large part because of their proximity to US markets. While the *enganchadores* initially focused their recruitment efforts on bilingual men, monolingual Mixtec speakers also made the journey north. Labor recruiters often provided free transportation to the northern fields, and at times advances on wages. Working conditions were notoriously bad. In the Culiacán valley migrant laborers from the Mixteca lived in squalid conditions, exposed to the elements and chemical fertilizers and pesticides.[36] The differential between the wages offered for agricultural labor in the north and the immiserated condition of many Mixtec communities in Oaxaca made the travails worthwhile for many.

Still others chose to migrate further north to the United States. The US's Bracero Program offered Mexicans legal guest worker status, particularly but not exclusively in agriculture. One such migrant was Vincente Ramírez. Born in a small town in the Silacayoapam district of the Mixteca, bordering the state of Guerrero, Ramírez was orphaned as a young child. He grew up working odd carpentry jobs and planting corn with an ox. At age twenty-five, Ramírez decided to try his chances in "El Norte" and enrolled in the Bracero Program. His first border crossing took place in 1955, and he eventually labored under three different bracero contracts. Among the different jobs Ramírez worked, one was picking lettuce in Salinas, California. Like many Mixtec migrants, Ramírez crossed the border various times over the course of his life, sometimes with authorization, other times without. In describing what motivated him to journey north, he invoked the poverty of his youth and the opportunities the program provided him and his family.[37] The Bracero Program was one more way in which Mixtec labor was integrated into the national and international economy, while it did little to integrate the region's own economic production.

By the time Ramírez first enrolled, the Bracero Program was over a decade old. It had begun in 1942, and the state of Oaxaca had issued its first bracero contracts in 1944. The program lasted until 1964, and roughly 4.5 million contracts were drawn up during the twenty-two years of its existence. In Oaxaca, the state's *subsecretario del trabajo* and an agent from the US Department of Labor set up the first contracting center in downtown Oaxaca City.[38] Officials placed a *convocatoria*, formal announcement, in Oaxacan newspapers to publicize the program. Local officials and government agencies often played a determinative role in the process, as they certified applicants' legal status. Initial stipulations required potential braceros to be at least twenty-one years of age, to not be *ejiditarios* (members of agrarian reform communities), and to pass a medical exam. Applicants were also asked to provide a birth certificate, something many from rural regions had trouble procuring. Oaxacan state officials frequently assisted potential braceros, producing birth certificates on the spot for in-need applicants. The arbitrary nature by which authorities meted out contracts, with some officials favoring applicants from their hometowns, reflected the persistence of communal ties in the state.

While US labor needs drove the Bracero Program, Mexican authorities generally embraced the initiative. These officials viewed it as a solution to the lack of employment in rural regions and as a modernizing tool for Mexico's rural population. National periodicals depicted Indigenous campesinos as ideal braceros, in need of not only employment but a cultural transformation away from their indigeneity. In Oaxaca, lack of Spanish language proficiency could constitute a barrier for potential braceros and Indigenous language speakers were more likely to migrate to the US without authorization.[39] Nonetheless, Oaxacans did enroll in the program. In the initial years it proved particularly popular in the central valleys and the Mixteca.[40] Whether through travel to commercial agriculture in northern Mexico, or authorized and unauthorized crossings into the United States, seasonal migration became a central survival strategy for many in the Mixteca and Oaxaca generally. This reality was reflected in the popular expression *andar de pata de perro* (to walk with dog paws, to be always on the move).[41]

The INI's voluntary resettlement initiative coincided with the final years of the Bracero Program. Both offered economic opportunities for highlanders. The two policies also shared an emphasis on a male head of household and breadwinner. The Bracero Program highlighted financial support for families as a key justification, even as it temporarily separated the male breadwinner from the family unit. The INI resettlement initiative in turn emphasized family units in the organization of new agricultural communities: for example, in 1963 resettling three groups of twenty-five families in three different areas of the Jamiltepec ejido: Los Charquitos, El Zarzal, and La Tuza.[42] Both programs placed women in subordinated positions to their male partners and centered the family unit as the salient category in public policy. If patriarchal norms united the two programs, what distinguished them was that one offered access to wage labor while the other offered land and permanent resettlement. This difference was particularly significant in the Mixteca Alta, where community membership and connection to place were highly valued.

Anatomy of a Failure: Environment, Infrastructure, and Local Opposition

While the highland and coastal regions of the Mixteca share common linguistic and cultural traits, their environments stand in stark contrast. The Mixteca Alta is dry, with erratic rainfall, cold temperatures due to high altitude, and often characterized by poor soil quality and high levels of erosion. This situation is in stark contrast to the tropical climates of the Costa Chica and Isthmus. Indeed, regional development studies repeatedly emphasized this juxtaposition. Some highland communities' rejection of the resettlement program explicitly invoked the coast's climate, saying there was little interest in moving to *tierra caliente*. The respective crops that the two environments supported also varied dramatically: cotton, coconuts, papaya, and mango on the coast, corn in the highlands. These distinct climates suggest a plausible explanation for the program's lack of popularity. There is a commonsense logic behind the notion that highlanders were ill-suited for a permanent transition to a tropical climate. But highlanders traveled to the tropical plains of Veracruz to work in the pineapple and sugarcane harvests, and the scalding temperatures of the Sinaloa fields did not deter them from laboring there.

If environmental factors do not fully explain the program's failure, perhaps the lack of infrastructure connecting the two regions played a role. Early INI officials, including Gonzalo Aguirre Beltrán, had called for the construction of new highways to connect the highlands with the Costa

Chica, but these were slow to arrive. Those from the Alta who resettled on the Isthmus could expect a two- or three-day journey: from their home communities to Tlaxiaco, from Tlaxiaco to Oaxaca City, and then on to Juchitán, before making the final leg of the trip to the new settlements.[43] Certainly, Oaxaca's forbidding topography was a factor in people's decisions to participate in the program, but given highlanders' ability to migrate on foot to Veracruz or travel 1,200 miles via bus to Sinaloa, this explanation reads as less than compelling.

In addition to the logistics of transporting people in large numbers—in 1963 alone INI authorities hoped to move two hundred families to the Isthmus—there was opposition to the new arrivals on the coast. While the La Tuza conflict was the most explosive, similar clashes appeared in almost every new settlement. Those from Nuyoó, who had so quickly and earnestly embraced the program, found themselves harassed by the local army detachment, which had taken the settlers' machetes away from them.[44] Locals also tried to force the resettled Nuyoó families into paying fees for the government-requisitioned land.[45] Federal officials set up another NCPA community, San José de Progreso, near Tututepec. The residents of San José, many relocated from Chalcatongo, found themselves attacked by Tututepec's municipal and *bienes comunales* (communal land) authorities, who opposed their presence.[46] As recounted in the case of La Tuza, opposition to the resettled highlanders could and often did turn violent. Communal land committees and municipal authorities dealt with competing interests over the land and frequently were controlled by caciques or powerful families. In La Tuza, INI officials claimed that such families mobilized the support of settlers from the neighboring state of Guerrero to gain control over the contested land.

Given the institute's presence on the Costa Chica since 1954, it was well aware of the African-descended communities located on the low-lying land between Jamiltepec and the Río Verde. Prominent researchers associated with the INI conducted studies of the Afro-Mexican population prior to the establishment of the Jamiltepec center. Gonzalo Aguirre Beltrán, a pioneer of Afro-Mexican studies, published on the topic in 1946 and again in 1948 with an ethnography of Cuajinicuilapa, Guerrero, a town located just northwest of Jamiltepec. His ethnography inspired more research on African-descended peoples in the area.[47] In 1957, Aguirre Beltrán estimated a total of 120,000 "Afromestizos" throughout the republic.[48] These studies reveal early indigenista attention to African-descended peoples, but at times they repeated long-standing colonial tropes of an African propensity for violence and aggression. The INI's Jamiltepec center extended agricultural assistance to such communities but did not develop specific programs for their "integration" or development in the way it did for the resettled highlanders.

Over the first decade of indigenista efforts on the Costa Chica, the center's relationship with Jamiltepec elites, in particular the Iglesias family, soured. Whereas Director Mijangos had collaborated, even socialized, with the family during the early years, by the mid-1960s the two were locked in conflict. Members of the Iglesias clan exploited their control of the Jamiltepec ejido to secure the best lands. Newcomers from Guerrero had also settled in the region to access better lands. At times they acted independently, but INI officials claimed that the family employed the Guerrense settlers to divide the ejido to their own advantage. Officials portrayed the Black population as also working at the Iglesias's behest. Doña Pancha denied such allegations. In a 1969 interview, she declared, "I am just an old lady. I took care of my seventeen children and they are all very well today. I am not a *limosnera* [beggar]. Everything I have I worked hard for." Doña Pancha denied being a cacique and claimed that her family's extensive holdings all fell within ejidal law. Nonetheless, she promised to bring seven hundred "negros" to presidential candidate Luis Echeverría's upcoming campaign stop in Pinotepa Nacional. This betrayed her ability to mobilize the local population.[49] In 1967, in order to deal with the increasingly fraught situation, INI officials brought the indefatigable Ramón Hernández López, who had left the highlands in 1965 to found the INI's new coordinating center in Michoacán, back to Oaxaca to lead their efforts on the coast.

The conflict with the Iglesias family was just one of the problems officials encountered in their resettlement efforts. As early as 1963, the program suffered from a lack of funds. Officials in Oaxaca reported that they had enough resources to support just five families moving to the coast.[50] Funding came from both state and federal sources, and given the multiple agencies involved, coordination between institutions complicated the program's implementation. This was a "high modernism" on the cheap, as the INI was often considered the caboose of the development train in Mexico. The lion's share of federal development dollars had gone to support commercial agriculture in the North, precisely where many from the Mixteca Alta now labored. Nor did indigenista policy challenge the existing patterns of unequal land tenure, a factor shaping both the highlands and the coast. Perhaps because of this confluence of interests and actors, and because regional development frameworks failed to address political and economic issues of inequality, federal officials intent on populating and developing the coast did not see the limitations of the project.

While logistics and financing certainly shaped the success of the project, the program was also limited by something more basic: the difference between land and labor. The resettlement program offered people land, agricultural credits, and permanent resettlement. Most highland communities rejected that offer.[51] Highlanders did, however, engage in seasonal migration for wage labor. Wage labor offered the possibility of increased income while maintaining, or at least allowing for the hope of maintaining, a connection to one's place of origin. While many people desire to maintain connection to home, Mixteca Alta communities' unique traditions, culture, and cosmovision make that dynamic stronger. Communal governance structures demand labor and service from their members, commitments that often define community members' individual identities and relationships. INI anthropologists had spent a decade or more analyzing and documenting local religious, cultural, and linguistic practices. And important indigenista officials, such as Ramón Hernández López, were themselves from the region and were bilingual in Mixtec and Spanish. That knowledge of highland culture and community relations appears to have had little impact on the conceptualization or implementation of the resettlement program. Permanent abandonment of their communities was too high a price for many from the highlands.

This is evident in the response of the *consejo de ancianos* (elders' council) of Magdalena Peñasco to Hernández's direct solicitation of their participation in the program. Despite the community's notorious poverty, the elders said they could not just abandon "their lands and saints."[52] The communal governance structure of most Mixtec communities, their connection to place, their beliefs in gods that inhabited the mountains around which they lived, and the corn harvest cycle's spiritual significance all shaped residents' survival choices in the 1960s. Magdalena's rejection of the INI program and sustained engagement with seasonal migration present a striking example of this. Studies of Mixtec migration have emphasized the grinding poverty and inequalities that compelled people to travel. That migration, often to work under some of the harshest labor

FIGURE 14. INI director Alfonso Caso meeting with palm weavers in Tlaxiaco, 1965.
Source: Instituto Nacional de los Pueblos Indígenas, Fototeca Nacho López, Hermanos Mayo.

conditions, was an Indigenous survival strategy.[53] This strategy was not unique to the Mixteca. Native peoples across the Americas engaged in similar tactics, while maintaining connections to home communities and Indigenous ways of being.[54] People from the Mixteca Alta took up seasonal wage labor as increasingly necessary for their survival. The resettlement program, while attractive to some, particularly those with long-standing ties to the coast, failed to recognize the significance of community membership in the Mixteca.

Conclusion

When indigenista officials arrived in the early 1950s, their institute was one of the few federal agencies with a presence in the region. As such they challenged existing authorities, many of whose power had gone unchecked in the first half of the century. INI leadership came from Mexico City, but their development work drew in local individuals, many of whom, like Ramón Hernández López, viewed the institute as a vehicle to improve the Mixteca. This generation often invoked a *mística indigenista*, a deeply felt personal commitment and dedication to Indigenous empowerment, to characterize their work, one that they claimed subsequent generations lacked. These pioneers transformed the Mixteca, though in ways they did not necessarily anticipate. State funding for Indigenous development never matched the expansive indigenista vision of change. Nor could this strand of development substantively alter the broader dynamics of capitalist growth in Mexico, which centralized production and employment in urbanizing cities and northern regions. Despite indigenista attention to local culture and language, federal planners rarely integrated local knowledge into their formulation of development policy.[55]

The INI's effort to "integrate" regions such as the Mixteca was an uphill battle. While regional development sought to transform and integrate the place into the larger nation, it primarily facilitated the integration of Mixtec labor into national and international markets.[56] The institute's public health, education, and road-building initiatives all facilitated this process. Mixtec communities elaborated migration strategies that at times engaged with and at other times rejected federal programs. They used seasonal migration as their own tool of development. These were strategies created out of necessity and hardship but nonetheless involved ingenuity and perseverance. In coming decades, those migration patterns became a mass phenomenon and shaped community life and politics.[57] This was an unintended consequence of regional development. Mixteca Alta communities engaged in such migration as a way to negotiate an increasingly interconnected economy, both nationally and internationally.

By the summer of 1968, INI officials on the coast were fighting a rearguard action to defend the few highland families who had chosen to relocate. As the conflict in La Tuza escalated, Hernández led the efforts to resolve the issue to the highlanders' benefit. He wrote INI national director Alfonso Caso and Oaxacan governor Rodolfo Brena Torres (1968–70), seeking their support. He also requested police protection for the Mixtec families. Here on the Costa Chica the INI challenged powerful, landed interests on behalf of landless campesinos. Indeed, Hernández had a personal history of political militancy, advocating left-wing politics in his youth and challenging conversative Tlaxiaco's Catholic officials during his tenure there. He and others understood their work in political terms, and indigenismo, as it was elaborated on the ground on the Costa Chica, was self-consciously anticolonial. Officials confronted what they sometimes referred to as "feudal" relations and sought to empower Indigenous campesinos. Nonetheless, there were moments in which the INI's interaction with its development targets replicated paternal, perhaps colonial, power relations, as they intervened on behalf of others.[58] That intervention frequently risked violence. In a meeting near Jamiltepec, in which INI officials, representing the relocated families, and the Iglesias family met to resolve the conflict, the discussion grew heated. As tempers flared, representatives of Doña Pancha physically assaulted Hernández.[59] In an effort to deescalate the conflict, Caso transferred Hernández to the coordinating center in Tlapa, Guerrero. This was one moment near the inauspicious end of INI's resettlement efforts. However, the institute's conflict with the Iglesias family did not end with Hernández's reassignment. In the coming years, INI employees who organized local campesinos into a cooperative came into conflict with the family once again. Jamiltepec experienced increased violence throughout the 1970s.[60]

On the horizon, a new generation of indigenista intellectuals, many shaped by the government's repression of the 1968 Mexico City student movement, called into question the work of Hernández and his generation. They claimed that INI policy itself was another iteration of colonial power directed toward Native peoples. While indigenista development had self-consciously sought to empower Indigenous actors and understand the origins of inequality, these young critics framed the state as an inheritor of colonial logics. They pointed to INI regional studies, which, while diverse, frequently invoked colonial legacies in their diagnoses of persistent poverty. While the resettlement program aimed to alleviate this situation, there were echoes of colonial logics at play on the Costa Chica, as the relocation of Indigenous populations had clear colonial precedents.[61] In contrast, Hernández, a Mixtec INI official who confronted mestizo elites that refused to respect federal authority, believed in leveraging federal authority to confront long-standing inequalities. The two generations in many respects were speaking past each other. Could the Mexican state be an agent of anticolonialism? Or was it in fact facilitating colonial relations? These questions shaped a dramatic rupture in indigenista thought in the years to come.

4

Indigenismo in the Age of Three Worlds
Oaxacan Youth and Mexico's Democratic Opening

> *The principal characteristic of Latin American development policy is a clear polarization between sectors: one that amply receives the benefits of development policy while another remains almost entirely marginalized from said benefits. In this last sector we can include Indigenous communities.*
> —Alejandro Marroquín, 1968¹

IN THE spring of 1968, delegates from throughout the Americas gathered in the colonial city of Pátzcuaro. Located in the Purépecha highlands of the southwestern state of Michoacán, the site was of symbolic importance. President Lázaro Cárdenas convened the first Inter-American Indigenista Congress here in 1940. That congress consolidated Mexico's leading role in indigenista policy and gave impetus to numerous national indigenista efforts throughout the hemisphere. Pátzcuaro's Indigenous past, its colonial aura, and its connection to the revered Cárdenas all contributed to its exalted position within PRI political culture. Here the Instituto Indigenista Interamericano returned to host its sixth congress in April 1968.² A growing division within the indigenista project was on display at the 1968 meetings. Carlos Guzmán Böckler, the Guatemalan representative, noted from the floor of the congress that the delegates were living in a time of changing values and "confrontation between generations." In a nod to the Cold War violence afflicting his home country, Guzmán Böckler argued that these new values were battling to rise to the surface in "a bath of blood and tears."³

The delegates traveled to the congress in the midst of rising global unrest. The months preceding the meetings witnessed the Tet Offensive against US forces in Vietnam and the assassination of Dr. Martin Luther King Jr. in Memphis, Tennessee. The political crisis that would eventually erupt into the Prague Spring was simmering in Czechoslovakia, and massive street mobilizations of students and workers rocked France in the month of May. In Mexico later that summer, many of the young anthropologists at the congress would immerse themselves in a youth movement centered in Mexico City. That movement, and its subsequent repression on October 2, resulted in a profound crisis in the relationship between intellectuals and the Mexican government.[4] In Brazil and Argentina, students demanding university autonomy and reform clashed with police in the month of June.[5] In August and September of that year, the Conference of Latin American Bishops met in Medellin, Colombia, where they declared their "preferential option for the poor." Inspired by Paulo Freire and currents of liberation theology, the assembled bishops contributed to the growing sense of urgency in the need to confront long-standing inequalities. Radical social change appeared not only possible but seemingly inevitable as countries as diverse as Cuba and the Congo challenged colonial relations and instituted agrarian reform.[6] These events percolated through Mexican dissident culture, shaping a generation that would challenge a regime that ruled in the name of revolution.[7]

The 1968 congress was a moment of continuity but also of change, in which a younger generation confronted long-standing indigenista positions with a renewed anticolonialism and new ideas about cultural rights and the role of the state. Indeed, this generation called into question many of the assumptions that undergirded the regional development projects of the previous decade such as those described in the preceding chapters. Rejecting notions of regional causes of Indigenous inequality, this generation emphasized ideas of dependent development and put forth global frameworks for theorizing Indigenous liberation. While this was part of the global 1968 moment, as others have observed, the political effervescence of that year reflected changes at work in preceding decades.[8] In the case of indigenista development, the debates at the Instituto Indigenista Interamericano's 1968 congress were symptomatic of the rise of a renewed Third-Worldist anticolonialism.

In this chapter I explore this rupture in the indigenista project through the experience of a group of Oaxacan youth trained as promotores bilingües, agents of development. The youth, educated at the Instituto de Investigación y Integración Social del Estado de Oaxaca (IIISEO) in Oaxaca City, returned to their home communities in the early 1970s to carry out a variety of development and education initiatives. There they confronted the limitations of institutional support for their work and began to call for their professionalization as teachers and control over their development and education projects. As they challenged the institutions that had trained them professionally, they articulated new theories of liberation that centered Indigenous peoples' unique cultural and historical experiences. In yet another unintended consequence of indigenista policy, the youth took advantage of a key period of reformism in Mexico, President Luis Echeverría's *apertura democrática* or democratic opening (1970–76).

In the wake of World War II, countries throughout the global South began to cast off European colonial power. From the struggle against British rule on the Indian subcontinent, to the Vietnamese fight against French occupation, to the varied movements against colonial rule in Africa, the Third World emerged as not merely a place but a "political project," as Vijay Prashad has put it.[9] The Americas were not immune to this phenomenon. Though formal independence from colonial powers was achieved by most Latin American countries in the first decades of the nineteenth century, the question of imperial power and exploitation remained central in the twentieth century as people struggled against authoritarian regimes, frequently supported by US or European interests. Countries from Asia, Africa, and the Americas came together in international forums to articulate alternative visions of development. The Non-Aligned Movement is the most famous example of this. In opposition to the United States and the Soviet Union, nonaligned countries sought to chart an independent path. Mexico, with its own tradition of internationalism, was a relative latecomer to this political formation. During the 1960s, President López Mateos, without officially joining the Movement, sought to ally Mexico with the participating countries and intervene in international debates.[10] Nonetheless, it was during President Echeverría's term that an explicit Third-Worldism came to define Mexican foreign policy and profoundly shape domestic dissent.

Mexico, though for much of the midcentury aligned politically and economically with its northern neighbor, the United States, came to play a leadership role in the 1970s Third World movement. President Echeverría revived economic nationalism domestically and through expanded diplomacy advocated for parallel policies internationally. By the early 1970s, the United Nations had become a forum where nonaligned countries had significant influence, even though the Security Council continued to be dominated by the victors of World War II. Given the reality of Third World nations' prominent role in international governance and the existence of leftist administrations in Cuba and Chile, President Echeverría sought to rehabilitate the PRI political project by aligning Mexico with this international trend.[11] While some observers have framed the Mexican government's reformism during this period as a strategy of co-optation of domestic dissent, an equally important story is how ordinary people took advantage of government discourse and opportunities and used them for their own ends.

President Echeverría was explicit about his break with previous administrations, stating that Mexico would shift from the period of "stabilizing development" associated with the Mexican Miracle to one of *desarrollo compartido*, or "shared development." Indeed, for a brief period both the Echeverría administration and some international institutions identified inequality itself as a barrier to development.[12] The democratic opening went beyond rhetoric. Federal authorities initiated a dramatic increase in social spending in all sectors, but particularly in education. The number of primary school teachers in Mexico doubled, and federal authorities expanded higher education, creating new academic programs and university systems, such as the Universidad Autónoma Metropolitana in Mexico City in 1974.[13] In addition, the federal government created new rural development agencies and policies to distribute land and combat poverty.[14] The voting age was lowered from twenty-one to eighteen.[15] Together these changes constituted an expansion of the state sector as the regime tried to accommodate a growing population pushing for increased economic and educational opportunities.[16] These measures, along with state intervention in industry and failed efforts at tax reform, constituted a dramatic attempt to reformulate and stabilize an aging political system.[17]

This broader context of decolonization and the attendant movements against racism called into question prior indigenista policy. Paradoxically, some of the leading critics of indigenista policy, such as Guillermo Bonfil Batalla, Margarita Nolasco, and Mercedes Olivera, achieved leadership positions in the INI and other Indigenous development initiatives during the 1970s. While these figures had been dissidents in the prior decade, and

FIGURE 15. The INI supported Conasupo, a state-sponsored food company, as it opened stores throughout the region. Here, a Conasupo-INI store in Magdalena Peñasco.
Source: Instituto Nacional de los Pueblos Indígenas, Fototeca Nacho López, Raúl Rocha.

Nolasco herself had participated in the 1968 Mexico City student movement, President Echeverría's *apertura democrática* welcomed many former opposition figures into government agencies, with some gaining top positions in the Indigenous development and education ministries. Indeed, Gonzalo Aguirre Beltrán, someone many dissidents held in high esteem, replaced Alfonso Caso as director of the INI in 1970, after Caso's death.

The Third-Worldist development model included reinvigorated rural development, land reform, and antipoverty programs as well as an incipient turn toward anticolonial pedagogy. During this period the target population of indigenista reforms increasingly invoked Native rights in their own political organizing. Teachers and campesinos combined traditional class-based rhetoric associated with 1930s agrarianism with invocations of indigeneity and connection to the land. Just as the government intensified its strategic invocations of Indigenous Mexico, dissidents, both within and outside state agencies, found Indigenous self-representation a meaningful way to speak to the moment. Furthermore, critics of official education models drew on anticolonial thinkers such as Franz Fanon and Albert Memmi as they analyzed federal policy.[18] The confluence of development models premised on Indigenous participation and the rise of a renewed anticolonial politics tended to shape individuals' and social movements' political rhetoric toward claims of rights and autonomy based on Indigenous ancestry. This coproduction occurred in Mexico but has parallels in Indigenous peoples' activism throughout the hemisphere. Officially, the INI shifted to promote an *indigenismo de participacion*, a participatory model of indigenismo. And in Oaxaca the democratic opening created opportunities for people to challenge state and federal authorities.

Oaxaca de Juárez: Conduit of Radicalism

The promotores' early instruction and politicization took place in Oaxaca City, which had grown substantially in the early 1970s. Beginning in the summer of 1968, a university movement there transformed the existing student federation, the Federación de Estudiantes Oaxaqueños, previously a pillar of PRI politics and a mechanism for political advancement, into a mobilized organization. The Oaxacan university movement had direct ties to events in the national capital, as many of its initiators had traveled to and even studied at UNAM.[19] Some of those students returned to form new organizations in Oaxaca, including the Bufete Popular Universitario and eventually the Coalición Obrero Campesino Estudiantil de Oaxaca (COCEO) in 1972. The activists sought to reform their university, UABJO, demanding democratic control of the university's administration and political autonomy. They eventually broadened their struggle to support independent trade unions in the state capital and peasant groups who were engaged in land seizures on the outskirts of the city.[20] Indeed, the COCEO would go on to play a crucial role in the overthrow of Oaxacan governor Manuel Zárate Aquino in 1977.

In this milieu the protest music of Cubans Silvio Rodríguez and Pablo Milanés intermingled with the classic *rancheras* of Pedro Infante and José Alfredo Jiménez.[21] The combination of *nueva trova* and Mexican *rancheras* speaks to the cultural power of the Cuban Revolution in Mexico and suggests the way in which youth embraced the cosmopolitanism of the global sixties alongside long-standing local traditions. The Oaxacan university students also relied on local cultural traditions in their mobilization for democratic reforms. During the last days of carnival in 1974, the Federación de Estudiantes Oaxaqueños organized its own *comparsa*, a costumed parade with bands, to promote its demands.[22] The bringing together of these local and global elements in Oaxacan protest culture suggests how events in provincial Mexico were shaped by new political cultures and discourses.

During the same period, a movement of youth and popular classes surged in the Isthmus town of Juchitán, culminating in the ouster of the PRI from the municipal government in 1981, one of the first such cases in the republic.[23] The Coalición Obrera, Campesina, Estudiantil del Istmo (COCEI), the organization that united the various struggles in Juchitán, built its strength through a Zapotec Indigenous identity along with traditions of leftist militancy. The COCEI organizers and activists in Oaxaca City established direct links to support each other, particularly against reprisals from the state government. These struggles were part of a broader generational conflict in which local PRI authorities, many of whom had participated in postrevolutionary state building, began to lose power, and population growth created a new generation of Indigenous youth.[24] The social pact that had successfully equated nation, party, and community in parts of Indigenous Mexico came undone in the 1970s as the state was forced to deal with a plethora of new actors.[25] In a place such as Oaxaca, with a long tradition of government negotiation with Indigenous leaders, this new generation leveraged the rhetoric of the democratic opening to challenge entrenched local authorities.

In addition to these generational conflicts, Catholic liberation theology, new strands of clandestine leftism, and an evolving official indigenista policy all contributed to a shift in the political environment of Indigenous Mexico. These forces had a particular impact in the southern states of Guerrero, Oaxaca, and Chiapas, each with relatively large Indigenous populations and high levels of rural poverty. While liberation theology became influential in Latin America generally during this period, Mexico's particular history of conservative church opposition to the postrevolutionary state meant that the doctrine remained a minority current within the country.[26] Indeed, Ernesto Corripio y Ahumada, the archbishop of Antequera, the archdiocese covering much of Oaxaca, was a staunch conservative, and as seen in chapter 2, Catholic opposition to federal authority produced violent clashes in the early 1960s.[27] Yet by the early years of the following decade a small number of Christian base communities were at work in the state capital, and liberation theology emerged at the institutional level through Bartolomé Carrasco Briseño, who replaced Corripio y Ahumada in 1976.[28]

Nor was the clandestine Left necessarily at odds with liberation theologians. The most notable example is the active collaboration of Archbishop Samuel Ruiz with Maoist organizers, many of them young northerners, in the organization of the 1974 Indigenous congress in San Cristóbal de las Casas, Chiapas.[29] In the aftermath of government repression of urban protests, and given the long-standing repression of rural agrarian movements, many came to view armed struggle as the only avenue for substantive social change. The most notable example of armed opposition during this period was that of the Partido de los Pobres in Guerrero, but in Oaxaca too a clandestine group, the Unión del Pueblo, took responsibility for multiple bombings in the state capital. Several armed groups were active in Chiapas, including the Fuerzas de Liberación Nacional, an organizational antecedent to the Ejército Zapatista de Liberación Nacional (EZLN).[30]

The government responded to the opposition with a *pan o palo*, bread or stick, strategy. Opposition forces that could be accommodated within state structures were dealt with through the *pan* approach; those that would not accommodate to PRI control were dealt with through targeted violence, the *palo*. Whereas state violence directed against Mexico City youth in 1968 has become iconic, the regime's use of the *pan* strategy was perhaps of greater significance. The democratic opening is most emblematic of this approach. Echeverría, who himself headed up the *palo* strategy as chief of the government in October of 1968, oversaw a liberalization in which government critics were welcomed into state agencies.[31] The president's rhetorical left turn and dramatic expansion of public spending responded to both domestic pressure and the changing context of the Cold War by presenting Mexico as a Third World nationalist government and an ally of countries such as Cuba and Chile.[32] These alliances helped transform Echeverría's image from PRI bureaucrat into progressive nationalist leader, an identity he played to by sporting *guayaberas* and sunglasses in his frequent travels throughout the republic.[33]

The late 1960s and 1970s saw military juntas come to power in Brazil and Argentina, to cite just two examples, and violent conflicts between leftist opposition and military regimes divided much of Central America. While the Mexican military never threatened the civilian leadership with a seizure of power, the differences between Mexico and its Latin American peers during the Cold War become less pronounced upon closer examination. For example, General Juan Velasco Alvarado seized power in a bloodless coup in Peru in October 1968, and while his was clearly a military government, he pursued a progressive nationalist agenda in ways similar to the efforts of Echeverría in Mexico.[34] Nor was Mexico immune to threats of civil war and military repression. Echeverría's foreign and domestic policies incurred conservative opposition, and rumors of military coups circulated in both the Mexican Right and Left.[35] His rhetoric and policies allowed conservative critics to paint him as akin to President Salvador Allende of Chile, whose state visit to Mexico in 1972 seemed to confirm their critique. Fears over left-wing terrorism drew on this international context, as well as on a small but significant domestic guerrilla threat. Kidnappings and armed attacks on businesses and government buildings occurred in cities throughout the republic. In the summer of 1972, as Oaxaca prepared to celebrate its annual Guelaguetza, a festival of regional music and dance, three bombs exploded throughout the city, killing one person.[36] Mexico, like its Latin American neighbors, experienced increased levels of political polarization and violence.

As part of this generalized political effervescence, in April 1975 the promotores bilingües occupied regional development centers throughout Oaxaca. From the Sierra Sur town of Miahuatlán, to the arid highlands of the Mixteca Alta, to the valley of the Papaloapan Dam project, these youth took control of INI coordinating centers and held them for more than a month. They demanded professional training and the creation of positions for themselves as federal teachers. Their banners accused the Mexican government of ethnocide against Native peoples, denouncing the regime's celebration of Indigenous culture as a mask for continued exploitation.[37]

The youth who occupied the development centers had been trained at the IIISEO, which embodied many of the changes wrought by the democratic opening. The institute embraced broadly anticolonial rhetoric and employed a generation of dissident social scientists to lead the effort to combat poverty in the state. Whereas previous federal education policy had relied primarily on normal school–trained teachers, during the 1970s officials shifted to rely more heavily on those with backgrounds in higher education. Yet the IIISEO was also rooted in a nineteenth-century Oaxacan tradition, the system of *pupilos*, wards, in which well-off Oaxaca City families took in Indigenous children from the countryside to work as *mozos*, servants, in their homes in exchange for the child's room and board and education expenses. One of Oaxaca City's prominent society members, Mariela Morales de Altamirano, had developed a reputation for taking in young girls for this purpose. Oaxacan governor Rodolfo Brena Torres (1962–68) offered to build on Morales's perceived success by creating an institute dedicated to the improvement of rural homes, the Escuela de Mejoradoras del Hogar Rural (EMHR). In 1964, Governor Brena Torres tapped Morales to run the EMHR.

The school trained the girls in a host of domestic skills as well as Spanish language literacy. In 1969, Víctor Bravo Ahuja became governor of Oaxaca and in that capacity presided over the annual graduation ceremony of the EMHR. After the performance of El Jarabe del Guajolote and Fandango Mixe, traditional Oaxacan dances, the governor dismissed the young women with the perfunctory words, "I hope that one day, thanks to all of you, every Oaxacan will speak the national language."[38] Celebrating Indigenous aesthetics while declaring the need for Spanish language proficiency was part of the indigenista tradition. In the coming years, the school started by Morales underwent an important transformation under the leadership of the new governor's wife, Gloria Ruiz de Bravo Ahuja, a linguist trained at the Colegio de México, one of the country's most prestigious educational centers.

The Bravo Ahujas were an up-and-coming political couple whose fortunes were tied to the *camarilla*, political faction, of Luis Echeverría. Víctor was from Tuxtepec, on the Oaxacan border with Veracruz. He attended the Instituto Politécnico Nacional (IPN) in Mexico City and began his political career in the northern city of Monterrey. Part of a new generation of PRI bureaucrats, Bravo Ahuja was connected to Mexico's technical education programs: prior to his term as governor he had served as director of technical education in the Secretaría de Educación Pública. While there in Mexico City, Gloria enrolled in the Colegio de México, known for its Spanish language linguistics program. Victor served as governor of Oaxaca for just two years, when, in 1970, incoming president Echeverría named him secretary of education.

The IIISEO was formally constituted in August 1969 on the EMHR's former campus, located on the banks of the Atoyac River on the western edge of Oaxaca City. Owing to the political connections of its founders, the institute received initial funding from private interests such as the Monterrey Group, industrialists from that northern city, and the financiers

Elías Souraski and Carlos Trouyet. These funds, along with support from UNESCO and Mexican federal and state agencies, made the IIISEO a veritable elite school for Indigenous youth. It sported the newest equipment and research supplies at its campus and new, imported Ford Broncos for the administrative staff.[39]

The founders of the institute sought to create an innovative agency that could confront the historic problems of Indigenous development. As director, Gloria Ruiz de Bravo Ahuja broke with long-held castellanización (Spanish language instruction) approaches to create a new method that she viewed as more effective. Whereas SEP and INI policy had focused on Spanish language literacy, often through *cartillas* with vocabulary words, Ruiz de Bravo Ahuja and the IIISEO pioneered a method that focused on oral acquisition of Spanish first, prior to literacy instruction.[40] Further, the IIISEO aimed to combine development and research, in contrast to the INI, which the former viewed as having reverted mainly to the distribution of resources.[41] The institute was based on a pyramidal structure that included research and advanced degrees (bachelor's, master's, and doctoral degrees in "social integration"), while its main thrust was the training of *promotores*, agents of change.[42] The IIISEO trained these *promotores*, strategically recruited from each of Oaxaca's Indigenous groups, and then sent them back to their home communities to serve as leaders in community development.

To test the new language method and to train the *promotores*, the institute recruited preschool-age children, called *portadores*, to invoke the notion of bearers of culture. Ruiz de Bravo Ahuja believed she needed children who were 100 percent monolingual in an Indigenous language and to that end interviewed them to test their language ability. Reportedly, with the young girls Ruiz de Bravo Ahuja would offer a doll from a collection she kept behind her desk only if they would say something for her in Spanish. If they were able to utter a semblance of Spanish, they were given the doll but were rejected from the program.[43] If they could not, or did not, speak Spanish, they were selected as participants. In this "scientific" experiment, Indigenous language proficiency was in a rare but increasingly common case an advantage, prioritized in this new model of development.

In addition to the *portadores*, Ruiz de Bravo Ahuja relied on a staff who had directly participated in the radical politics of 1968 to carry out the mission of the institute. It consisted of social scientists and university-educated youth, almost all from Mexico City and abroad, with a handful

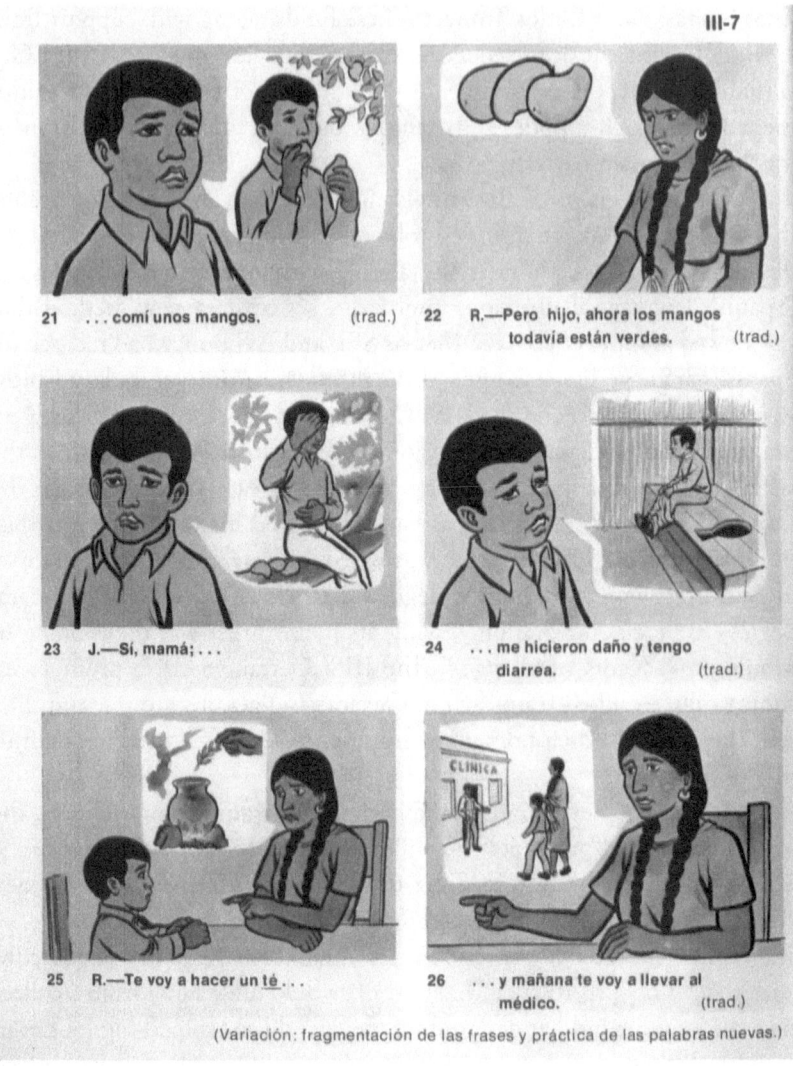

FIGURE 16. Lesson 7 of the IIISEO method for Spanish language teaching in Oaxaca. *Source:* Gloria Bravo Ahuja, *La enseñanza del español a los indígenas mexicanos* (Mexico City: El Colegio de México, 1977).

originating from the state of Oaxaca itself. Tasked to lead the research component of the IIISEO was Margarita Nolasco, a prominent anthropologist. Nolasco's generation had ruthlessly critiqued federal Indigenous policy in the preceding years; yet, as part of the democratic opening, she, like many of her cohort, gained an administrative position within a development agency. The essays collected in the 1970 publication *De eso que llaman antropología mexicana* became the clarion call of this generation, launching a trenchant critique of indigenista thought and policy. The authors argued that indigenista intellectuals continued a colonial practice of studying Indians in isolation and that such studies were particularly indefensible from a theoretical viewpoint.[44] Comparing themselves favorably to Bartolomé de las Casas and dissident Catholic orders of the colonial period, the authors denounced indigenista practice, arguing that "the anthropologist . . . is a technician in the manipulation of Indians."[45] Drawing theoretical support from figures ranging from Rodolfo Stavenhagen to Pablo González Casanova and from Herbert Marcuse to Andre Gunder Frank, Nolasco would argue that "indigenismo has always been a colonialist anthropology, devoted to the knowledge and thus use of the dominated."[46]

This critique formed part of a broader rupture in the social sciences generally, in which poverty and inequality became central concerns. In a Cold War context where modernization appeared to have failed to address these issues in both the United States and Latin America, social scientists initiated major studies to investigate the apparent dilemma. This shift in the framing of poverty and inequality was intimately connected to the rise of anticolonial and antiracist politics.[47] Oscar Lewis's ethnographic work published in 1959 in English as *Five Families: Mexican Case Studies in the Culture of Poverty* was perhaps the most emblematic and influential single book in this shift. By the early 1960s, Latin American social scientists, influenced by their own nationalist traditions and various currents of Marxism, had begun to articulate a counterexplanation to modernization theory's conceptualization of unequal economic development. Rather than positing an explanation based on deficit—the alleged lack of integration into modern economic activity—these intellectuals argued that so-called developing economies were deeply integrated into the world economy, some claimed from the colonial period forward, but that this integration was on fundamentally unequal terms.[48]

The implication for indigenista policy was clear: rural schoolteachers and other indigenista agents had been engaged in nothing less than ethnocide, in which Native peoples were forced into a homogenizing assimilation process, losing both cultural knowledge and language. Nolasco, as the head of the IIISEO research program, oriented the institute's activities around her structural explanations of rural and ethnic subordination. In addition, she supervised the "scientific" selection of promotores based on levels of monolingualism in each language group. Among the staff was Gerry Morris, a US-born Catholic priest who had worked with Ivan Illich in Cuernavaca, Morelos, outside of Mexico City. There, at the Centro Intercultural de Documentación, Illich and his colleagues promoted educational ideals that were critical of institutionalization and rigid classroom-focused models and instead encouraged the creativity of youth.[49] Illich and the center had a close relationship with the archbishop of Cuernavaca, Sergio Méndez Arceo, a prominent liberation theologian. Popular among the students, Morris taught by example through his work with the monolingual portadores selected by Ruiz de Bravo Ahuja.

Anticolonialism also spurred a renewed interest in linguistics.[50] Mexican linguists had had relatively little interest in studying the country's Indigenous languages. Indeed, a US evangelical organization, the Summer Institute of Linguistics (SIL), was responsible for much of the linguistic research done on Mexico's Native languages in previous decades. A key component of the IIISEO mission was a linguistic program that involved the cataloguing of Oaxaca's Native languages as well as an effort to develop effective methods for teaching Spanish language acquisition. Two institutions, the Colegio de México and the University of Texas at Austin, supported this goal through visiting personnel and material support.[51] The IIISEO's guiding principle was the integration of Indigenous regions and peoples into national society and economic activity without the loss of their Indigenous culture. This notion clearly derived from Nolasco's leadership but also from a broader coalescence of ideas regarding race, culture, and language during the early 1970s.[52] While Ruiz de Bravo Ahuja's objectives formed part of a shift in official indigenista policy and an effort to reformulate government institutions, the staff she counted on to carry this out were engaged in New Left politics and in turn shared and debated those ideas with their students.

Recruiting Indigenous Youth

Eva Ruiz was from the small town of Santa Inés de Zaragoza, a Mixtec community in the arid Nochixtlán valley, just north of Oaxaca City. She had finished primary school and had no money to continue her studies, so her uncle encouraged her to travel to Oaxaca City to sit for the IIISEO entrance exam, which she did successfully. In contrast, Santiago Salazar claimed his mother had tricked him into enrolling in the IIISEO. Salazar was from San Juan Teita, a community in the Mixteca Alta that had no more than five hundred residents and still functioned by usos y costumbres. In the fall of 1969 his mother, already taking his sister to the entrance exam, asked Santiago to accompany them on horseback to the nearest town. Upon arrival, she encouraged him to travel all the way to Oaxaca City and apply as well, which he did successfully. Two years later, Felipe Feria, another would-be promotor, would take a similar journey, traveling for three days on foot through the Sierra Madre del Sur to enroll in the institute.

All were responding to an official convocation sent out by the IIISEO to municipal authorities. The notice targeted specific regions for recruitment because of their relatively high levels of Indigenous language monolingualism. The requirements for enrollment were strict: the youth had to be between seventeen and twenty-one years of age, have completed six years of primary school (a major accomplishment in Oaxacan communities, which, if they had a primary school, often lacked instruction through the sixth grade), be bilingual in Spanish and their native language, and pass an entrance exam.[53] Out of the roughly five hundred youth who applied the first fall, only one hundred were selected, a majority of whom were young women, with a total of eighty-seven ultimately matriculating.[54] This female majority was a unique occurrence in a national context where male teachers had dominated rural education efforts.

Upon acceptance, the youth enrolled in a ten-month residential program. There was a strict separation of male and female students, as some Indigenous communities were particularly concerned about the commingling of their young girls with male students. The curriculum focused on a host of practical skills, including carpentry, domestic organization, sewing, elementary electronics, nutrition, basic linguistics, and, most importantly, Spanish language instruction. In addition, the students were asked to record their native languages in the school's linguistic laboratory. All of this, along with the occasional Catholic mass that *la maestra* Mariela encouraged them to attend, was required.

What differentiated the IIISEO curriculum from those of previous Indigenous education efforts were the courses offered on rural economy and the social sciences. It was in these disciplines that the youth were introduced to the concepts of inequality, exploitation, and dependency. Nolasco brought with her students from the ENAH to conduct research and train the young promotores. Among them were Alberto González Pintos, Héctor Manuel Popoca, and Hilario Aguilar, all of whom would go on to serve as advisers to the promotores in the struggle for professionalization. Indeed, the promotores' official charge was to break relations of domination in the countryside, often identified as exploitative relations between commercial centers and neighboring Native communities, and to engage in consciousness-raising among the communities they served.[55] In this way New Left politics engaged with the question of Indigenous liberation through both state activities and independent initiatives.

This training was broader and more advanced than that given to promotores employed by the INI, who received at most one month of preparation before being sent to communities as agents of development. The skills in which IIISEO youth were trained led some to label themselves *todólogos*, or experts in everything. Students were allowed to return home for vacations, yet many spent the entire ten months in Oaxaca City, as they could not afford the trip.[56] While the youth were groomed as agents of development, Oaxaca City, like much of the Americas at the time, was experiencing a new wave of dissidence directed at social and political change. After completing their training, the promotores were sent back to their home communities to collect population data for the institute's research component and to spur community development. While most focused on teaching Spanish language to preschool-age children, they were also tasked with many other activities. For example, the promotores sought to train municipal authorities in basic administrative skills, show them how to send telegrams, teach them to compose official letters to state agencies, and negotiate land conflicts (all too common in Oaxaca). The catchall term for these activities was *gestoría* (negotiation on behalf of clients for official purposes). The goal was to empower communities to organize for their own interests and to facilitate their access to government services. In some cases, the promotores were the only state agents in the town, while in others they worked alongside rural schoolteachers or INI development agents.

In general, the home communities warmly received their returning youth. Having gone away, earned an education, and come back to help, they were often viewed as respected sons and daughters of the community who brought with them needed skills and knowledge. One challenge was that in communities where status was often determined by marriage and positions occupied in the system of usos y costumbres, young, single promotores, particularly women, had difficulty gaining respect.[57] Yet their ability to solve basic problems with knowledge about state law and health care (including childbirth) meant they were called upon frequently. Despite their broad training, many ended up specializing in one service, usually language instruction to preschool-age youth, agricultural support, or community health.[58] In their work, they at times came into conflict with local authorities, and some primary school teachers viewed their activities outside the classroom as a challenge to their own authority.[59] More significantly, the promotores, whether from the IIISEO or the INI, often constituted a threat to caciques and they aligned themselves with movements for land reform and against entrenched local authorities.[60]

For their services the promotores were paid between 600 and 800 pesos a month, roughly equivalent to the daily minimum wage of 19 pesos, with no vacation or other time off.[61] Notably, they were not considered full-time state employees and thus had no access to federal health and social security services. Since they were single youth in their late teens and early twenties, administrators believed they did not need a larger salary, particularly in rural Oaxacan communities where little remunerated employment existed. The institutional expectations appear to have been that the youth were volunteers in their communities, though there is also evidence that the administrators knew the wages were insufficient.[62] While rural schoolteachers had traditionally engaged in community activities in addition to their work in the classroom, the promotores were placed directly into the broader community from the outset and brought with them a new vision of social change. This positioning allowed them to build close ties to the communities they served.

These communities were undergoing significant economic and demographic changes. One of the poorest states in Mexico, Oaxaca had a population of roughly two million people at the time, a majority of whom belonged to one of the state's sixteen officially recognized Indigenous groups.[63] Over half of the state's population supported itself through small-scale agriculture.[64] Because of the state's rugged topography, few regions were ripe for large-scale monoculture, with the exception of parts of the Pacific coast and the fertile valley bordering the state of Veracruz, where Governor Bravo Ahuja's family held large tracts of land. In mountainous regions such as the Mixteca Alta, which lacked both arable land and water, the growing population could not sustain itself. The INI's main development work in the region consisted of importing corn at subsidized rates to fight malnutrition. Under these circumstances, in the 1970s rural Oaxaca experienced a rise in agrarian conflicts and struggles over land.

While some violent conflicts revolved around long-standing inter-community disputes, others were struggles for land reform that involved poor campesinos and the violent responses of *guardias blancas*, armed groups in the pay of large landholders.[65] Echeverría's 1970 presidential campaign rhetoric had recognized the reality of rising inequality, particularly the problems facing the Mexican countryside, and the candidate had promised a more balanced distribution of the fruits of the Revolution. Young Oaxacans took Echeverría at his word, campaigning for changes big and small. On the Costa Chica in particular, violent confrontation erupted in 1973 between campesinos and the Iglesias Meza family of Jamiltepec.[66] By mid-decade there emerged a growing cohesion among dissident forces. Urban squatters, known locally as *paracaidistas*, engaged in land seizures on the outskirts of Oaxaca City. And in nearly every corner of the state, the organized poor sought access to land and government support.

During the democratic opening, federal authorities frequently opted for a strategy of negotiation and concessions to Oaxacan dissident forces, yet state authorities preferred a harder line.[67] Following Bravo Ahuja's departure in 1970, interim governor Fernando Gómez Sandoval was succeeded in 1974 by Manuel Zárate Aquino. From the beginning of his term, Zárate Aquino, a Oaxacan lawyer and PRI politician, sought to directly confront dissident activity in the state. Shortly after assuming power he employed military force to suppress municipal elections that did not favor the PRI.[68] Given federal authorities' proclivity to negotiate conflict, President Echeverría and the governor were often at odds over how to respond to the polarizing struggles around rural land, the growing urban squatters' movement, and conflicts at UABJO.

Indigenismo Occupied

The educated and politicized youth were sent to geographically isolated communities facing material deprivation. They quickly joined this broader political dissidence, moving to the center of ongoing struggles over land and confrontations with local authoritarian politics. Better trained and more politically astute than their INI counterparts, they often came into conflict with INI promotores, whose numbers expanded after President Echeverría substantially increased the INI's national budget. Yet the

IIISEO youth lacked the material support to carry out their tasks. Trained in carpentry and animal husbandry, they often did not have basic building materials or animal feed.[69] In spite of ample funding, the institute, focusing as it did on research and educational missions, lacked resources for projects involving significant capital input. The promotores complained of overwork, no vacations, poor pay, no compensation for their transportation costs, and a complete lack of job security.[70] Perhaps more significantly, the promotores' increased expectations, developed through their technical training and reading of protest movements throughout the Americas, tended to make more piecemeal reforms seem insufficient. The IIISEO had created conditions in which well-trained Indigenous youth had learned to think critically about the problems they and their communities faced, but the material support to address those very problems was missing.

President Echeverría's reforms created the space and opportunity for youth to engage with new ideas of anticolonialism and antiracism. Applied anthropology at the service of Echeverría's developmentalism was a conduit for political radicalization. As one promotor put it, describing the role of their instructors: "That progressive orientation helped us to better understand the political and socioeconomic dynamics of the communities, . . . let's say, the cultural question, the way of understanding things, the cosmology of the communities, all of that."[71] Thus applied anthropology was a key part of the intellectual development of this new generation in Indigenous Mexico. The radicalization of the period, far from being a purely middle-class or urban affair, included Indigenous youth who actively consumed and articulated their own version of New Left politics. These agents of modernization often developed alterative visions of social change as they collaborated with official development and education initiatives.[72] This was an unanticipated but consequential result of indigenismo.

Along with the IIISEO's official curriculum, staff offered parallel courses on alternative themes, including a broad range of Marxist literature.[73] These courses, taught by IIISEO staff, visiting "volunteer teachers" from the ENAH, the Escuela Nacional de Agricultura at Chapingo (the national agricultural school), and the national universities in Mexico City (UNAM and the Instituto Politécnico Nacional), had a profound impact on the youth. Santiago Salazar remembers reading a variety of Marxist literature, including interpretations of Karl Marx's *Capital*, provided by Ernest Mandel and Marta Harnecker. Eleazar García Ortega, a promotor from the central valleys, recalls that among the theorists of the various

Marxist currents, from Trotskyism to Maoism, the Peruvian intellectual José Carlos Mariátegui was most influential: "He said we have a socialism that comes from our own lands. He described this as an Indian socialism, as *indianismo*, not the official indigenismo. . . . Mariátegui is the first to articulate it as a project for the future, not just as the past, not just the dead glorious Indian, etc. No, he proposed an Indian socialism as a project for humanity."[74] In such ways the youth made sense of their particular situation through debates and ideas articulated on a global level.

Another political inspiration for the newly radicalized Oaxacan youth was the Peruvian peasant leader Hugo Blanco. As a Quechua-speaking Trotskyist, Blanco represented a New Left politics that spoke directly to the specific conditions of Latin America.[75] While ultimately a failure, his 1962 uprising in the department of Cuzco remained symbolic of agrarian radicalism in the second half of the century. In Oaxaca, Blanco exemplified the struggle for "Indigenous liberation," a struggle intimately tied to questions of class and exploitation.[76]

For the Oaxacans inspired to follow this lead, the logistics of organizing themselves, dispersed as they were throughout the state, were daunting.[77] How to address shared complaints? How to create a space to discuss their work experiences and grievances? The initiative came in 1971 from the first generation of promotores, thirteen of whom were trained as *técnicos de integración social*, in effect supervisors of the others in the field. These técnicos led the initial organizing efforts in 1973, calling regional meetings in which the promotores were brought together to discuss grievances and strategies for redress. In the Mixteca Alta, the técnicos used basketball tournaments, a product of postrevolutionary public health reform, to organize their coworkers.[78] These tournaments provided the space for preliminary discussions, but eventually the técnicos took a more provocative path, using their authority to call "official" regional meetings that all promotores were compelled to attend. At these meetings they would discuss the campaign to form a collective organization.[79]

By April 1974, the promotores had achieved enough group cohesion and commitment to seize control of the IIISEO campus. They occupied the institute's administrative offices for fifteen days, resulting in the April 23 signing of an official agreement between the IIISEO administration and the promotores' new organization, eventually named La Coalición de Promotores Culturales Bilingües.[80] The agreement detailed a number of labor rights, including the creation of *plazas de base*, permanent positions, for the promotores and their incorporation into the SEP's Dirección General de Educación Extraescolar en el Medio Indígena (DGEEMI). This struggle, along with other efforts by promotores pertaining to the INI, resulted in an expansion of Indigenous education through the creation of permanent positions for bilingual teachers on a national level.[81]

Peace at the institute did not last long. By November of 1974, rumors abounded that the IIISEO youth would stage another action, this time more dramatic.[82] The Coalition—shorthand for the promotores' organization—had developed direct relationships with other dissident groups, officially forming part of the COCEO, which itself had links to the COCEI in Juchitán. Only a few months after signing the initial agreement, the promotores argued that the institute's administration had not respected what had been established. In particular, they complained that the administration engaged in intimidation and reprisals, arbitrarily changing the assignments of the promotores—to communities outside their language areas—and that seven of the técnicos, in other words half their leadership, had been fired. On March 30, 1975, twelve promotores were arrested in Oaxaca City for passing out literature detailing their demands. Federal agents, conducting surveillance of the conflict, noted the slogans the protesters raised, including, "We are not folklore, we are not just for tourism—this is about exploitation."[83] After local police took them into custody, a large crowd, numbering in the hundreds and organized by the COCEO, gathered outside police headquarters to demand the promotores' release. The protesters chanted, "Zárate Aquino, Pinochet!" comparing the state governor to the leader of the 1973 military coup against President Salvador Allende of Chile. Eventually the governor ordered the protesters' release.

The broader context of opposition to the state government and mass mobilization provided crucial leverage to the promotores' struggle. The broad-based opposition movement increasingly referred to the governor, himself an ally of a "Third-Worldist" president, and the state police forces as "fascists" and denounced what they described as torture suffered at the hands of the latter. In response, authorities deployed local police and army units against youth and student demonstrations in the state capital. PRI politicians and business associations organized their own large-scale demonstrations, busing in rural Oaxacans to demonstrate support for the governor and denounce the opposition.[84]

Just after the arrest and release of the protesters, the Coalition initiated their most dramatic action to date. Early in April 1975, they struck four INI coordinating centers simultaneously, occupying office buildings and warehouses and paralyzing the institute's activities for the entire month. While security agents stressed that no violence occurred in these actions, former participants noted that violence, mainly directed at the occupiers, was a constant reality.[85] Those occupying the Miahuatlán coordinating center faced attacks by the center's staff, armed with machetes.[86] The promotores sought public support and sympathy by organizing nighttime meetings in the central plazas of Huautla de Jiménez, Miahuatlán, and Tlaxiaco, speaking to the gathered crowds of their own struggle and exposing the alleged corruption of indigenista agencies.[87] To help them survive, the promotores occupying the Tuxtepec center, located in an agriculturally rich region, sent cash and supplies to comrades in need at other locations.[88] All of this aimed to pressure both IIISEO officials and the SEP to meet the Coalition's demands.

To gain support and further publicize the strike, the Coalition's leadership traveled to the Escuela Nacional de Agricultura at Chapingo, on the outskirts of Mexico City. Chapingo had a long history of agrarian research and education and at the end of the 1960s underwent a major expansion with the creation of a postgraduate program, part of the broader growth in higher education. There, various New Left currents competed for students' allegiance. Eleazar García Ortega, Santiago Salazar, and Pedro "El Chino" Santiago Méndez canvassed the campus *boteando*, asking for donations and solidarity. As they passed through the halls a young agrarian economist, Francisco Abardía Moros, invited them into his classroom to make their pitch.[89] It was there that the promotores met Fernando Soberanes, a student from the northern state of Sinaloa. The leaders eventually invited Soberanes and Abardía to serve as official advisers to the coalition. The two accepted and joined the promotores' organizing efforts back in Oaxaca. The Coalition had successfully built a collaborative relationship between their organization and New Left forces in the country's capital.

The official rhetoric of the democratic opening, its language of dialogue and acknowledgment of grievances, was clearly useful to the promotores, but they also critiqued it as insufficient and as inherently limited by timidity and half measures. They highlighted what they viewed as the hypocrisy of the Mexican state that spoke of "vindicating the Indian," yet acted with utter "paternalism" toward Indigenous youth who articulated their own ideas and acted upon them. This effort is evidenced in the leaflets the Coalition distributed in April of 1975 outside the *palacio del gobierno* in the state capital in which they decried how authorities "foolishly think it is possible to develop an Indigenous community without confronting caciques, monopolies, and landlords, a confrontation that is utterly political. This situation reveals the contradictory character of the Mexican government that ends up frightened of its own demagoguery."[90] Here the federal government's own rhetoric provided ammunition for these youth, who turned it against local elites.[91]

Eva Ruiz led the occupation of the Miahuatlán center. Despite their numeric majority, women had remained a minority within the Coalition's leadership. They nonetheless faced similar levels of government repression. In a COCEO demonstration the following February, out of the eighty-one people detained by police, forty-three were women activists from the IIISEO and the state normal school.[92] In Miahuatlán, Ruiz played a decisive role in holding together the occupation. She faced off against armed INI employees, who were angered by the actions of the IIISEO youth, and dealt with internal tensions between the promotores and their allies. One radical university student, armed with a pistol and targeted by those outside as an agitator, was disarmed by a group of promotoras in an effort to deescalate the conflict. Once the student was secretly hustled out of the center at three in the morning, Ruiz rallied the remaining comrades to continue the occupation by convincing them that if even one center fell into the hands of the administration, it would be the end of their strike.[93]

The IIISEO youth were successful in winning their demands for the reinstatement of the supervisors, SEP recognition of their organizational structure, and placement within the Dirección General de Educación Normal.[94] Their struggle was part of a broader political uprising involving youth and independent trade unions, which gave material and political support to one another. For example, Rafael Gasca Iturribarría, a UABJO student leader, took up the promotores' demands in a meeting with Zárate Aquino in front of two hundred other students. This, along with a direct meeting with President Echeverría during his visit to Oaxaca in May 1975, contributed to the authorities' eventual recognition of their organizational structure and demands.[95] In this case federal power was marshaled to back up youth demands and limit the state government's repressive approach.

The promotores' work gained national attention not only from authorities forced to deal with their labor demands but also from the Mexico City media. In the winter of 1976, Paco Ignacio Taibo II, a young writer from a prominent literary family and a participant in the 1968 student movement, traveled to Oaxaca to witness the promotores' organizing. In an article for *El Universal*, Taibo described a community meeting conducted in Mixtec in the town of El Oro, Nuxaá. Among the topics on the agenda were collective projects such as the building of garden plots to improve nutrition as well as the construction of terraces to protect the soil from erosion. These projects would improve material conditions and also build community organization. As one promotor argued, "Collective work doesn't have as its main goal just the construction of particular projects; rather, it serves to reinforce the confidence of the community in itself, to strengthen ourselves, to not remain isolated but to strengthen our unity."[96]

The Coalition sought to improve not only their own professional status but also the self-organization, consciousness, and dignity of the communities they served. In this way the New Left's politics of consciousness-raising directly connected to the survival strategies of Indigenous communities themselves. Their struggle, along with PRI high politics, contributed to the shuttering of the IIISEO in 1977.[97] The most significant achievement of the Coalition, which by then had been renamed the Coalición de Maestros y Promotores Indígenas de Oaxaca (CMPIO), was the establishment of institutional independence for their group within the SEP in 1975. In later years, they used that autonomy to develop alternative classroom practices and teacher training, anchored in their community activism.

Conclusion

Mexico's democratic opening was both a response to and an attempt to get ahead of grassroots demands for change. During President Echeverría's term many social movements and individual activists learned exactly how the state operated and negotiated the terms of their relationship to state agencies with considerable political savvy.[98] While examples of armed opposition to the PRI and government control—the struggles of the Jaramillistas in Morelos and the campaigns of Genaro Vásquez and Lucio Cabañas in the state of Guerrero—might be more iconic, it was in these quotidian struggles to determine the terms of one's incorporation into state structures that power was most frequently contested.[99] The promotores' struggles for professionalization and control over the schools in which they served were about determining their relationship to state power on their own terms.

The youths' engagement with New Left politics, specifically anticolonialism and antiracism, was central to their mobilization. Those politics provided a language with which they challenged the IIISEO administration; they argued that they had been used as *conejillos de indias*, guinea pigs, for Gloria Ruiz de Bravo Ahuja's doctorate. Their relationship to their instructors, however, many of whom encouraged them in their critical reflection, was not always such strident opposition. As María Luisa Acevedo Conde, who worked closely with the youth, recounted, "The first thing we taught them, let me say it to you in one word, was to think. To not accept things as they were."[100] As a development agency based in the state capital, the IIISEO not only put youth from disparate Indigenous communities in dialogue with each other but also placed them within the vibrant politics of Oaxaca City. There a dissident politics rooted in a youth culture that transcended national boundaries grew beyond university politics. The anthropologists and other social scientists on staff at the IIISEO constituted yet another ingredient in this political effervescence. As one promotor noted, referring to his experience at the institute, "They planted in us a seed of unrest."[101]

Placing these youth within a constellation of politics that spans the Third-Worldist moment reveals how Mexico's democratic opening was part of a global phenomenon. The period of Third World advance internationally and of Echeverría's domestic democratic opening was short-lived. The oil boom, off which much of the global South alliance was based, faltered. The political alliances necessary in OPEC were fragile, and its weakness undermined initiatives such as the New International Economic Order.[102] Leftist governments, such as Chile, fell to coups and military dictatorships. And the postindependence political formations were susceptible to corruption and authoritarianism. Domestically, Echeverría struggled to build political coalitions that could defend his reform agenda. While he could funnel oil wealth into development and antipoverty programs such as Conasupo, the state-run food enterprise, he was unable to fix stagnant national economic output.[103] Hostile business interests opposed much of his agenda, and many on the left saw the PRI, even in its Third-Worldist garb, as nothing more than an instrument of authoritarianism. Echeverría's reformism suffered from enemies on the left and the right, and he ended his presidency in 1976 embattled.

Nonetheless, Mexico's democratic opening and Third World rhetoric created opportunities for change at the level of official politics and grassroots activism. Moreover, the shift in official indigenista discourse presented opportunities that Oaxacan youth seized to demand alternative education and development models. The pluralism one associates with this generation, be it efforts at consciousness-raising, Freirian education models, or women's rights, also included a component that pointed the way toward an Indigenous resurgence in the Americas. The roots of that resurgence lay in the intersection of state-led development and New Left cultural pluralism.[104] In the years to come, teachers from the Indigenous education sector were at the forefront of an explosive dissident trade union movement. That movement challenged not only PRI control of trade unions but also policies of austerity. As the federal government backed away from state-led development, teachers such as those in the CMPIO organized the strongest opposition.

5

Bilingual Teachers at the Front
The Rise of Dissident Trade Unionism and the Neoliberal Order

Pero si todos trabajamos juntos
seremos juntos mucho más
Vámonos juntando todos,
Vámonos juntando más
   If we all work together,
   We will be so much more
   Let's bring everyone together
   Let's bring in even more
      —"Vámonos juntando todos,"
      Jaime Martínez Luna, 1988[1]

SINCE 1922, the Secretaría de Educación Pública's stately headquarters have been located in the historic center of Mexico City. Originally built in 1594 to house La Encarnación convent, the structure underwent multiple renovations over the centuries. In the aftermath of the 1910 Revolution, the building was once again remodeled for its new role as the center of postrevolutionary education reform. From here, Mexico's first secretary of education, José Vasconcelos, organized the government's large-scale project of rural education to unite a diverse and fractured nation. Among the building's impressive facades and neoclassic design, what catches the eye today are a series of Diego Rivera murals in two interior courtyards. In over two hundred individual panels, Rivera depicted scenes of rural agriculture, markets, and street vendors, alongside the revolutionary struggles of workers, teachers, and campesinos. Completed in 1928, the murals

FIGURE 17. Diego Rivera, *Patio del trabajo* panels in the Secretaría de Educación Pública, Mexico City, 1923–24.
Source: Photographs by author.

visually crystallize postrevolutionary indigenista discourse. Combining images of revolutionary struggle along with invocations of a socialist future, Rivera made an argument about Mexico's past, its national character, as well as its future. Commissioned by Vasconcelos himself, the frescos illustrate the government's self-representation as one made by and for the people.[2] Rivera's radicalism, housed within a government ministry, reflects the tensions and instability of a postrevolutionary order that sought to channel and control mass, collective action. This tension remained central to twentieth-century Mexican politics.

Fifty years after the murals' completion, in November 1978, roughly 150 Oaxacan teachers and their allies surreptitiously entered the SEP's offices. Arriving in groups of four or five so as to not attract attention, they eventually assembled in one of the central courtyards. There they were surrounded by what would have been familiar images from their home state: Oaxacan weavers, dye makers, and sugar cutters, along with idyllic landscapes from the Isthmus of Tehuantepec. This was by no means the first time protesters had occupied the ministry's offices, but it was one of the earliest times that they did so as self-identified Indigenous actors.

Those assembled in the patio were members of the Coalición de Maestros y Promotores Indígenas de Oaxaca (CMPIO), the same group of teachers profiled in chapter 4. That November they demanded respect for their hard-won autonomy as an independent school district, an arrangement now put in jeopardy by President José López Portillo's (1976–82) education reforms. Santiago Salazar, a CMPIO leader from the Mixteca Alta, led the action. Once they had massed inside, he convened a rally to demand an audience with the secretary of education.[3] Standing atop the steps of the patio, Salazar had Rivera's depiction of a rural schoolteacher and an armed revolutionary to his right, and the women of the Oaxacan Isthmus to his left. To pressure education officials, Salazar and his comrades continued their protest for four days. During the occupation, they toured the building, contemplated the murals, and chatted with security guards over the contents of Rivera's panels. The protesters could not count on support from the SNTE, the national teachers' union. Not yet full members, in the years to come CMPIO activists fought for inclusion as a

FIGURE 18. Santiago Salazar leading an occupation of the Secretaría de Educación Pública offices in Mexico City, 1978.
Source: Personal Papers, Santiago Salazar.

union delegation within the Oaxacan local, Sección 22. By November 25 the protesters had won their demands for autonomy and democratic control of their school district.[4] The CMPIO's district consisted of a group of preschool and primary schools scattered throughout the state, most often in its most remote and linguistically diverse regions.

The teachers' actions were a portent of things to come. The ministry's reforms sought to modernize its operations, which had grown exponentially in the previous years and had become unwieldy, according to reformers. Most SEP functions continued to take place in the central offices, and the president's stated goal of "deconcentration" was in effect an expansion of the ministry's bureaucratic structure and institutional functions down to the state government level. These reforms coincided with an incipient national shift toward austerity. Despite Mexico's discovery of oil off its Gulf Coast in 1971, rising inflation and the 1976 peso devaluation meant that ordinary Mexicans struggled to make ends meet. The hardship of the economic crisis for teachers was compounded by the poor implementation of decentralization, which resulted in widespread delays in the distribution of paychecks. The reforms also caused a division between SEP officials and SNTE leadership, who had worked closely during the previous presidential administration. By the end of the decade, this breach, along with the broader economic situation, created the context in which a massive dissident teacher trade union movement developed. The movement included union locals across the republic but was strongest in the southern states of Chiapas and Oaxaca. The militant bilingual teachers who occupied the ministry's offices in 1978 had honed their political and mobilization skills over the preceding years and provided crucial leadership and energy to the emerging dissident movement.

These teachers' experience tells us much about the unanticipated consequences of indigenista policy. Originally contracted as promotores bilingües in the 1960s and 1970s, they eventually demanded professionalization as teachers. As recounted in the preceding chapter, by the mid-1970s many were officially incorporated into the SEP. But they were incorporated on an unequal basis. They did not have the professional training that normal school–educated teachers received. Nor did they have effective representation in their union local, Sección 22. Even SEP nomenclature, which labeled subministries *educación formal* (formal education) and *educación indígena* (Indigenous education), reflected this inequality. The employment category of *maestro bilingüe* implied Indigenous language proficiency and was often racialized as Indigenous, regardless of the self-identification of the individual. These teachers continued to challenge this structural inequality and in so doing defied education authorities and, at times, their trade union colleagues.

The struggle to democratize the SNTE coincided with broader forces of liberalization in Mexico such as the late 1970s electoral reforms and the swelling of civic engagement in the aftermath of the 1985 Mexico City earthquake. Scholarship on the teachers' movement has thus emphasized its democratic character and role within the larger process of democratization in Mexico.[5] Social scientists have stressed the struggle to transform and democratize the internal functioning of the SNTE. As in many government agencies and organizations, vertical patron-client relations and cronyism were central to the functioning of the SNTE. While I pay attention to these dynamics, my focus is on the questions of equity that the union movement raised for its Indigenous members. I ask how participation in the struggle opened space to challenge anti-Indigenous views within the education sector and society at large. Contemporary trade union voices often invoke the Indigenous character of their membership as a key element of union strength, equating indigeneity with traditions of resistance. Here I examine the relationship between indigeneity and 1980s trade union culture. In so doing, I place the movement within the history of indigenismo, arguing that bilingual teachers were far from passive recipients of government efforts and campaigned for their own visions of education, development, and equality.

In addition, I revisit the emergence of a series of political and economic reforms that scholars typically associate with austerity and the rise of neoliberalism. The 1982 Mexican debt crisis, which involved the forgiveness of the country's foreign debt in exchange for structural adjustment policies, was an iconic moment in the global emergence of neoliberalism.[6] In turn, twelve years later, the 1994 Zapatista rebellion in the neighboring state of Chiapas, launched in opposition to the signing of the North American Free Trade Agreement (NAFTA), was one of the most iconic rejections of that neoliberal order. I argue, however, that the dissident teachers' movement, emerging at the end of the 1970s, was the first sustained resistance to neoliberal reform. While the movement responded to the specific problems of a PRI-dominated political system and trade union leadership, it was also an explicit rejection of this global economic phenomenon. That movement's most dynamic sector consisted of bilingual teachers from southern Mexico.

The Debt Crisis and the Neoliberal Turn in Latin America

The 1982 Mexican debt crisis originated in mid-1970s international lending and related development models. The glut of petrodollars in global financial markets had led financial institutions to encourage borrowing by developing countries. During Luis Echeverría's presidency, the federal government took advantage of these borrowed funds and revenue from rising oil prices to increase state spending and expand public sector employment. Officially termed *desarrollo compartido*, the state's program of "shared development" allocated state funds to combat economic inequality and targeted rural sectors for increased state support. This policy simultaneously sought to rejuvenate the Mexican political system through the incorporation of the growing population into state-backed industries and popular organizations. When President José López Portillo assumed office in 1976, he attempted early on to maintain some continuity with Echeverría's model of economic governance and political reform. To do so, López Portillo continued to expand state enterprises, such as Conasupo, the state-run food company, and accelerated electoral and media reform, such as permitting increased competition in municipal elections. But this period of government expansion did not last long.

As the steep rise in global oil prices in the 1970s pushed up inflation rates around the world, nominal interest rates began to increase rapidly. These higher interest rates sharply increased the costliness of servicing the loans developing countries had taken out. Mexico and other Latin American governments faced skyrocketing costs of servicing their debt, growing unemployment, and high rates of inflation. Mexico's mounting debt, which rose from $6.8 billion in 1972 to $58 billion by 1982, meant that the "shared development" model was increasingly untenable.[7] In response to the crisis, authorities devalued the peso in 1976, the first devaluation in over two decades. The following year they instituted wage caps in the public sector, including for teachers, and curtailed public spending. In 1978, federal authorities announced the first-ever value-added tax in Mexico, to be implemented in 1980. These economic problems and the disastrous policies adopted to address them led many to refer to the 1980s in Latin America as the "Lost Decade."

The effects of this Lost Decade varied given the political and social contexts of the countries in the hemisphere. In Chile, which had undergone a US-backed coup in 1973, the military junta initiated large-scale austerity and privatization, closing universities and reversing land reform.[8] As a result, by the early 1980s the country became the poster child for the achievements of neoliberal reform, albeit at the cost of thousands of lives of Chilean dissidents. Venezuela, itself an oil exporter that had attracted migrants from across Latin America in the previous decade, saw its middle class hollow out as devaluation ravaged people's spending power. The social turbulence unleased in that country, particularly after its 1983 currency devaluation, culminated in the 1989 Caracazo, an urban uprising violently crushed by the government. In turn, the military dictatorship in Brazil, which had racked up large amounts of debt in its own development efforts, slowly lost its grip on power at the beginning of the decade. A trade union–led dissident movement there challenged austerity and authoritarianism until the military government fell in 1985. Given these dynamics, scholars and commentators have frequently framed neoliberalism as hatched by US intellectuals and policy makers and imposed through Latin American military regimes. This interpretation has merit but fails to fully account for events in Mexico. The Mexican case instead reveals how national elites and policy makers at the end of the 1970s debated how to respond the debt crisis and chose to implement austerity measures. During the López Portillo administration the PRI was internally divided on this issue, but a section of party leadership moved toward an embrace of the neoliberal model.

This crisis hit rural Mexico particularly hard. During the previous decade, the Echeverría administration implemented new supports for small producers in the countryside. In the late 1960s agricultural productivity began to decrease, and by 1974 Mexico switched from a net exporter of agricultural goods to a net importer.[9] Federal authorities therefore sought to exert themselves once again in the countryside, and programs such as Conasupo aimed to bolster small-scale agricultural production through initiatives such as *bodegas rurales*. By the end of the decade federal officials encountered a problem. With declining oil prices and rising national debt, they chose to roll back state-led development and agricultural supports for small producers. In effect, federal support for the rural sector expanded dramatically and then contracted in less than a decade.

Oaxacans increasingly turned to migration to navigate the crisis. Migration networks established in previous decades became important outlets, what political scientists sometimes term "safety valves," for the accelerated agricultural crisis at the end of the 1970s. As described in chapter 3, those networks had their roots in the midcentury, as commercial agriculture in northern Mexico boomed, and large numbers of Oaxacans, particularly men, traveled north to the states of Baja California, Sonora, and Sinaloa to work the fields.[10] While this migration included nearly all of rural Mexico, Oaxacan migrants, given their relative material impoverishment, lack of Spanish language skills, and traditions of internal migration, often worked in the most low-paid and dangerous jobs. This rural crisis and rising levels of migration formed the context for an upsurge of dissident politics in the state.

By the late 1970s, Oaxaca, like much of the rest of the country, had experienced a wave of social mobilization and unrest.[11] During the second half of the decade, rural-to-urban migration transformed the state capital's politics and culture. Squatter movements campaigned for public services and the regularization of newly formed communities on the outskirts of the capital. Land invasions led by young organizers, some aligned with currents within the ruling party, some opposed, took place in Tuxtepec, near the border with Veracruz, as well as on Oaxaca's Pacific coast.[12] In the capital, dissidents organized through the COCEO, of which the CMPIO was a part, continued to demand change from state officials. The violent repression of demonstrations in Oaxaca City, during which state police opened fire on demonstrators and killed multiple people, eventually triggered federal intervention.[13] Just three months into the presidential term of López Portillo (1976–82), on March 3, 1977, governor Zárate Aquino agreed to step down. The president and his secretary of government, Jesús Reyes Heroles, orchestrated the governor's replacement with Eliseo Jiménez Ruiz, a military general who had just overseen a scorched-earth campaign against rural guerrillas in the state of Guerrero.[14] Just four years later on the Isthmus of Tehuantepec, the COCEI defeated the PRI in Juchitán's municipal elections. While the optimism Oaxacans felt after the ouster of Zárate Aquino was tempered by the arrival of the general, popular opinion was decidedly with dissidents. Indeed, the most militant sections of the teachers' movement were often led by those who had participated in this 1970s activism.[15]

Vanguardia Revolucionaria and Federal Education Reform

As described in chapter 4, over the course of his term President Echeverría had doubled the number of primary school teachers serving rural

Mexico and had instituted new systems of secondary and higher education. As the 1917 Constitution guaranteed union rights, these new teachers automatically became members of the national union. The SNTE grew out of the consolidation of various education worker unions in 1943 and had an extensive tradition of political activism. During its first few decades, multiple political currents competed for influence within the union, notwithstanding its integration into the PRI corporate structure. Dissident movements, such as the Movimiento Revolucionario Magisterial, which emerged in Mexico City and had ties to the Partido Comunista Mexicano, exerted strong influence.[16] However, the overarching trend was that the SNTE became an avenue for mobility within the PRI system, a so-called transmission belt, as teachers frequently became municipal presidents and might move vertically to positions within the PRI party structure or state and federal governments.[17] Reformers denounced this party- and government-controlled leadership as *charrista*, a system in which union bosses ruled undemocratically and often through violent means. This alliance between the ruling party and the SNTE was strengthened, one might say exacerbated, during Echeverría's term. In 1972, as the president sought to install allies in top trade union positions, he supported a "coup" of SNTE leadership. The faction Echeverría threw his support behind came to be known as Vanguardia Revolucionaria.[18] Led by Carlos Jonguitud Barrios, Vanguardia, as its name suggests, imagined itself as the leading edge of the entire teachers' union, not a mere faction or caucus.

Vanguardia Revolucionaria was also part of President Echeverría's Third-Worldist reinvention of the PRI. Under Jonguitud Barrio's leadership, the SNTE embraced the president's rhetoric of progressive nationalism and Third World solidarity. Federal authorities invested heavily in education, and SNTE leadership responded in kind, presenting flattering portrayals of the president in their publications and aligning themselves with his policies. Nationally this invocation of Third World solidarity created opportunities for dissidents to exploit. Peasants seized land and invoked Echeverría's own words. Students campaigned for education reform though similar strategies. Indeed, the government's emphasis on "participatory indigenismo" proved useful to bilingual teachers campaigning for their own rights and professionalization.[19] The CMPIO activists who occupied SEP offices in 1978 were part of this contested expansion of Indigenous education. Conversely, inside the union Vanguardia Revolucionaria oversaw a centralization of power and increasingly limited the ability of other currents or factions to raise criticism. The space for dissent within the union decreased as the government's largesse, in the form of an influx of funding and the creation of numerous nonteaching positions, allowed leaders to practice growing levels of patronage and corruption.[20] This arrangement further facilitated the ability of the national SNTE leadership to influence education policy and control SEP administrative positions.

When López Portillo assumed office in 1976, he identified two major problems within the education sector. The first was that the increases in state spending that had funded the expansion of the SEP ran up against the fiscal constraints of rising inflation and a serious economic downturn. The second was that the expansion in the numbers of teachers placed strains on the SEP's highly centralized bureaucratic structure. If teachers had a problem with their pay or had other administrative complaints, they were forced to travel to Mexico City to resolve them, regardless of their proximity to the nation's capital. López Portillo began his term by appointing Porfirio Muñoz Ledo as secretary of education. Muñoz Ledo had served in the Echeverría administration and was associated with the progressive wing of the PRI. His ministerial appointment appeared to portend a continuity between the Echeverría and López Portillo administrations. But Muñoz Ledo served just one year as secretary before he was forced out of the job. Speculation existed as to the motives for his removal; some suggested it was part of the president's desire to distance himself from his predecessor.[21] According to Muñoz Ledo, López Portillo told him there was "a lack of balance in the government," suggesting that the secretary had too high of a public profile.[22] Given the promptness of the subsequent reforms, the sacking suggests substantive policy differences and an unequivocal shift to austerity. In his brief tenure, Muñoz Ledo proposed a dramatic increase in the education budget, advocated more robust union rights for university workers, and endorsed bilingual-bicultural policies. Indeed, he claimed to have advocated for López Portillo to be an "education president" rather than an "oil president."[23] Muñoz Ledo's proposals were a continuation of Echeverría's policies but also reflected a broader vision of investing oil wealth into education and development.

López Portillo chose a different path. He dismissed Muñoz Ledo, who took up various diplomatic posts abroad, in what was part of a long tradition of exiling out-of-favor PRI officials. In March 1978 the deconcentration reform began. This was a clear break with the Echeverría administration. The reforms sparked a split between SEP officials and national SNTE leadership, whose interests were threatened by the proposed bureaucratic shake-up. As SEP administrative functions would be distributed throughout the republic, SNTE control over such bureaucratic procedures could be weakened. This growing split between SEP officials and SNTE leaders was compounded by problems with the rollout of the decentralization. The delegation of administrative functions to state-level offices caused months-long delays in the distribution of teachers' paychecks. In addition, as a response to inflation, federal officials instituted wage caps for public workers. Teachers in states such as Oaxaca often waited months to receive what were supposed to be regular biweekly payments.[24] Throughout the republic, teachers began to demand a solution to the problem of delayed payments as well as a salary increase to offset the rising cost of living. Far from resolving the administrative problems within the SEP, the reforms only added to them and created instability within union leadership.

The Oaxacan SNTE local, Sección 22, was at the center of the fight to transform the teachers' union. While the movement emerged on the national scene in 1980, as early as 1977 federal authorities were aware that opposition was brewing against the leadership of Sección 22. On June 9, 1977, Policía Judicial officers, supported by elements of the army, conducted a counternarcotics campaign on the southeastern edge of the central valleys of Oaxaca, a region well known for marijuana cultivation. After an aerial fumigation of the plants, two government helicopters landed in the town of San Juan Lachigalla in pursuit of local growers.[25] Police and soldiers searched nearby houses, all of which appeared abandoned, until they came upon the local school director, Ausencia Jiménez Martínez, and a teacher, René Velázquez Vázquez. With guns drawn, agents approached the teachers and interrogated them for upwards of two hours. Jiménez and Velázquez later denounced the incident, in an official complaint to the secretary general of Sección 22, stating they had been detained, held at gunpoint, and humiliated. However, for federal agents the incident was significant—not for the information it revealed about marijuana production or transportation but rather for what it exposed regarding internal trade union politics. As they summarized: "There is dissatisfaction and disquiet among elements of the teachers in the state because their leader, Professor Mayrén, used the organization as a springboard for his candidacy for local deputy with the PRI."[26] Security agents emphasized that the close ties between trade union positions and PRI political advancement were generating opposition within the ranks of the Oaxacan local.

In Oaxaca, with a relatively small private sector and limited industrialization, the education system was the largest employer in the state. Indeed, Sección 22 was the largest trade union, with roughly 26,000 members working throughout the state at the beginning of the 1980s. The union's size conferred upon teachers exceptional power and influence in state and local politics. While teachers had a history of dissidence, with active currents of the Movimiento Revolucionario Magisterial and the Partido Popular Socialista, by the 1970s Sección 22 had become a pillar of PRI politics. The ousted governor, Manuel Zárate Aquino, had supported the local Vanguardia Revolucionaria leadership.[27] Teachers who advanced in the ranks of union leadership frequently used their positions to gain power within the PRI political apparatus. A prime example of this dynamic was the Sección 22 secretary general, David Mayrén Rodríguez, who security officials acknowledged was using the union as a "springboard" to a state congressional seat. While Vanguardia Revolucionaria was strong throughout the state, particularly on the Isthmus and in the Mixteca, opposition had emerged in the central valleys. These dissidents began to protest the delayed paychecks and wage caps and pressed Mayrén Rodríguez to do more, but local leaders remained hesitant to challenge national SNTE authority. What was true for other public sector unions, namely that their "historic relation to the state not only hindered but undermined their resistance to neoliberalism," was equally true in the education sector and evidenced in the SNTE's inability to effectively confront austerity.[28]

The growing tensions within Sección 22 were on full display at its January 1980 congress. Held in Huajuapan de León, in the Mixteca Baja, 294 representatives from across the state gathered to select their new leadership. Mayrén Rodríguez, the outgoing secretary general, along with Ernesto Aguilar Flores, a member of the national SNTE leadership, presided over the meetings. However, the congress proceedings were interrupted by the surprise visit of the national SNTE secretary general, José Luis Andrade Ibarra, a close ally of Jonguitud Barrios. In a show of the union boss's political and economic clout, Andrade Ibarra arrived by plane from Mexico City. He addressed the assembled delegates, encouraging "unity" and ending his speech with the characteristic rhetoric of Vanguardia Revolucionaria, "Teachers are education of and for the people!"[29] His visit no doubt sought to ensure the victory of his preferred candidate, Fernando

Maldonado Robles, and signaled to dissidents that the national union leadership took their activities seriously.[30] Two hours after touching down in Huajuapan de León, Andrade Ibarra was back on his plane to Mexico City, and by the end of the congress, a closed session of delegates chose Maldonado as the next secretary general. Maldonado quickly became an emblematic symbol of the symbiotic relationship between the PRI and Sección 22. Just three months after assuming leadership of the union, Maldonado was named secretary general of the state PRI as well.[31] The blatant political corruption of the union leadership along with frustrations over austerity and lack of consistent paychecks proved an explosive mixture.

While discontent over union democracy and delayed wages produced increasingly visible conflicts within the entire union, Indigenous educators faced unique challenges and had their own specific complaints. These grievances grew out of the long history of Indigenous education. After the 1910 Revolution, reformers famously expanded the country's public education system into the countryside, offering secular and social justice–oriented curricula as a benefit of the Revolution.[32] That universal project necessarily raised questions of Indigenous difference as SEP officials confronted the cultural and linguistic diversity of the countryside.[33] Policy makers' solutions were often haphazard, and serving Indigenous populations was of secondary importance—at best—to the broad sweep of education policy. As we have seen, this meant those charged with Indigenous education at midcentury, promotores bilingües, began their careers without normal school training. Frequently recruited to work in their home communities, the promotores were young and typically had little more than a primary or secondary education. Contracted on the basis of their bilingualism, fluency in a Native language and Spanish, the promotores worked without a *plaza de base* and were therefore paid poorly and had no rights to benefits or union membership. In contrast, federal teachers frequently attended rural normal school and had more extensive training, better pay, and union membership.[34] Because of the piecemeal and halting way in which the promoters were contracted, federal schoolteachers often viewed them as second-class teachers.

This institutional inequality combined with broader prejudices that equated indigeneity with ignorance, poverty, and rural isolation. Like the young bilingual radio teachers of the 1950s and 1960s described in chapter 2, the promotores bilingües were frequently maligned by their colleagues and derogatorily labeled as *huarachudos* for the thick sandals that were common among bilingual instructors. The fact that they tended children and served in schools in the most rural and impoverished sectors of the state only seemed to confirm the prejudice of their colleagues. But these inequalities were increasingly unacceptable to young teachers. In August of 1979 the CMPIO initiated efforts to organize other bilingual teachers into a broad front, to make demands for further professionalization. They mobilized throughout the state. In Tuxtepec, on Oaxaca's border with Veracruz, they initiated a strike in response to the murder of their bilingual school's director, and in the winter months of 1979 and 1980, bilingual teachers in the Mixteca Alta demanded higher wages.[35] They engaged in a two-front struggle, one for respect and equality within the teaching profession and the other for democratization of the union itself.

Women had historically been a minority within rural and Indigenous education sectors. This underrepresentation was in part a reflection of Indigenous communities' specific gender norms, which often involved gendered divisions of communal labor. The rural nature of the work also meant teachers frequently traveled great distances to serve their schools, a task all the more challenging for women, who were often expected to rear their own children and attend to other domestic labor. However, with the 1970s expansion of the education system, this imbalance slowly began to change. A majority of the first generation of the CMPIO's *promotores bilingües* were women because of that organization's historic connection to the EMHR. Many of these *promotoras*, such as Eva Ruiz, went on to serve in key roles in the political and professional struggles of the CMPIO. INI *promotores*, on the other hand, remained majority men. While there was an overall rise in women teachers within Sección 22 over the course of the following decades, its leadership, both *charrista* and dissident, remained dominated by men.

At the beginning of the 1980s there was broad consensus that teacher pay in Oaxaca was a problem. All public sector workers' wages suffered from rising inflation. And the situation faced by bilingual teachers was more dire: their salaries averaged 3,500 pesos a month, far less than the 5,000-peso average teacher salary in the state. In addition, they faced worse working conditions, often traveling on foot to far-flung communities with poor infrastructure, inadequate school facilities, and minimal supplies. Not only dissidents but Vanguardia figures such as Mayrén Rodríguez and Oaxacan SEP delegate Salvador Nuñez Ledezma denounced the poor conditions.³⁶ Despite Sección 22 leadership's acknowledgment of pay problems, they took no substantive action to challenge the SEP on the issue, providing dissidents with ample opportunity to denounce their leaders' timidity. Even federal intelligence agents, who monitored teacher politics with detailed attention, predicted that the lack of union democracy and long pay delays could potentially produce a powerful opposition movement.³⁷ On May 1, 1980, that prediction proved right as the teacher opposition made its first public demonstration in the streets of Oaxaca City.

The Rise of a Teachers' Insurgency

May Day parades have a long history in Mexico. The postrevolutionary state embraced the holiday as one of its own, and state-sponsored unions used the day to publicly demonstrate their strength and fealty to the ruling party. In the Oaxacan capital, the traditional route of the May Day parade traversed the colonial downtown, culminating at the Zócalo, where workers filed past the Palacio de Gobierno and the official delegation, headed by the governor. The 1980 celebrations, however, were anything but typical. While the festivities began as usual, with Governor Eliseo Jiménez Ruiz officiating from a balcony overlooking the Zócalo, trouble loomed for officials that spring afternoon. Dissident teachers seized on the festivities to publicize their fight. Toward the end of the march, as the teachers' contingent, roughly three thousand of the estimated twenty thousand attendees, approached the Zócalo, state police allowed Sección 22 leadership to pass but blocked dissident teachers who raised chants critical of their leadership and the PRI. With slogans of "El maestro honrado jamás será diputado" (The honorable teacher will never be a congressman) and "País petrolero, el maestro sin dinero" (Country of oil, teachers without money), the dissidents challenged the union's unfailing loyalty to the governing party and its policies of austerity.³⁸ The assembled crowds applauded the protesters as scattered fights broke out between teachers and state police. This was the worst-case scenario for PRI and SNTE officials, who had sought to muffle the growing demands for change.

Here, in the center of Oaxaca City, with the public and media watching, a teacher insurgency was born. The dissident movement gained momentum in the coming weeks, sidestepping official union leadership by organizing public assemblies and meetings at private homes. In two weeks, the dissidents successfully forced secretary general Maldonado to step down from his position and, after a month-and-a-half-long strike, negotiated a 22 percent salary increase. While wage raises were key elements of the movement's demands, a range of other grievances created a groundswell of support. In addition to the poor working conditions faced by teachers serving Oaxaca's disparate rural communities, sexual harassment and abuse of women teachers by education and union officials motivated many.[39] Ultimately, the question of union democracy emerged as the most urgent demand for dissidents and the most threatening to union and party officials.

From the May Day action forward, bilingual teachers played a decisive role in the movement. Ignacio Santiago Pérez, who came from a ranchería on the outskirts of San Andrés Nuxiño in the Mixteca Alta, entered the profession a year prior to the birth of the insurgency. His hometown subsisted on small-scale farming, and in the 1960s many of its members had begun to migrate to Mexico City for work. Santiago's town had lacked a school of its own, so he began work as a teacher by organizing Spanish language lessons for first and second graders of the community. In addition to the collective issue of delayed paychecks, what motivated Santiago's participation in the movement was the fact that while bilingual teachers paid union dues, they had very little representation within Sección 22's decision-making bodies.[40] This was due to the lack of delegational representation of Indigenous education within the local's internal structures. Santiago also attributed this lack of meaningful participation to two forms of discrimination bilingual teachers suffered, one "racial" and one "professional."[41] For their indigeneity, they suffered discrimination from society at large but were also looked down upon by their colleagues, who viewed them as less professionally qualified than teachers in *educación formal*. While some teachers in the Indigenous education sector had accommodated themselves to this institutional inequality, young bilingual teachers such as Santiago viewed it as a problem to be overcome. Shortly after beginning his career, Santiago joined the new Seccíon 22 assemblies and by 1981 had become secretary general of his regional delegation. His rapid rise in elected leadership demonstrates the movement's transformation of internal union culture and the opportunities it created for young bilingual teachers.

These existing tensions in the education system sparked parallel teachers' struggles throughout the country. Teacher activism was driven by the overall expansion of the education system, the poor implementation of decentralization, and a corrupt and passive union leadership.

The Coordinadora Nacional de Trabajadores de la Educación (CNTE) coalesced in 1979 to direct the dissident movement nationally. It was in Oaxaca that the CNTE would have the most success in challenging Vanguardia's power. CNTE strategies involved bypassing the existing union structures to create new forms of direct democratic control. Teacher activists did this through the implementation of direct regional representation, based on public assemblies of teachers from given areas. These teachers elected representatives, *delegados*, and alternates who were to implement their decisions in state assemblies. This practice ran contrary to previous top-down methods in which state-wide leaders selected the next generation of union leadership on the basis of fealty to the ruling party and union officials. Dissidents combined the above forms of direct participation with close collaboration with *padres de familia*, parents' organizations. In this context, regional representation within the union served to counter the vertically organized power Vanguardia had exercised. That grassroots strategy was key to the dissident seizure of control of Sección 22 in February of 1982. That month the state assembly elected Pedro Martínez Noriega secretary general of the local, the first dissident to hold the office. The outpouring of grassroots activity forced the old guard to respect the results of the election. Vanguardia Revolucionaria still had a presence in the state-wide leadership but had lost its hegemonic control over the union structure. Bilingual teachers played a key role in organizing the regional assemblies and electing opponents of charrista practices.

Local Vanguardia leadership saw bilingual teachers as a threat to their control of the union well prior to the emergence of the teachers' insurgency. Young bilingual teachers had mobilized to convert contract positions into formalized ones within the education and union structure since the mid-1970s. Given their explicit exclusion from the union, these independent struggles threatened Vanguardista power, as they frequently mobilized outside union structures. In addition, young teachers allied with independent left-wing activists, often veterans of university-based politics and other struggles for independent unions. The CMPIO was one such political group of bilingual teachers. The Coalition functioned as both a school district and, by 1982, an official union delegation. This dynamic, of independent leftist politics emerging as a force within official trade unions, was a growing phenomenon at the time. Groups such as Línea Proletaria, a Maoist-oriented organization active nationally, similarly challenged charrista leadership within the steelworkers' union.[42] Given its political orientation and its decade-long struggle to join the union, the CMPIO provided crucial leadership to the expanding democratic movement. It prioritized the regional practices of democratic representatives and employed a rotating leadership style internally.[43] Reflecting on the struggle in 1984, Santiago Salazar, a leader of the 1978 occupation of the SEP's headquarters, framed the collective principles and democratic practices of the movement as a reflection of its Indigenous base: "We act in ways very similar to our Indigenous communities and this is the key characteristic of our coalition."[44] In this instance, leftist politics and indigeneity served as strategic and discursive tools in the teachers' insurgency.

The dissidents won control over Sección 22 shortly before a major economic crisis. From 1981 to 1982, inflation in Mexico soared from 26 percent to 100 percent.[45] Oil prices, which had been at record-high levels in the mid-1970s, hollowed out at the beginning of the 1980s, and authorities made a number of desperate efforts to address the crisis. One was to conduct a series of further peso devaluations. And in what would become the defining moment of the debt crisis in the hemisphere, in August 1982 federal officials announced a default on the foreign debt. That was followed by López Portillo's final major act as president, the nationalization of the banks in September of that year. After a relatively uncontested presidential election, Miguel de la Madrid (1982–88) of the ruling party took office in December. De la Madrid's reversal of the previous two administrations' policies was quick and decisive. He oversaw the large-scale privatization of state-owned industries and began once again to service Mexico's foreign debt.[46] Thus the dissident teachers' movement achieved limited power over union structures precisely as full neoliberal reform arrived on the national stage. While dissidents now controlled Sección 22, they faced an uphill battle, both to retain their control on the state level and to challenge charrista leadership nationally.

Authoritarian power is slow to die in Mexico. In the years following, Vanguardia activists used every method imaginable to reassert control over Sección 22. Local and national Vanguardia figures employed bribery, corruption, bureaucratic manipulation, violence, and murder in their effort to recoup control over what had been a key source of their power. Indeed, when Jonguitud Barrios, the de facto permanent leader of the SNTE and Vanguardia, was asked at a press conference about the deaths of dissident teachers during this period, he caustically joked that they were tragic accidents bound to occur, a comment that mocked the dead and threatened activist teachers.⁴⁷ Isaías Sánchez López, a veteran teacher from Santiago Yosondúa, described how Vanguardistas had assembled bilingual teachers from the Mixteca Alta and offered them positions as supervisors and school directors, credit lines, medicine, and even cars in exchange for their loyalty.⁴⁸ These Vanguardistas, most likely sent from the SNTE's Comité Ejecutivo Nacional in Mexico City, canvassed Oaxaca looking to break the dissident union's strength. Roberto Villalana Castillejos, a rare figure who was at once a member of the PRI and an opponent of the Vanguardistas, described such activists as *reivindicadores* for their efforts to recuperate Vanguardia Revolucionaria's image.⁴⁹ Their targeting of bilingual teachers in their efforts to reassert control of Sección 22 speaks to the bilingual teachers' strategic weight in coalescing the dissident movement.

By the fall of 1983, Oaxacan dissidents appeared to be on their heels. The COCEI's insurgent movement on the Isthmus of Tehuantepec successfully defeated the PRI in municipal elections in 1981. Yet state and federal authorities deployed a series of strategies to try to undermine the movement.⁵⁰ The state government, headed by General Jiménez Ruiz, sought to destroy the dissident municipality, going so far as to legally abolish the city government's functions in August 1983. In this context, the Vanguardistas attempted their most dramatic action to date to regain control of the union local. On October 24, 1983, more than seventy Vanguardista activists seized Sección 22's headquarters, located just off the Zócalo in downtown Oaxaca City. In the process they took a handful of office workers hostage. The move, which aimed to seize administrative control of the union, proved a severe miscalculation. Word of the occupation quickly spread, and movement leadership decided to surround the building. Within hours, thousands of militant and angry teachers had encircled the offices on Armenta y López Street. Over the next two days, some of the Vanguardistas tried unsuccessfully to escape. The state government then negotiated a resolution to the conflict. The movement eventually agreed to a government proposal of peacefully removing the occupiers. At 1:00 a.m. state officials, with police and transport at the ready, removed the remaining Vanguardistas.⁵¹ Activists speculated as to the motives of the occupiers: some argued that they were directly supported by Governor Jiménez Ruiz, while others suggested they were part of a broader federal plan to undermine the movement. Either way, the incident demonstrated the dissidents' determination and their readiness to fight every attempted return to the status quo.

While contemporary trade union activists and scholarly accounts have emphasized bilingual teachers were always *los que iban al frente* (those at the front of the movement), the Indigenous education sector was not without internal divisions of its own. Younger teachers were quick to take up the struggle, while some older bilingual teachers either avoided participation or outright opposed it. Ramón Hernández López, for example, the pioneer of bilingual instruction in the Mixteca Alta whose work was described in chapters 2 and 3, had by the 1970s become subdirector general of the Indigenous education subministry, the DGEEMI. He was critical of the rise of the teacher insurgency and claimed that the movement took teachers out of the classroom and abandoned the communities they served.[52] Another figure who typified the sector of Indigenous education aligned with Vanguardia Revolucionaria was Antolín Osorio Nicolás. Born in 1945 near the town of Chalcatongo, Osorio was seventeen years old when he entered the teaching profession. Osorio first served as a *promotor bilingüe* in the INI's experimental radio school program in the early 1960s. He himself had struggled to learn Spanish, arriving at primary school monolingual in his native Mixtec. Given his own difficulties with the language—he continued to speak an accented Spanish throughout his life—Osorio sympathized with his students' plight. He later described how he spoke in Mixtec with students to put them at ease in the classroom. By 1972, with almost ten years of service under his belt, Osorio became a union leader, and by 1975 served as a supervisor, overseeing a school district in the Mixteca Baja.[53]

Osorio's union leadership went hand in hand with more administrative responsibilities. In May 1979 he led a group of promotores bilingües that struck against the promotores' union, a struggle that landed him a position as director.[54] Just one year later, however, in April 1980, Osorio found himself on the wrong side of the swelling opposition to Vanguardia control of Sección 22. Dissidents mounted a successful campaign that removed him from his position as director.[55] While this conflict, which Osorio described as *un detalle* (a complication), revealed his association with the Vanguardia tendency, he later dismissed the incident with the colloquialism "Cría cuervos y te sacarán los ojos" (Raise crows and get your eyes pecked out). In his view, the insurgency was no more than political infighting within the union, not a struggle for Indigenous empowerment or democracy. Perhaps because of the timing of when they joined the union, figures such as Osorio understood advancement individually, while

Santiago, who had joined during a collective upsurge, viewed these older teachers as having accommodated themselves to institutional inequalities. While Osorio reflected a minority position within the *educación indígena* during the insurgency, his case demonstrates that there was no automatic affinity between Indigenous educators and the dissident teachers' struggle.

Through the mid-1980s, the movement grew, both in Oaxaca and nationally, expanding its tactics to pressure federal authorities for democratization of the SNTE and for wage increases. Given the broader context of economic insecurity and the eroding legitimacy of PRI officials, Oaxacan public opinion was decidedly with the teachers. This is evidenced in the numerous teacher-led marches and caravans from Oaxaca to the nation's capital. When teachers came home after these marches, they were regularly greeted as returning heroes. In 1986, they organized one such caravan in which they walked from Oaxaca to the national capital, a more than three-hundred-mile journey that took twenty days to complete. As Victor Raúl Martínez Vásquez, a scholar and participant, observed, the movement relied not only on a politics of solidarity but also on a "sense of stoic sacrifice." Broad swaths of Oaxacan society supported the movement, whose ideological breadth spanned the Far Left, dissident *priístas*, and those inspired by liberation theology. Indeed, many Oaxacan priests spoke in favor of the movement. Fernando Soberanes, a CMPIO activist who had been recruited to the movement while a student at the Chapingo agricultural school, played a leadership role in the march.[56] The caravan culminated in Mexico City, where teachers began a hunger strike to highlight their struggle. The nation's capital was already beset by its own crisis when the teachers arrived. A year prior, in September 1985, Mexico City had been rocked by a massive earthquake that killed thousands and left millions sleeping in the street. The city saw an explosion of citizen activism as local and national officials failed to respond adequately. Entire neighborhoods came together to search for survivors and provide communal support.[57] The teachers' movement connected to this already mobilized and angry environment.

The 1988 Presidential Elections and the Fall of Jonguitut Barrios

This swelling opposition to the PRI was on full display in the 1988 presidential elections. The ruling party picked Harvard-educated technocrat Carlos Salinas de Gotari as its candidate, while opponents coalesced around the popular former mayor of Mexico City, Cuauhtémoc Cárdenas, who ran on the Partido de la Revolución Democrática (PRD) ticket. Frustration with austerity, decreased purchasing power, and impoverishment of middle-class life, along with anger at the ruling party's apparent abandonment of a twenty-year social pact that exchanged rising standards of living for continued PRI rule, fueled Cárdenas's campaign. Over the spring and early summer, Cárdenas was ahead in most polls, but during the election night a "glitch" brought the electoral computing system down, and when it turned back on, Salinas emerged as the narrow victor. The 1988 elections were one of the most tightly contested in the PRI's history, and Cárdenas was in all likelihood robbed of his rightful victory. President Salinas would go on to oversee the large-scale privatization, and in many cases shuttering, of state industries. The expansion of privatization and the neoliberal agenda thus eked their way to power through fraud and electoral manipulation. While the International Monetary Fund and the World Bank praised Mexico for these policies, few in these institutions commented on how they came at the expense of electoral democracy.[58]

By 1989, the national dissident movement had gained significant strength. However, the Oaxacans were still battling to fully remove the remaining Vanguardia officials from the leadership of Sección 22. To that end, dissidents organized a *congreso magisterial* (teachers' congress) to elect a new leadership. As in previous springs, teachers declared an indefinite strike to pressure authorities to meet their demands. During precongress meetings in Oaxaca City at the Centro Regional de Educación Normal de Oaxaca, delegates successfully rejected any Vanguardia participation in state-level leadership. Sección 22 was finally free of Vanguardia control, a remarkable accomplishment that took over a decade to achieve. This meant the CNTE-aligned dissidents had full administrative power over the union local, a feat no other local in the republic had accomplished at that point.

One of Sección 22's long-standing demands had been the removal of Jonguitud Barrios from SNTE leadership. The dissidents' decade-long struggle against Vanguardia Revolucionaria now coincided with President Salinas's assault on trade unions nationally. Salinas administration officials moved against entrenched union leadership, most notably within the Sindicato de Trabajadores Petroleros de la República Mexicana, the national oil workers' union, and did not hesitate to employ the military against trade unions.[59] In this context and under direct pressure from the president, Jonguitud Barrios finally stepped down. In turn, Elba Esther Gordillo replaced Refugio Araujo del Ángel as SNTE secretary general. On a national level, the 1989 change in SNTE leadership was a Pyrrhic victory. While Jonguitud Barrios formally lost power, the negotiated replacement of the secretary general with Gordillo marked a continuation of charrista control. Gordillo, who rose through the Vanguardista ranks with the support of Jonguitud Barrios for much of her career, went on to oversee large-scale corruption within the union. Her ill-gotten personal wealth and ability to consistently align herself with powerful politicians became potent symbols of SNTE corruption. She was eventually arrested in 2013 on charges of embezzlement. While the Oaxacan dissidents had successfully wrested control of their local from Vanguardia Revolucionaria, they faced seemingly intractable charrista control over the national union, now aligned with a large-scale neoliberal assault.[60]

Sección 22 celebrated its democratization and referred to itself as *el magisterio democrático*, the democratic teachers' movement. This served to galvanize its base but also to present a contrast to Gordillo and the national SNTE. In turn, much of the scholarship on the movement emphasized the democratic character of the struggle, in terms of both internal trade union culture and the movement's impact on Mexican society more broadly. In the early years of the insurgency, grassroots democratic practices expanded the social base of the movement and served as a bulwark against Vanguardia attacks. However, internal democratic culture within Sección 22 was often partial and temporary, particularly when judged over subsequent decades.[61] In 1992, Sección 22 successfully negotiated with then-governor Diódoro Carrasco Altamirano (1992–98) for the union's full control over the Instituto Estatal de Educación Pública de Oaxaca, the state ministry of education. This apparent victory allowed for an increasing lack of transparency and increasing corruption within union leadership, albeit with a base still committed to the movement's ideals. This mixed record is understandable, as the dissidents confronted a long history and entrenched culture of authoritarian practices and union corruption. Unlike autonomist movements that looked to create space outside the state, the Oaxacan struggle sought to transform a pillar of PRI control, no small task.

The other major outcome of the union struggle was increased equity for the Indigenous education sector. Bilingual teachers leveraged the dissident movement to confront long-standing inequalities. By putting their jobs, and at times their lives, on the line, bilingual teachers challenged the notion that they were second-class educators. As Isaías Sánchez López recalled, "There we are all together, and so the federal teacher saw the Indigenous teacher enter the movement with enthusiasm. . . . From that point on we were accepted by the federal teachers; of course it was slow, not fast, little by little the idea that the federal teacher is over here and the Indigenous over there has been erased, but it was a slow process."[62] Bilingual teachers' increased participation in union leadership was another marker of these successes. As we will see in the next chapter, a minority of teachers campaigned for pedagogical practices aimed at strengthening Indigenous linguistic and cultural diversity.[63] The union movement as a whole, even the dissident wing, was not uniformly supportive of Indigenous colleagues as Indigenous activists. An unresolved dilemma existed within the teachers' insurgency. It created opportunities for equality but also prioritized a union culture that valorized mestizo practices long associated with the federal teacher. An uneasy tension remained between the bilingual teachers' cultural and linguistic activism and their participation in the broader union struggle.

Conclusion

From its emergence as a public force, the dissident teachers' movement consistently opposed charrista trade unionism and austerity. The demands for democratization of their union and wage increases for its members went hand in hand. Indeed, the dissidents argued, Vanguardia Revolucionaria's fealty to the government meant they were unwilling to fight for better pay. Over the course of the 1980s, the Oaxacan movement successfully democratized Sección 22 and achieved salary increases. While they contributed to the fall of Vanguardia officials nationally, the movement also coincided with President Salinas's efforts to assert control over trade union leadership.[64] Salinas's efforts sought to facilitate privatization, the opposite of what dissident teachers had campaigned for. Dissidents therefore were successful in transforming their union local but faced an uphill battle in tackling the SNTE nationally. It was the largest trade union in the Americas, and its leadership was reshuffled but not defeated under President Salinas.

Economic hardships compounded by austerity measures provided the material basis of the movement. Indeed by 1977, well prior to the 1982 debt crisis, austerity was on the table as a solution to the government's untenable development model. This was not a preordained outcome or foreign imposition but rather the product of a series of discrete decisions by Mexican policy makers. López Portillo's sacking of Muñoz Ledo as secretary of education was one such decision, as it indicated a turn away from robust federal support of public education.[65] The teachers' resistance to austerity measures points to the necessity of abandoning facile distinctions between the *sexenio* of López Portillo and that of Miguel de la Madrid. As Roger Bartra pointed out during debates over how to understand the September 1982 bank nationalization, the traditional dichotomy of "national popular" and "neoliberal" frameworks does not always elucidate how austerity developed within PRI governments.[66] Various factions within the ruling party embraced neoliberalism as a response to specific political and economic conjunctures.

Key to the political and social weight of the teachers' struggle was the role played by its bilingual members. As previous chapters make clear, these teachers were part of a long history of indigenista development and education efforts. From the postrevolutionary period forward, the indigenista project discursively embraced the pre-Hispanic past and elements of indigeneity. Rivera's SEP murals are a clear visual articulation of that project. For the first half of the century, that indigenista discourse was attached to policies of state-led development. By the end of the 1970s, authorities began to abandon the view that federal government could act as an agent of a more equitable development. But the murals remained. Art historians have rightly critiqued the SEP frescoes for their romantic treatment of the Indigenous subject.[67] Indeed, they reflect the double bind of indigenismo, at once valorizing Indigenous cultures while fixing them to a pre-Hispanic past and the natural world. But the murals are also part of a contested indigenista experience. Public art and government rhetoric provided ammunition for dissidents in a way that continued to be productive into the late twentieth century. The teachers who occupied the SEP's patio in 1978, who challenged their union leadership in downtown Oaxaca City in 1980, and who marched with blistered feet in 1986 to the nation's capital all constituted an unanticipated outcome of indigenismo.

Over the course of the 1980s, as dissidents confronted their union leaders and government austerity, major changes were afoot within the indigenista and *educación indígena* bureaucracies. At the grassroots level, teacher activists drew on New Left and Third-Worldist ideas of cultural and social emancipation to construct alternative pedagogies. At the level of national policy, dissident anthropologists took up positions within the respective INI and the SEP administrations and helped usher in a shift toward what was termed bilingual-bicultural education and *etnodesarrollo*, ethnic development. Collectively, these policies constituted a robust shift toward multiculturalism. Mexico was not alone in this. Countries throughout the hemisphere embraced multicultural polices at the end of the century. In chapter 6, I examine this shift at both the institutional and grassroots levels.

6

Anticolonialism in the Classroom
The Institutionalization of Multiculturalism

DURING HIS high school years Marcos Abraham Cruz Bautista used the backroom of a Tlaxiaco warehouse as his bedroom. In the mornings he cleaned the local INI offices, and in the afternoons he attended classes. Cruz spent his formative years working this way, eventually moving from the position of night watchman to subdirector and then director of Conasupo-IMSS warehouses, a federal food distribution program, throughout the Mixteca Alta. Born in 1949 in San Juan Mixtepec, roughly twenty-five miles west of Tlaxiaco, Cruz had moved to the district capital to finish primary school. Initially, he found work with a local merchant, Rufino San Juan. The young Cruz carried the merchant's goods to the Tlaxiaco market early each morning and tended the showers that San Juan rented to travelers, splitting wood and feeding the fires that heated the water. He eventually won an INI scholarship to support his studies, and through a combination of odd jobs and scholarships he completed high school in 1974. Cruz's educational and professional trajectories were tied to the expanding indigenista development efforts of the period. He won scholarships based on academic performance and fluency in his native Mixtec. Later he found employment in the growing INI and Conasupo programs. In late 1978, after working for the INI in the Mixteca Alta towns of San Juan Bautista Coixtlahuaca and Nochixtlán, Cruz heard tell of scholarships for a new *licenciatura* (bachelor's program) and eagerly applied.

Cruz was accepted into a three-year ethnolinguistics program whose founding principle was etnodesarrollo, or ethnic development. Etnodesarrollo was an educational and development model that valorized ethnicity

FIGURE 19. The INI-Conasupo warehouse in Tlaxiaco.
Source: Instituto Nacional de los Pueblos Indígenas, Fototeca Nacho López, Raúl Rocha.

and the self-activity of Indigenous peoples in defense of their own cultures, languages, and communities. Led by many of Mexico's most prominent indigenista figures, notably Guillermo Bonfil Batalla, the program was located in the auspicious setting of Pátzcuaro, Michoacán, and trained Indigenous linguists to conduct research on their own languages. The Pátzcuaro program was one component of a broader institutional shift toward what reformers termed bilingual-bicultural education.

Over the course of the 1970s, anthropologists throughout the Americas had united around the concept of ethnocide, the notion that Native peoples had experienced a form of cultural genocide. Through continent-wide conversations regarding Native peoples' relationship to nation-states, these figures imagined a state-facilitated revalorization and restoration of Native languages and cultures. By the beginning of the 1980s, Mexico's SEP institutionalized these ideas in a series of reforms. In the context of indigenista policy, officials increasingly termed the new orientation *indigenismo de participación*, participatory indigenismo. In this delicate balance, anthropologists who sympathized with Native peoples would leverage state resources and agencies to facilitate "Indigenous liberation." This was both an old and a new idea. Throughout the indigenista experience, a minority current had advocated the inherent value of Indigenous languages and cultures and the need to support the self-determination of those marked as Indigenous. Institutions such as the SEP and the INI now officially embraced such ideas, even if their implementation was uneven.

These cultural rights frameworks also took center stage internationally. Intellectuals, activists, and policy makers increasingly employed the language of "rights" to defend populations considered marginal or oppressed. The expansion and evolution of international institutions such as the United Nations meant activists increasingly sought to use international law in order to achieve their objectives. The emphasis on cultural rights thus emerged alongside a growing human rights discourse.[1] As evidenced in the preceding chapter, the 1980s was also a period of rising levels of social inequality. Scholars have debated the relationship between the emergence of human and cultural rights discourses alongside this increased inequality. One interpretation has focused on elite savviness, in which government officials conceded to robust cultural pluralism or human rights rhetoric while maintaining—indeed often increasing—existing social inequities. Guatemala is a prime example of this dynamic, in which politicians tied to the former military dictatorship came to embrace Mayan cultural rights.[2] Another interpretation posits that grassroots activists gave up on discussions of social inequality and accepted watered-down versions of inclusion, in this case official multiculturalism.[3] Here I consider this broader question through the institutionalization of multicultural education reform. In contrast to the above accounts, I underscore continuities as opposed to rupture in the rise of official multiculturalism. Rather than a theory of abandonment, I suggest coproduction as a better model for understanding the emergence of the hemispheric multicultural moment. I do so by underscoring its origins in New Left and Third-Worldist activism.

The 1980s in Mexico was a period of economic crisis and political conflict. As recounted in the previous chapter, federal authorities had begun to embrace policies of austerity at the end of the previous decade. The 1982 debt crisis then proved even more damaging. By the following year, the devaluation of the peso meant severe hardship for ordinary Mexicans. However, the PRI, which oversaw neoliberal reform in the country, continued to employ the language of the 1910 Revolution and to portray itself as an ally to the Latin American Left. Officials invoked the country's long-standing support for Cuba as an example of its revolutionary credentials. More concretely, federal officials welcomed dissidents fleeing South American military regimes and violent civil wars in Central America. Exiles from across the hemisphere found Mexico City a refuge from political persecution and violence. President Miguel de la Madrid (1982–88), like PRI officials before him, had to navigate competing tendencies within the party. He appointed prominent PRI functionary Jesús Reyes Heroles as his secretary of education. Reyes Heroles, who served the previous administration as secretary of government, was most famous for facilitating the 1977 electoral reforms. President de la Madrid and Reyes Heroles (until his death in 1985) oversaw a series of austerity-oriented economic policies. They also eventually moved to sideline many of the ruling party's more left-wing functionaries.

To head the INI, the president appointed Salomón Nahmad Sitton (b. 1935). A Mexican anthropologist of Syrian descent, Nahmad trained at the ENAH in the 1950s alongside figures such as Margarita Nolasco and Luis Reyes. From 1978 until his 1982 INI appointment, Nahmad had directed the SEP's new subministry of Indigenous education, the Dirección General de Educación Indígena (DGEI). Under Nahmad's leadership, the DGEI promoted bilingual-bicultural education. During his tenure as DGEI director, he earned a reputation as an advocate of Indigenous languages and as an adept public servant. In 1982, when de la Madrid tapped Nahmad to serve as INI director, the anthropologist advocated for Indigenous leadership within indigenista agencies. As he explained to Bonfil Batalla, "It is now the time that the Indigenous themselves assume political control of their development."[4] Nahmad framed these policies around the notion of Indigenous peoples' agency, and the ethnolinguistics program occupied a key position within this broader strategy. He imagined the graduates would then lead INI programs and offices, including the agency's dozens of regional coordinating centers dispersed throughout the republic. But his tenure at the helm of the institute was short-lived. He encountered opposition to his policy proposals at all levels, from Vanguardia Revolucionaria union leaders to presidential cabinet members. This conflict eventually led to Nahmad's 1983 ouster as INI director and a five-month stint in jail on allegations of financial mismanagement.[5] This tumult within the indigenista bureaucracy demonstrates the high stakes and contested nature of Mexico's multicultural reforms.

The government's turn toward multiculturalism also met with opposition from the Mexican Left. Critics denounced the Pátzcuaro program as "bourgeois populism," arguing that its focus on ethnicity over questions of class and class struggle served to distract from a broader revolutionary project.[6] These critics made class-first arguments, contending that the

FIGURE 20. From left, Ramón Hernández López, Gonzalo Aguirre Beltrán, and Salomón Nahmad Sitton, 1972.
Source: Instituto Nacional de los Pueblos Indígenas, Fototeca Nacho López, Ramón Hernández.

federal government promoted ethnic politics as a way to demobilize and divide Mexicans. Defenders of the policies appeared to make identitarian claims, emphasizing ethnic or cultural standpoints over all else. But the lines between these two positions were frequently blurred, and education policy and classroom practice were two entirely separate things. Indeed, those involved in multicultural reform had a diversity of ideas, as did the intended subjects of their policies. Left critics also failed to see how policies of etnodesarrollo did reckon with questions of social inequality.[7] As will become evident, those behind multicultural reform, both policy makers and grassroots activists, saw inequality as an urgent issue, but framed that inequality as falling along ethnic and racial lines. Furthermore they understood global inequalities as fundamentally legacies of colonialism. These ideas were part and parcel of the Third-Worldist political and economic project of the 1970s. Many of the most ambitious policy initiatives of that moment, such as Mexico's advocacy of the 1974 New International Economic Order, had been foreclosed by the early 1980s. Nonetheless, that Third-Worldist project shaped Indigenous education reform.

The Pátzcuaro Ethnolinguistic Program

Marcos Abraham Cruz Bautista arrived in Pátzcuaro in the summer of 1979. "I just went for the degree, whatever it was," he recounted, "because I didn't have the means to study."[8] Nahmad and Rodolfo Stavenhagen, a Mexican sociologist dedicated to Indigenous empowerment, led the effort to create a pioneering group of Indigenous linguists. INI leaders, including then director Ignacio Ovalle Fernández, along with others from the Centro de Investigaciones Superiores del Instituto Nacional de Antropología e Historia, and the DGEI, created the Programa de Licenciatura en Etnolingüística. The program trained just one class of students before relocating to the state of Tlaxcala for its second entering class.[9] Along with fluency in Spanish and their native language, prospective students were to hold normal school degrees or a minimum of secondary education. For the first class, officials selected eighty-one students, sixty-seven of whom enrolled.[10] The majority were men, with only seven women in the original cohort. This gender gap conformed with long-standing trends in Indigenous education. The program selected students from seven language groups, chosen on the basis of perceived demographic importance and the availability of qualified instructors: Nahuatl, Mayan, Mixtec, Otomi, Purépecha, Tononaco, and Zapotec.[11]

Classes began at the Centro Regional de Educación Fundamental para la América campus on July 2, 1979. The program brought together an impressive and eclectic array of scholars. Luis Reyes, a Nahuatl intellectual, served as program coordinator and proved influential for many of the students. The majority of the teaching staff were from Mexico City, including Bonfil Batalla and Maria del Carmen Nava Nava. Program leaders also convened a diverse group of scholars to visit Pátzcuaro as guest lecturers and thesis advisers. Evelyn Hu Dehart, a recent PhD from the University of Texas at Austin, offered classes in the program before going on to publish multiple books on the Yaqui of northern Mexico. Marshall Durbin, who had previous experience training Indigenous linguists, served as head of the linguistics section. Peter Worsley, an influential British anthropologist associated with the *New Left Review* who helped popularize the concept of the Third World, also taught in Pátzcuaro. The Guatemalan Carlos Guzmán Böckler, one of the youthful dissidents at the 1968 Inter-American Indigenista Congress, visited the program with his longtime collaborator, French anthropologist Jean-Loup Herbert. Bonfil Batalla and Guzmán Böckler jointly taught the introductory course of social anthropology. Carlos Monsiváis, the famed literary critic, visited and spoke with students about Mexican cinema.[12] All traveled to southwestern Mexico to collaborate with and help shape a new generation of Indigenous linguists in training.

The Pátzcuaro curriculum consisted of three years of formal coursework, workshops organized by ethnicity, and fieldwork. Typical courses covered such topics as "Introducción a etnohistoria," "Teorías de las etenias," and "Dominación criolla-mestiza."[13] While the program emphasized themes of culture and ethnicity, courses such as "Teoría y práctica de la auto gestión" and "Problemas étnicos contemporáneos" also addressed questions of class and economic power. When Guzmán-Böckler taught theories of social class, he introduced students not only to the work of Karl Marx and Frederick Engels but also to that of George Lukacs, Nicos Poulantzas, and Mao Zedong. In "Theories of Ethnicity," students examined case studies including the Mapuche of southern Chile, religious missions in Brazil, the conflict between Eritrea and Ethiopia, and the Negritud movement.[14] Over half of each semester's coursework focused on linguistics, and in "Semantica II" there was a unit on "Marxism and linguistics." To complete the program, students wrote a thesis based on fieldwork, some of which the SEP and INI published as a series.[15]

The interdisciplinary curriculum consisted of three major fields of study: linguistics, history, and social anthropology. One of the instructors, Nemesio Rodríguez, edited a multivolume series of texts for the students titled *Imperialismo y descolonización*. Rodríguez compiled the series with a focus on Third World politics, racial discrimination, and self-determination. He framed the volume's distinct case studies with the overarching argument that Western political hegemony was in crisis. Rodríguez cited myriad examples of colonized and formerly colonized countries, from China to Mozambique, as evidence of a global anticolonial movement. The touchstone cases included Vietnam and the Philippines, and he highlighted works by the West African revolutionary Amílcar Cabral. The volumes included essays critical the Soviet Union and its allies, what Rodríguez termed the "bureaucratic Left." This series sought to situate Mexico's Indigenous peoples within a constellation of anticolonial politics, always emphasizing the role of culture in struggles for liberation. This

FIGURE 21. The cover of *Imperialismo y descolonización*, volume 2, featured in the Ethnolinguistic Program.
Source: Marcos Abraham Cruz Bautista, Personal Papers.

was a Third-Worldist multiculturalism that framed Indigenous liberation as part of a global anticolonial struggle.

By placing Indigenous issues in dialogue with global South struggles for cultural and political emancipation, the instructors reframed indigenista thought. The emphasis here was not to study Indigenous peoples in isolation, or in connection to pre-Hispanic civilizations, but rather to think of them as colonized and exploited populations like those of sub-Saharan Africa or Indonesia. The texts framed colonialism as relying on ethnic divisions in order to perpetuate and sustain itself. This was a departure from the more folkloric traditions within Mexican anthropology associated with the ENAH. While the Pátzcuaro program exposed students to a multiplicity of perspectives, all emphasized decolonization. Instructors did not present ethnicity as a static concept, but they prioritized it as a key component of liberation struggles. For the leaders of the program, such as Bonfil Batalla, decolonization and liberation could be achieved within the limits of the Mexican nation-state, but the curriculum also included anticapitalist critiques of economics and society.

In this context, the SEP officially severed its relationship with the SIL in September 1979.[16] A US-based evangelical missionary organization dedicated to translating the Bible, the SIL became enmeshed in controversy in the 1970s. In Mexico the organization had enjoyed a privileged position, signing a *convenio*, official agreement to collaborate, with the SEP during President Lázaro Cárdenas's term (1934–40). While the relationship between a secular nationalist government and foreign evangelical linguists had always been a delicate one, by the 1970s anthropologists and Indigenous rights activists looked upon the SIL in a new light. In the polarized Cold War context, from which the SIL was not entirely separate—particularly in its operations in Southeast Asia and South America—academics, journalists, and activists questioned the group's intentions and financing.[17] Some claimed the SIL was a front operation for the US Central Intelligence Agency, others denounced them for their evangelization efforts. The SIL was not officially engaged in missionary work, for the *convenio* with the Mexican government explicitly prohibited them from establishing churches. Nonetheless, for many, the mere presence of foreign missionaries engaged in linguistic research with the official backing of the state was increasingly unpalatable.

In October 1975, the First National Congress of Indigenous Peoples, held in Pátzcuaro, issued a public statement in opposition to the SIL.[18]

Pressure built against the organization at the Second Barbados Conference in 1977. Sponsored by the World Council of Churches and the Programme to Combat Racism, the meeting brought together Indigenous activists and sympathetic anthropologists from across the Americas. At the first conference, held in 1971, anthropologists had begun to articulate self-criticism concerning their own relationship to Native communities.[19] Six years later, in their continuing effort to support "Indigenous liberation," the Mexican participants Bonfil Batalla, Miguel Alberto Bartolomé, and Stefano Varese took advantage of the international audience provided by the event to denounce the SIL's work in their country, which they argued contributed to the further division of Indigenous peoples. The rising tide of criticism targeted not only the alleged cultural imperialism of the SIL but also its linguistic work. The anthropologists suggested the organization's development of distinct vocabularies and pedagogical materials for variants within Native languages constituted a divide-and-conquer strategy.[20] The 1979 severing of the *convenio* was a dramatic and symbolic victory for the new indigenista administrators and forced the SIL's staff of some 140 people to slowly leave the country by the end of 1980.[21]

The multicultural reformers intended to replace SIL linguists with the graduates of the Pátzcuaro program. Indeed, many Pátzcuaro graduates went on to engage in activities that indigenista authorities had envisioned. Some did so through official agencies such as the INI and the SEP, while others chose to conduct their research outside official institutions. As Cruz recounted of his Pátzcuaro experience, "It changed my way of being, I began to be radical in terms of union politics, similar to culture, and slowly I began to learn how to do research on my own language, about my own culture, about my own people, that changed my life."[22] Cruz's emphasis on the transformative nature of his experience is echoed by other program participants.[23] For Cruz, the idea of valorizing the Indigenous elements of his self was a radical notion, even though he had benefited from indigenista fellowships and employment in his youth. At Pátzcuaro, he felt valorized precisely for these traits. Whereas much of his prior schooling and social world had shunned Native language and culture as representing poverty and ignorance, in Pátzcuaro his instructors affirmed Indigenous language and culture as intrinsically valuable. Through the curriculum and classroom instruction, Cruz's Mixtec culture was placed within a rich historical context dating to pre-Hispanic times and a vibrant contemporary struggle against colonialism internationally. Indigeneity went from being a source of isolation and impoverishment to being a powerful personal and political tool for fully realizing one's self in the world.

Juan Julián Caballero (b. 1949), another Mixtec student at Pátzcuaro, wrote his graduating thesis on the detrimental role rural teachers played in the destruction of Indigenous culture. Drawing on his own experience as an INI bilingual promoter and later as a teacher, Julián Caballero's thesis served as a kind of self-indictment. He recounted his own "bitter experience" of primary school education in the 1950s. His teachers favored Spanish-speaking students over those students who were more comfortable in Mixtec and they used rote repetition in the classroom. Julián Caballero's need to work as a seasonal laborer in the nearby coffee fincas frequently interrupted his studies. Finishing primary school in 1964, he took a job as an INI bilingual promoter in 1967. Despite the INI's injunctions to use Mixtec as a bridge to the castellanización of students, without adequate training Julián Caballero reverted to the same techniques his own teachers had used: corporal punishment and Spanish language repetition exercises.[24] At Pátzcuaro, he and his colleagues were trained to reverse these trends in education history, a daunting assignment.

The ethnolinguistic program was in effect another pilot project, similar to the Mixteca Alta radio school program, in which federal agencies gave a limited amount of funding and administrative space to a group of committed indigenistas and academics interested in alternative models of Indigenous development. Training just two generations of students, the program exposed the yawning gap between the stated goal of overturning colonial power dynamics and the meager institutional support offered. Some contemporary Left critics viewed its focus on ethnicity as a distraction, arguing that the state was deliberately leading Indigenous youth away from the politics of class and social revolution.[25] Indeed, Cruz noted that some students felt uncomfortable with the program's emphasis on ethnic consciousness and eventually quit. But the program's curriculum and students' subsequent experiences tell a more complex story. The curriculum and staff represented a range of ideas, many of them in dialogue with long-standing debates on the left regarding social class, ethnicity, and race. And as Cruz recounted, he became more, not less, involved in trade union activism after the conversations that began in Pátzcuaro. In the case of the other Mixtec participants, in 1989 Julián Caballero helped to found a civic association, Ve'e Tu'un Savi, which sought to promote a unified

Mixtec vocabulary and the collection of oral narratives for language revitalization.[26] For program officials, it was largely a success in that it trained a cadre of Indigenous educators who went on to work in the SEP's Indigenous education sector or developed their own projects of linguistic and cultural revitalization. The program's fate was tied to the precarious economic context of the 1980s, in which the state moved to slash government spending in education and rural development.

The Institutionalization of Multicultural Education

Pátzcuaro was just one piece in a broader reorganization and reform of Indigenous education in Mexico. The new Indigenous education subministry, the DGEI, oversaw curriculum design, pedagogical training, and the supervision of *escuelas albergues,* Indigenous boarding schools. The subministry's explicit charge was the supervision of educational services for monolingual Indigenous communities and Spanish language instruction. Even though Nahmad and others involved in the early administration of the subministry advocated a radical multiculturalism, there was no explicit reference to instruction in Native languages in the DGEI official charter. Instead, there was an emphasis on castellanización or Spanish language acquisition.[27] This could have been due to inertia in the revision of policy documents or a continued ambivalence among top-level administrators as to the competing demands within Indigenous education of national integration versus cultural preservation.

Much like the long-standing debates regarding the utility of instruction in Native languages, controversy surrounded the creation of the new subministry. Some dissident teachers worried that with the bureaucratic reshuffling of the SEP, the dissolution of the DGEEMI, and the subsequent creation of the DGEI, an agency specifically dedicated to Indigenous education might be eliminated.[28] Since the postrevolutionary period, the SEP's subministry dedicated to serving Indigenous students went through a series of name changes and bureaucratic transformations. The DGEEMI (1971–78) began to embrace bilingual methods, and the creation of the DGEI further institutionalized that approach. It in turn created a new type of residential school, escuelas albergues. INI officials, who had pioneered bilingual pedagogies at midcentury, often encountered resistance to such methods from local SEP officials and federal schoolteachers.[29] With the creation of the DGEI, the INI and SEP's efforts were linked more closely. Federal administrators were unified by an embrace of bilingual-bicultural pedagogy. Concretely, that approach meant that in DGEI preschools and primary schools, children were to be instructed in both their native language and Spanish and to work with culturally relevant didactic materials.

The subministry's first self-assessment underscored the gap between the reformers' goals and the reality they faced. In 1979 the DGEI reported that out of the estimated seven hundred thousand Indigenous primary-age children in the country, fewer than half were attending school and just twelve thousand had completed the sixth grade. Oaxaca was the state with the largest demand for Indigenous preschool and primary school education. The subministry therefore devoted the greatest share of its budget to the state. Neighboring Chiapas received the second-largest portion of funds. In terms of teacher training, out of the roughly eleven thousand bilingual teachers and promoters, 30 percent were said to have normal school training, 50 percent secondary education, and 20 percent only a primary school education. The subministry identified this lack of teacher training as a key problem, along with inadequate teacher supervision and inadequate distribution of didactic materials.[30] Particularly as the system had expanded, the SEP contracted teachers without the sufficient preparation in order to meet rising demand. Because of this dynamic the subministry created in-service teacher training programs in Mexico City as well in state capitals. For reformers such as Nahmad, this reality required a major overhaul of the ministry's functions.

The new subministry's responsibilities fell into three main areas: the castellanización of monolingual Indigenous children of preschool age, the training of primary school teachers, and adult education and literacy instruction. The castellanización efforts were conducted through both residential schools and traditional schools by staff specifically trained for such work. According to the subministry's requirements, the *castellanizadores* were to be of "Indigenous origin (bilingual)," to have completed secondary school, and to speak the languages of the students they would be responsible for.[31] While an enormous gap had long existed between stated policy and classroom practice, and prior Indigenous education efforts had employed bilingual staff, the subministry's official commitment to employing only bilingual personnel reflected a new institutional consensus regarding the need for and desirability of bilingual instruction.

The subministry began by recruiting roughly two thousand new *castellanizadores*. Under the DGEI's supervision, they were trained in two different pedagogical methods: one developed by US linguist Morris Swadesh, "Juegos para Aprender Español," and the other associated with the Centro de Investigación para la Integración Social in Mexico City, termed "Enseñanza del Español a Hablantes de Lengua Indígena."[32] Both stressed oral proficiency in Spanish as opposed to traditional literacy approaches, while Swadesh's method aimed for literacy in vernacular languages as well. Trained in one of the two methods during a two-month program, the instructors were then sent into service in the classroom.[33] Their charge was to promote ethnic identity while teaching the national language to monolingual children.[34]

Indigenous boarding schools, termed *internados,* dated back to postrevolutionary state-building efforts. As in other countries, critics condemned Mexican boarding schools for taking Indigenous children out of their cultural environment and for their hostility to children's specific language and cultural practices. In part because of such critiques, officials closed or converted them into escuelas albergues, so-called hostel schools. In contrast to full-time residential schools, albergues allowed parents in far-flung rural communities to send their children to school during the week, where they were provided room and board, but where they would also return home to their families on weekends. Officials believed this would maintain cultural ties between children and their parents. This innovation, along with the injunction that members of Indigenous communities staff the escuelas albergues, gave the schools a different connotation.[35] In 1978, the subministry oversaw a significant expansion of the *albergue* system, adding three hundred new schools to the roughly nine hundred in operation nationally.[36] The multicultural reforms in residential schools sought to alter but not abolish a long-standing instrument of Indigenous education.

Another key change was the creation and distribution of didactic materials in Native languages.[37] During the early 1980s the subministry produced its first bilingual-bicultural textbooks. These books were explicitly framed as part of an anticolonial pedagogical project. For example, the first-grade Mixtec textbook, *Tutu sa'an ñuu savi: Mi libro mixteco-primer grado*, introduced students to the word *kiti* and broke it into its two component syllables, *ki* and *ti*. *Kiti* means animal in Mixtec. With familiar images of a goat, a pig, a turkey, and a burro, the bilingual-bicultural objective was to first teach students in their own language and introduce Spanish language instruction in second grade. *Tutu sa'an ñuu savi* began with words and images students knew, broke them into their component syllables, and used those as the basis to form other words. This pedagogical strategy fostered literacy in Indigenous languages first, in this case Tlaxiaco-East Mixtec, before exposure to a second language. Given the primarily oral nature of Oaxacan languages in the late twentieth century, this objective was an ambitious one.

The subministry produced these texts in twenty-two different languages as well as their multiple dialectical variants. The books employed drawings and photographs deemed culturally relevant. *Tutu sa'an ñuu savi*, for example, contained images of nature, photographs of typical houses in the Mixtec Alta, local parents and children, and scenes of agriculture. Whereas previous bilingual pedagogical materials were often mere translations of existing Spanish language texts, these texts were grounded in the

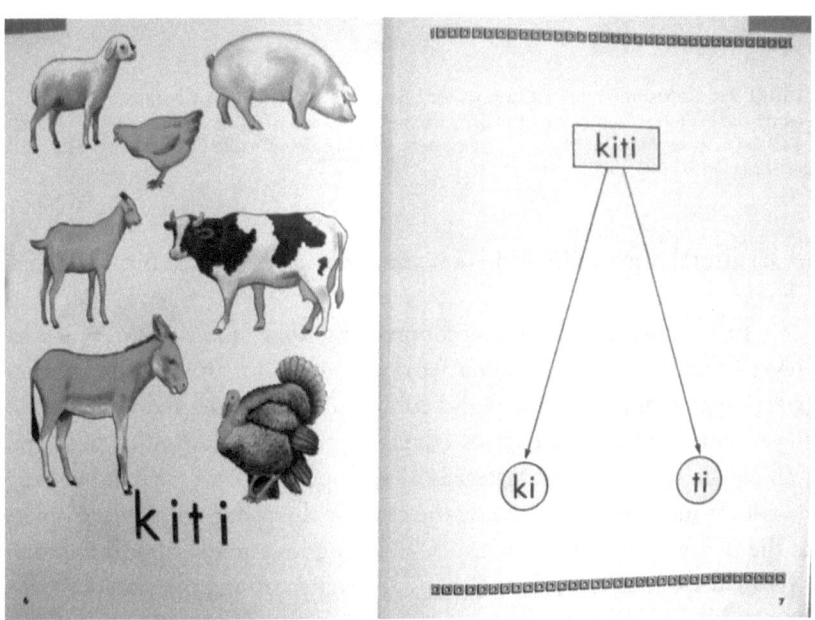

FIGURE 22. Anticolonial pedagogy for first-grade students.
Source: Gabina Reyes Bautista and Pauala Fería Barrios, *Manuel para la enseñanza de lecto-escritura en lengua mixteca: Libro del maestro, primer grado, Tlaxiaco Este, Oaxaca* (Mexico City: Secretaría de Educación Pública, 1985).

FIGURE 23. Culturally relevant images for first-grade students in the Mixteca Alta.
Source: Gabina Reyes Bautista and Pauala Fería Barrios, *Manuel para la enseñanza de lecto-escritura en lengua mixteca: Libro del maestro, primer grado, Tlaxiaco Este, Oaxaca* (Mexico City: Secretaría de Educación Pública, 1985).

local cultural context. Indeed, *Tutu sa'an ñuu savi* contained not one Spanish word.

In the teacher's manual accompanying *Tutu sa'an ñuu savi*, Gabina Reyes Bautista and Pauala Fería Barrios noted, "To survive, our cultures had to take refuge in families and communites for more than 450 years." Reyes and Fería critiqued prior education models as assimilationist and framed the new didactic materials as responding to the demands of the people. While the authors made the case for the pedagogical effectiveness of the bilingual-bicultural method, including instruction of arithmetic in Mixtec, they went beyond utilitarian arguments, making the case for the inherent value of Indigenous languages and cultures. "There is no such thing as primitive languages," they argued, and noted that while "the West" had made contributions to modern civilization, so too had Native peoples.[38] They highlighted Native peoples' "rational" use of natural resources and stewardship of the environment, communitarian systems of production, traditional medicine, and unique ways of understanding the world. Reyes and Fería encouraged teachers to be creative in their approach, to rely on the local communities, to value their students as individuals, and to share their results and suggestions with the authors.[39]

Dilemmas of Anticolonial Pedagogy

These transformations took place precisely as teachers in Oaxaca and throughout the republic challenged education and union authorities on multiple fronts. Indeed, as noted in chapter 5, the piecemeal expansion of the Indigenous education sector meant that newly contracted bilingual teachers played key roles in the democratization of Sección 22 of the SNTE. However, the union struggle often prioritized political contributions and participation over innovative classroom practice. Teachers involved in the dissident movement at times died in mysterious or unexplained circumstances.[40] Their colleagues knew that those who had perished in car crashes on Oaxaca's lonely backroads, or in shootouts at local bars, were most likely victims of Vanguardia Revolucionaria's paid assassins. These deaths underscored the life-and-death struggle teachers faced. This dynamic meant that many teacher activists often prioritized union organizing over any other activity, including work in the classroom.

Nor did the broader economic context contribute to innovative education practices. As the crisis in Mexican agriculture deepened and as federal authorities pulled subsidies and other supports from small producers, rural economic hardship became more dire. Large numbers of Oaxacans migrated to points north, including the United States. In this situation, the teaching profession became one of the few forms of remunerated employment left in rural communities. The education sector itself offered paths for individual advancement, in which a teacher could hope to become head of a school district, take on other administrative duties, and be transferred to a district capital and eventually the state capital, Oaxaca City. This "up and out" dynamic, facilitated through union participation and professional advancement, did not necessarily advance the goals of bilingual-bicultural education. Indeed, these dynamics mirrored broader forces that often undermined the preservation of Native language practices.

The 1980s was a period of economic crisis, debt, and stagnation throughout the hemisphere. Violent civil wars raged in Central America, and South American military juntas, while embattled, remained in power. While electoral democracy would be restored throughout much of the region by the early 1990s, the persistence of high levels of inequality and poverty alongside diminished political possibilities gave the end of the century a decidedly bleak outlook.[41] National governments and international financial institutions ushered in a round of free trade agreements and structural adjustment policies. While their advocates touted their effectiveness at the national level, rural regions such as Oaxaca continued to experience agricultural decline and high rates of emigration. Indeed, the crisis in rural agriculture caused a spike in Mexican migration to the United States. These policies disproportionately affected Oaxacans, and particularly Indigenous people.

In the final decades of the century, Oaxaca was one of the two most impoverished states in Mexico. According to official statistics, it had the highest level of "marginalization" after the neighboring state of Chiapas. While definitions of poverty are socially and culturally bound, a number of indicators reflect the precarity and vulnerability Oaxacans faced. The state's illiteracy rate of 27.5 percent was more than double the national average of 12.4 percent. Educational access and enrollment were limited, particularly in predominantly Indigenous regions. Many Oaxacans continued to live in dirt-floor structures without indoor plumbing or access to potable water. Most alarming, infant mortality rates among the Indigenous population remained egregiously high. All of the 159 Oaxacan municipalities with infant mortality rates of at least 60 percent were majority Indigenous.[42] This reality provided the basis for popular support of the dissident teachers' movement but also fueled large-scale out-migration.

While there was a persistence of rural poverty in Oaxaca, Indigenous life in the state was far from homogeneous. Too often commentators have equated indigeneity and poverty, as if one were synonymous with the other. There was a high correlation between the Indigenous regions and levels of social precarity, but class differences existed throughout the state and within Indigenous communities. Take the Isthmus town of Juchitán: an urban and commercial center with a considerable business class, Juchitán had preserved quotidian Zapotec language practices throughout the twentieth century. Schoolteachers, business people, and municipal politicians conducted much of their professional lives in Zapotec. This cross-class phenomenon on the Isthmus constituted a major outlier in the social scientific data on poverty in the state.[43] Oaxaca's highland regions were where the rural crisis was felt most acutely. This heterogeneity demonstrates how questions of indigeneity were always tied to relative power, whether local, national, or global. The project of multicultural education reform, one that was building for decades, was implemented precisely in this context of economic crisis and out-migration. That project's origins were in previous decades, but it achieved institutional power precisely at a moment of economic restructuring. That conjuncture meant that multicultural reform at times was experienced as a top-down project, rather than one emanating from grassroots demands.

A 1982 independent assessment of the Indigenous education subministry raised fundamental questions regarding the reformers' multicultural vision. Stefano Varese, who led the study alongside the Argentine researchers Nemesio Rodríguez and Maria Inés Laje, was no enemy of multicultural reform. Varese had in fact helped denounce the SIL, and Rodríguez and Laje had worked in the Pátzcuaro program. Their assessment, though conducted just four years after the creation of the DGEI, was grim. They noted that bilingual teachers frequently employed Spanish-only instruction rather than bilingual methods, that they were often assigned to communities outside their language capabilities, and that many official bilingual materials were still mere translations of Spanish language textbooks. In addition, the reformed residential schools continued to break the cultural connection of children with their home communities.

Perhaps more damningly, Rodríguez and Laje noted that bilingual teachers "express a lack of self-worth for belonging to the system, whose theoretical and ideological premises they do not fully understand." The researchers argued that this produced a dynamic in which teachers ended up repeating the methods used in non-Indigenous schools, noting that this "mimicking dynamic upends from its own roots the very purpose of specialized education for Indigenous populations."[44] These problems were perhaps not surprising given the broader history of rural education that for decades stressed castellanización at the expense of Native languages. But the specific criticisms also point to a more fundamental problem that reformers faced, namely the "inverse relation" between so-called ethnic consciousness and formal schooling.[45] The authors noted that bilingual educators with higher levels of education had less appreciation for Native language and culture. In other words, the very people most formally capable of carrying out bilingual instruction had little interest in doing so.

If multicultural reform struggled to achieve its ends at the local level, it also encountered challenges within top administrative circles. For example, the victory against the SIL was short-lived. The organization was eventually allowed to return to the country, albeit without its former official status. The incoming de la Madrid administration took a less-than-approving view of Nahmad's hostility to the group. When Nahmad assumed control of the INI in 1982, he learned that the government had cut the institute's budget. He quickly found himself in tense negotiations with Secretary of Education Reyes Heroles over the SIL, the budget, and a proposal for a constitutional amendment to recognize Indigenous languages. The president and Reyes Heroles had hoped for a "yes man" in Nahmad but instead found a stubborn anthropologist committed to implementing ideas he and his cohort had developed over the course of two decades. After a conflict regarding the nomination of Yaqui activists to run the INI's coordinating center in the state of Sonora, Nahmad found himself a victim of a budgetary audit and was eventually accused of financial irregularities involving a family member. He was apprehended in his INI office, knowing full well his fate, and spent roughly five months in jail before being released. Nahmad's rise and sudden fall demonstrate the persistence of authoritarianism within the PRI political system. The INI had always been a part of a political apparatus that could facilitate individual advancement. When Nahmad did not respond to the normal institutional pressures, he was removed. His arrest signaled that reformers had reached the upper limits of possible change within the institutions.

The conflicts within the indigenista bureaucracy also betrayed a fundamental weakness and limitation of multicultural reform, namely its top-down nature. The pluralist ideas and programs reformers implemented through federal agencies also ran up against the larger societal dynamics that persisted in equating indigeneity with cultural backwardness and poverty. While there were persistent problems of capacity in the Indigenous education sector, namely a deficit of both the production and the distribution of culturally relevant didactic materials along with insufficient teacher training and support, persistent anti-Indigenous sentiment also proved detrimental.

This was particularly true in the Mixteca Alta, where little material basis existed for Indigenous resurgence. Membership in a particular community or town often proved more salient than any pan-Mixtec subjectivity. Within the Mixteca Alta there were substantive differences between the language practices of individual towns: in one Mixtec might be spoken only in a whisper by town elders, while in another it was spoken with pride by its youth. On the Isthmus language practices were quite different. There, being and speaking Zapotec experienced a full resurgence. The Mixteca Alta's persistent material impoverishment meant that outmigration, often to regions of commercial agriculture, was one of the few avenues for material survival. The teacher trade union movement, which facilitated bilingual teachers' participation and professional development, had an ambivalent relationship to multicultural education reform. While the union movement opened up opportunities for bilingual teachers to articulate their own demands, it often prioritized a union culture that sidelined questions of indigeneity. And neither the dissident movement nor federal education reform could fully challenge a context in which the teaching profession was frequently viewed as a route out of community impoverishment, through individual advancement and migration to urban centers.

Multiculturalism from Below

These multiple structural barriers did not deter a minority of teachers and their allies from putting into practice alternative and anticolonial pedagogies. The Coalición de Maestros y Promotores Indígenas de Oaxaca (CMPIO) was at the forefront of this movement. The Coalition controlled their own *jefatura de zona*, school district, which allowed them more autonomy in developing alternative classroom practices. As described in chapter 5, they formed a highly mobilized and politicized current within the broader teachers' movement. Indeed, the CMPIO prided itself in having formally joined the dissident CNTE prior to Sección 22 itself.[46] The Coalition combined union militancy with an increasing focus on alternative pedagogies and close collaboration with the communities they served. With their roots in the IIISEO development agency, CMPIO teachers typically served Oaxaca's most marginalized and Indigenous monolingual communities. In the 1980s, the Coalition, like other sections of the teachers' movement, suffered violent attacks by those allied with the Vanguardia Revolucionaria.

One teacher who joined the Coalition was Alverino López López. From the Mixteca Alta town of El Oro, Nuxaá, López began teaching in 1986. In his youth, he assisted his family by tending sheep and helping his father in the production of *carbón*, or charcoal. Prior to becoming a teacher López spent time working at a hotel in the neighboring town of Nochixtlán and later at a clothing stand and at a juice and sandwich shop. He studied briefly to be an agricultural agronomist before eventually deciding to follow his brother into the teaching profession. López's initial training as a teacher was brief. He arrived late for a three-month course in Temescal, Tuxtepec, near the border with Veracruz. Like many in the Indigenous education sector, he had completed only secondary school. While the training in Temescal was short and fairly orthodox, there was a focus on creating didactic materials in one's native language—Mixtec, in López's case. He eventually landed a job teaching second grade in his hometown.[47]

After working in the primary school for about three years, López began to attend in-service programs for teachers to continue their studies. He started preparing for his *bachillerato*, high school degree. It was then that he was first exposed to the theories of Paulo Freire and Célestin Freinet. At times referred to as the modern school movement, the Freinet model emphasized inquiry- and work-based learning. While López found Freire's theories interesting, he struggled to connect them with his classroom practice. It was when he began studies at a local campus of the Universidad Pedagógica Nacional that he became more involved in anticolonial pedagogy. As López recounts, the most important insight he took away from his experiences there was to "start with community knowledge." He learned about lunar cycles and how they relate to agricultural cycles. He focused on developing mathematics teaching materials in Mixtec, whose number system is based on integrals of twenty. He learned how to develop particular topics for the students, and lesson plans focused on local plants and animals. This training differed from that offered at the more traditional rural normal schools, particularly in its focus on history and anthropology and the revindication of Indigenous cultures.[48]

López's anticolonial training occurred in the midst of intense and sometimes deadly internal union struggles. Over the course of the decade, he and his comrades traveled frequently to Mexico City to demand the ouster of Jonguitud Barrios from the SNTE. They succeeded in 1989. However, within the movement, bilingual teachers faced another struggle. No teacher from the Indigenous education sector had ever served as secretary general of Sección 22, and few had held any other leadership positions. The union discriminated against bilingual teachers in multiple ways.

They had no access to *cargos*, official leadership positions that offered extra pay, and they faced daily slights from colleagues in *educación formal*, who dismissed them as *los bilingües*, to the parents of students. As López summarized, "There is a lot of discrimination against those from Indigenous backgrounds, a lot of discrimination."[49]

These inequalities within the union did not stop CMPIO teachers from participating in the movement. As seen in chapter 5, they were most often at the forefront of the struggle. However, Coalition teachers had an alternative pedagogical project that distinguished them even from colleagues within *educación indígena*. They increasingly focused on issues of classroom instruction and developed specific pedagogies to meet the needs of the communities and children they served. By the early 1990s, the CMPIO put forward a state-wide education proposal focused on *técnicas Freinet*. This was a deliberate effort to move away from methods of rote repetition that frequently dominated education in rural Oaxaca. Coalition teachers experimented with taking students outside the classroom and into the community for class projects. This at times provoked opposition from parents, who thought education should reflect their own experiences. Even fellow teachers, who saw the extra work and effort required by such models, viewed them as a threat to their own status within the union.

Because of their unique pedagogical mission, as well as political formation, Coalition teachers had a tense relationship with the broader union movement. Sección 22 comprised teachers from a variety of political tendencies, including those connected to the PRI, as well as various Far Left currents. The CMPIO's origins in the IIISEO provided them with a unique professional and political orientation. Indeed, their slogan "Por la liberación del Indígena" was visible on banners and in their propaganda as early as 1974. Coalition teachers read widely from such theorists as Marta Harnecker, the Peruvian Trotskyist and peasant leader Hugo Blanco, and José Carlos Mariátegui. Their politics evolved over more than three decades of activism. Early on, the group's political discourse underscored members' indigeneity and relationship to their home communities, but they did not call for language revitalization. It was in the 1980s that they increasingly emphasized language activism and cultural preservation. Their experience demonstrates a continuity between a New Left project and the rise of cultural rights frameworks.

The relationships forged within Coalition organizing required members to think about the particularities of the communities they served and at the same time articulate a vision for the broader transformation of society. Francisco Abardía Moros, a university student from Mexico City who joined the Coalition as an adviser in 1976, is just one example of this dynamic. His path to Oaxaca, and over a decade of experience collaborating with bilingual teachers, underscore the unexpected links between New Left politics and the rise of Indigenous resurgence movements. As described in chapter 4, Abardía was born in Mexico City in 1948, the child of Spanish republican refugees. He grew up singing "La Marseillaise" in Spanish expatriate schools. He eventually made his way to the UNAM, where he studied economics and immersed himself in student politics. He befriended major figures of the 1968 student movement, some of whom would go on to become public intellectuals, including Armando Bartra, Rolando Cordera, and Paco Ignacio Taibo II. Like other student activists, Abardía was forced into hiding during the post-1968 government repression. He eventually returned to Mexico City and found a job teaching nearby at the Universidad Autónoma de Chapingo, the national agricultural university.

It was at Chapingo in 1975 that Abardía would have his first encounter with the CMPIO. Members had traveled to the Chapingo campus to seek political support and funds for their struggle. Among those who walked the halls soliciting support was Servando Vérulo Aparicio López. Born in 1952, Aparicio grew up in the Mixteca Alta town of San Lucas Yosonicaje. During his youth, Yosonicaje had few schools and was a twelve-hour walk to the district capital, Tlaxiaco. Aparicio's father was a campesino who never left his hometown but had participated in a national literacy campaign and thus knew how to read and write a bit of Spanish.[50] His father died while Aparicio was still a child. Perhaps because of his father's experience, the family encouraged Aparicio to continue his studies. The soft-spoken young man eventually left Yosonicaje and trained at the IIISEO to become a promotor bilingüe. This is how Aparicio found himself in Chapingo, visiting classrooms and sharing the Coalition's stories.[51]

The CMPIO's efforts were a success. Not only were they able to fund-raise, but they made connections with activist students as well as Abardía. They eventually convinced Fernando Soberanes, a student from the northern state of Sinaloa, to also join them as an official adviser to the movement. By 1976, Abardía had taken a leave of absence from his teaching job, which would later become permanent, and moved to Oaxaca. It was some time thereafter that he found himself listening to something that to his ears was "un pinche discutidero de la chingada," an unintelligible gaggle of voices. He was in a community assembly in Oaxaca's Sierra Mixe and had just proposed the construction of a new preschool. Abardía and his CMPIO colleagues were doing work sanctioned by the state, the promotion of new schools and literacy projects, but were acting independently. They controlled the schools and promoted their own vision of community development. Eventually the assembly quieted, and the authorities turned to Abardía and said, "Well, they say no" (Pues, dicen que no). Abardía was astonished. Where was the vote? Who was the president presumably running the meeting? As was the custom of the Mixes' and other Indigenous communities, they had relied on a process of consensus, in which small group discussions led to a generalized collective decision. Abardía's colleague explained to him, "No seas tarugo," don't be stupid, they had already come to consensus.[52]

This encounter between a leftist militant from Mexico City and an Indigenous community may appear to confirm many common assumptions about the nature of leftist organizing in the Americas. Urban activists may have been inspired by counterculture visions of Indians as promoted by writers such as Carlos Castañeda, but when they confronted actual Indigenous community structures, they were confounded and confused. Abardía, inspired by New Left ideologies, may well have held different romanticisms, perhaps that of a revolutionary peasantry, but was equally confounded. Nonetheless, this moment of incomprehension, in which people were speaking entirely different languages, is significant for another reason. It was not just a moment of incomprehension but also one of solidarity and learning. It was a productive moment of difference.[53] While Abardía's collaboration with the CMPIO reflected the broader inequalities of the world, it also generated new forms of politics and visions for alternative futures. As he described his initial arrival in Oaxaca and collaboration with the Coalition, "That beautiful part of community, they opened our eyes to that. Like somone who gives you a fucking book full of colors, right? They say to you, look, *cabrón* . . . Wow, this is what you are inviting me to? A culture very different from my own as a city rat."[54] While teachers and their allies collaborated on unequal terms and from distinct social positions, they fostered bonds of solidarity and took steps toward confronting social hierarchies. They articulated notions of dignity, solidarity, and equality in similar ways. It was in these moments of incomprehension, collaboration, and learning that activists developed what would eventually be termed a politics of Indigenous resurgence.[55]

Conclusion

Given Oaxaca's diversity, resurgent politics took different forms in particular localities. On the Isthmus of Tehuantepec, the COCEI combined Zapotec culture and language with left-wing politics to win control of the Juchitán municipal government in 1981. The COCEI continued to confront an openly hostile state administrations in the years following. Their electoral success proved short-lived, but their model of Zapotec-based politics inspired others. Those engaged in resurgent politics frequently fought for autonomous control of town governments and challenged local authoritarian officials. In the Mixteca, among Triqui communities, the Movimiento de Unificación de Lucha Triqui emerged to oppose violent political repression in the region and remained a central player in state politics in subsequent decades. Catholic organizing in the state was not immune to Indigenous resurgence, and parts of the church hierarchy, along with grassroots lay activists, embraced what they called Indigenous theology. Language too was a key terrain of resurgent politics, with various groups and individuals engaged in activism for linguistic preservation or revival. This took the form of organizing conferences on the creation of a pan-Mixtec alphabet as well as Mazatec song-writing contests.[56] While the form of resurgent politics varied, without question indigeneity took center stage at the end of the century, whether in militant political confrontations or more narrowly "cultural" activities and programming.

At the beginning of the 1990s, Oaxacan officials, including Governor Carrasco, introduced legislation aimed at bolstering Indigenous rights in the state. The proposals, including legal recognition of Indigenous linguistic diversity and the practice of usos y costumbres in Oaxacan communities, were a far cry from some of the more radical initiatives advocated by Guillermo Bonfil Batalla and Salomón Nahmad Sitton. Through the Pátzcuaro ethnolinguistic program, they had sought to place Indigenous professionals in directing roles at federal agencies. At the same time, grassroots actors, including the CMPIO, campaigned for student-centered education models that valorized Indigenous culture and language.

In December 1995, Sección 22 officially voted to endorse the CMPIO's "Movimiento pedagógico" initiative. That officials and activists moved to adopt multicultural policies in a context of continued economic austerity does not demonstrate a necessary affinity between cultural rights and neoliberalism. Indeed, as we have seen over the course of this chapter, an array of grassroots actors, leftist intellectuals, and academics working in federal agencies from the 1970s through the 1980s contributed to projects that fell into the category of cultural rights. More specifically, New Left activists that engaged in anticolonial, Third-Worldist politics articulated their own forms of multiculturalism, at times inside and at times outside state institutions.[57] Rather than a story of activists abandoning questions of inequality, one sees a mutual construction of cultural rights frameworks. Mixtec linguists Juan Julián Caballero and Marcos Abraham Cruz Bautista developed Indigenous language initiatives, at times in opposition to official multiculturalism, at times working alongside it. Alverino López López and other CMPIO teachers demonstrate the complicated relationship between the trade union movement and questions of cultural revival. As committed trade unionists they struggled against policies of austerity while also challenging their colleagues' anti-Indigenous views. While officials such as Governor Carrasco may have endorsed cultural rights cynically, in an effort at superficial inclusion, Mexican multicultural policies also originated in an eclipsed Third-Worldist project. They were not a mere liberal veneer to a neoliberal order. We misunderstand the past, and the present, if we accept the neoliberal assumption that cultural revindications are necessarily detached from struggles against inequality. While neoliberal governance models framed them in such a way, that was not how many practitioners understood them.

Conclusion

The Entangled Histories of Recognition and Resurgence

ON A sunny morning in July 1993, hundreds of dancers and musicians gathered for the Guelaguetza de los Lunes del Cerro on a hill overlooking downtown Oaxaca City. Organized by the state government, the annual festival presents regional dance and music from across Oaxaca. Thousands of national and international tourists were in attendance. That morning the tourists ascended the steep hill on which the auditorium sits. They protected themselves from the intense sun with palm hats, some bearing the Coca-Cola logo. Begun in 1932, the festival features dress, music, and dance from the state's seven official regions. In the Danza de la Pluma to the Danza del Diablo, the performers represented Oaxaca's diverse cultures in front of the governor and assembled crowds. Maribel Roque, from an ejido near Tuxtepec, served as that year's Diosa Centéotl (corn goddess). Carrying a staff and circling the stage, Roque welcomed the attendees to Oaxaca's "most important festival." On the stage of honor sat the king and queen of Spain, Juan Carlos I and Sophia, alongside President Carlos Salinas de Gotari (1988–94). The Guatemalan activist and Nobel Peace prizewinner Rigoberta Menchú Tum sat to the president's left. The state governor, Diódoro Carrasco Altamirano, served as official host. Roque and the other performers thanked the governor and greeted his special guests before beginning the show.

This performance of indigeneity for politicians and tourists appears nearly as caricature. The deference paid to President Salinas and state officials, the presence of Spanish royalty, and a tourist economy based on the folklorization of Indigenous culture all suggest cultural violence and

FIGURE 24. From left, King Juan Carlos I, President Carlos Salinas de Gotari, and Rigoberta Menchú Tum attending the 1993 Guelaguetza in Oaxaca City.
Source: *El Sur* (Juchitán, Oaxaca), 1993. Courtesy la Hemeroteca Pública de Oaxaca Néstor Sánchez Hernández.

persistent colonial oppression. A former Mixe festival participant, Donaldo Monterrubio, denounced it as "una exhibición de indios," an exhibition of Indians. Not only did the government commodify Indigenous aesthetics, most seats in the auditorium were ticketed at high prices, but the organization of the event itself was fraught with PRI politics. Communities connected to particular ruling party officials had greater access to the festivities. The gendered nature of the performances cannot be overlooked either, with women's *trajes* serving as symbols of particular regions and cultures.[1] Nor was President Salinas's attendance incidental. In 1992 governments across the hemisphere had celebrated the five-hundredth anniversary of European arrival to the Americas. One year after the anniversary, Salinas chose to attend flanked by the Spanish royalty and Menchú. The Guelaguetza allowed the president to cloak himself in Menchú's reputation as an Indigenous activist and to welcome her to the country's Indigenous South.[2] The commercial nature of the event and the political cover it afforded Salinas crystallize what critics have termed neoliberal multiculturalism. At the festival, neoliberal politicians presided over the commodification of Oaxaca's diverse communities and cultural traditions.

The Guelaguetza has a singular history, dating to Mexico's postrevolutionary period and the Oaxacan government's effort to unify a fractious state. Yet its 1993 incarnation formed part of the broader multicultural turn. Throughout the 1980s, activists mobilized for Indigenous rights, government recognition, and at times autonomy. In 1992, while many Latin American governments touted the five-hundredth anniversary in nationalist rhetoric, activists denounced the Quinto Centenario, with the phrase "No hay nada de que festejar" (There is nothing to celebrate).[3] The debates regarding the anniversary were part of tensions brewing over previous decades. Across the hemisphere, national governments, as well as international organizations, increasingly recognized the "cultural rights" of Native peoples in official rhetoric and policy. Perhaps the most significant example of this was the International Labour Organization's Convention 169, written in 1989 and ratified by the Mexican government in 1990. Convention 169 obligates signatory governments to respect Indigenous peoples' cultures, lifeways, land, and access to natural recourses. Bolivian Indigenous rights advocates had pioneered bilingual intercultural education in the late 1980s, and by 1994 the Bolivian government had adopted it as official policy. In Guatemala, as its decades-long civil war wound down, government officials and activists increasingly advocated for official recognition of Mayan peoples in government and educational policy. In the north, Canada adopted constitutional reforms that recognized "aboriginal rights" in 1982 and by 1995 conceded First Nations' right to self-government. While mainstream discourse in the United States focused on "diversity," US institutions too were part of the global turn to multiculturalism, what philosopher Charles Taylor termed a "politics of recognition."[4] By the end of the century, multiculturalism, despite some opposition, had become hegemonic.

In Mexico multiculturalism drew on long-standing nationalist traditions. While the postrevolutionary state had consistently invoked the pre-Hispanic past and Native cultures in its patriotic rhetoric, that project celebrated *mestizaje*. And while *mestizaje* rhetorically embraced biological and culture mixture, it ultimately denigrated indigeneity and Blackness and favored assimilation toward whiteness. Some figures within the indigenista tradition had critiqued *mestizaje* and advocated a more robust form of cultural pluralism. Perhaps the most significant Mexican voice for a radical multiculturalism was that of Guillermo Bonfil Batalla, whose 1987 book *México profundo: Una civilización negada*, drew on the long indigenista tradition to denounce persistent discrimination, internal colonialism, and what he viewed as a "civilizational" conflict between Mesoamerican peoples and Western society.⁵ In *México profundo* Bonfil Batalla advocated for an embrace of the Mesoamerican heritage of the country, suggesting that non-Natives should learn Indigenous languages and cultural knowledge. While his ideas were not taken up in full by Mexican institutions, elements of his program were visible in post-1993 official discourse.

The January 1994 Zapatista uprising sparked another wave of multicultural reform. Led by the EZLN, insurgents seized control of a series of municipalities in the Chiapas highlands and captured the attention of the world. While a number of reforms were already under way in the 1980s, as described in chapter 6, it was in the aftermath of the 1994 uprising and subsequent negotiations between the Zapatistas and federal authorities that Indigenous rights legislation took center stage. The San Andrés Accords, as yet unsigned, provided for a number of cultural rights, including access to government services and education in one's native language, along with autonomy for Mexico's Native peoples. In 1996, the SEP officially embraced "bilingual intercultural education."⁶ By 2001, federal legislators reformed Article 2 of the Constitution to recognize the "pluricultural" nature of the republic. Mexico, a pioneer of indigenista policy in the hemisphere, here appeared to lead once again in the shift toward multiculturalism.⁷

While the Chiapas uprising spurred a series of multicultural reforms at the federal level, Oaxacan officials had taken steps toward such reform years earlier. In 1990 Governor Heladio Ramírez López (1986–92) spearheaded two amendments to the state constitution, recognizing the "pluriethnic" nature of the territory and calling for respect of Indigenous communities' traditional practices. Four years later, on March 2, 1994, Governor Carrasco Altamirano traveled to Guelatao, Oaxaca, the birthplace of Mexico's famed nineteenth-century president Benito Juárez, to propose two further Indigenous rights legislative initiatives. One was the official recognition and institutionalization of usos y costumbres, Indigenous customary law, which many Oaxacan communities had in practice used for centuries. The other was a law guaranteeing Indigenous rights. In 1995 both were incorporated into the state constitution.⁸ The first of these reforms in effect legalized what had been de facto local practice in many Indigenous communities, and the second was a liberal invocation of juridical equality and access that has yet to be fully implemented.

For some observers, the twin dynamic of an embrace of cultural rights alongside deepening social inequalities constituted a paradox. How was it that the seemingly progressive reforms of cultural recognition, respect for difference, and acknowledgment of Native peoples' place in the nation could emerge alongside a deepening of capitalist power and persistent inequalities? In this framing, the politics of the Guelaguetza were contradictory, a celebration of indigeneity overseen by an austerity-minded president. However, the paradox may be less contradictory than it originally appears. Other moments of capitalist expansion have gone hand in hand with political and social reform. The bourgeois revolutions of the eighteenth and early nineteenth centuries brought with them both an expansion of capitalist power and a simultaneous embrace of political rights and new notions of citizenship. Rather than a paradox, the rise of neoliberal multiculturalism was another, albeit distinct, moment in the longer history of capitalism.

Other critics scoffed at the notion of any paradox inherent in neoliberal multiculturalism. Instead they argued that the term itself was a tautology. Neoliberalism by its very nature was multicultural, and multiculturalism had inevitably been neoliberal. In this understanding, recognition of cultural rights merely served to entrap people in a "grid of intelligibility."[9] National governments along with international development and trade organizations celebrated cultural difference while overseeing neoliberal economic and political reform. These critics argued for a fundamental affinity between market logic and multiculturalism. Whereas nineteenth-century reformers and twentieth-century modernizers focused on national economic integration and linguistic unification, cultural heterogeneity was now compatible with the logic of late capitalism. Cultural difference had ceased to be a threat to the nation-state. Rather, it represented a further market specialization for capital. No contradiction here, merely unfettered market logic. In this sense, at the end of the twentieth century neoliberal multiculturalism appeared as a model of full-spectrum governance and market capture.[10]

The multicultural order also had its defenders. Liberal advocates depicted such policies as a natural evolution within a universalist political order. In this view, democratic societies based on individual rights require "equal recognition" to function properly. Multiculturalism addresses the absence of such equal recognition through policies of "cultural survival," or legal guarantees of cultural recognition.[11] Dene philosopher Glen Sean

Coulthard has criticized this approach, arguing that it reproduces social dynamics Indigenous people have sought to transcend and that the politics of recognition are little more than a "re-articulation of colonialism."[12] Coulthard argues that "mutual" recognition is impossible in colonial contexts, where Native peoples often require recognition from the dominant society while this same society requires no such reciprocal recognition. In this perspective the Guelaguetza, in which performers don Native dress and dance for non-Native audiences, is a prime example of colonized people facing "an externally determined and devalued conception" of themselves.[13]

These critics highlight multiculturalism's limitations. Such policies have frequently meant the folklorization of Native cultures, freezing particular cultural practices in time as "essential" components of Native life rooted in the past. Scholars aligned with activist struggles have understandably stressed the limitations of the multicultural order as they seek to transform it. In formulating their critiques, many have failed to reckon with the contested history of multicultural reform. As we have seen in Oaxaca, these policies often emerged as concessions to struggles waged by activists for whom recognition meant not so much state approval as the creation of spaces for individual and community empowerment. Indigenous anticolonial politics advocated for education models that embraced Native language and knowledge, as well as development projects that allowed for local control. Multiculturalism was not just an effective system of neoliberal governance. In Oaxaca it was also a concession made to activist demands. While the entirety of those anticolonial visions was not achieved, scholarly cynicism should not blind us to the accomplishments of those alternative visions.

Writing against Narratives of Defeat

Nor should the limitations of official multiculturalism obscure the history that produced it. That history and the related but distinct rise of movements of Indigenous resurgence are crucial to a comprehensive view of the past as well as the project of imagining alternative futures. As revealed over the course of this book, multiculturalism and Indigenous resurgence have an entangled history. While this experience reflects the particularities of Oaxaca, a place whose impressive diversity lends itself to the descriptor of *todo un mundo*, a world unto itself, the dynamics at play were particular neither to Oaxaca nor to Mexico. Over the course of the twentieth century in the Americas three main processes contributed to the twin rise of official multiculturalism and a politics of Indigenous resurgence: midcentury development models, New Left antiracism and anticolonialism, and grassroots struggles around education reform. Underscoring the political struggles that surrounded these three processes reveals the Third-Worldist origins of official multiculturalism, as well as the continuities between 1970s radical politics and the Indigenous resurgence of subsequent decades.

Development, for all of the debates it has inspired, was fundamentally a state attempt to resolve historically produced inequalities. While it evolved over the course of the century, one current focused on Native peoples' particular relationship to modernization. Though policy makers frequently framed Indigenous cultures and language as barriers to development, antithetical to modernization, dissidents challenged these binary frameworks, arguing for models that did not force Native peoples to shed a part of themselves in order to engage with modern politics or economics. Development thinking and policy varied in their theorization and implementation, but a plurality of midcentury models emphasized the need for local brokers who could ensure the success and "buy-in" of the targeted populations.[14] Because development frequently figured its subject in spatial terms, officials focused on regions marked as poor or Indigenous, with these descriptors often viewed as synonymous. This meant Native peoples engaged directly with development thinking. We have seen the alternative models that emerged out of this dialogue, such as the theory of etnodesarrollo described in chapter 6. Mexico's international advocacy of the New International Economic Order reflected the notion that the colonial legacy had to be reckoned with, not only domestically, but through international law and trade agreements. Development as such became the terrain on which much of Native and Indigenous politics played out over the second half of the century.

If development configured the terrain of Indigenous politics, new theories of antiracism and anticolonialism introduced an incendiary spark. While the twentieth century witnessed a first wave of anticolonial thought in the aftermath of World War I and the Mexican and Russian revolutions, decolonization in Africa and Asia brought about a second wave of anticolonialism. As the *promotores* profiled in chapter 4 demonstrate,

Indigenous youth reconsidered their personal and community contexts in light of colonial relations and what came to be a prominent theory, that of internal colonialism. Throughout the hemisphere, the question of the colonial legacy and what constituted anticolonial politics was raised again and again. This was evident in the 1968 Inter-American Indigenista Congress held in Pátzcuaro. Young anthropologists and activists denounced the previous generation of indigenista intellectuals for facilitating internal colonialism. Alfonso Caso's death in 1970, along with President Echeverría's rhetorical leftward shift, created the opportunity for this new generation of indigenista figures to put their ideas into practice. Simultaneously, in the United States young people organizing with the American Indian Movement challenged corrupt, clientelist tribal governments working in collusion with the Bureau of Indian Affairs. First Nations activists challenged the Canadian government's long-standing assimilationist policies and denounced its publication of its 1969 White Paper. In 1971, the World Council of Churches, Indigenous activists, and sympathetic anthropologists published the Barbados Declaration, calling on governments to respect and support Indigenous demands for cultural and social liberation. Mexican anthropologists and activists played a decisive role in that conference, helping to draft and publish the final document.[15] This political ferment was part and parcel of New Left radicalism and constituted a new moment of leftist politics' grappling with colonial legacies, indigeneity, and new paths toward liberation.

Indigenista development was a two-pronged project, prioritizing rural agricultural reform and education. In postrevolutionary Mexico, the promise of secular, public, universal education necessarily raised questions of Indigenous difference. Postrevolutionary education officials, with notable exceptions, emphasized the need to teach the national language, Spanish, to a heterogeneous and multilingual population. While SEP administrators such as Rafael Ramírez were famous for their injunctions to prohibit Indigenous languages in the classroom, education officials were not immune to the radicalism of the 1930s, and a prominent minority articulated more pluralist approaches to Mexico's linguistic diversity. The official policy of universal public education raised the possibility of increased representation of indigeneity. As midcentury officials sought to expand educational offerings, they increasingly relied on bilingual promotores. From Isaias Sánchez López's work as a radio teacher in the 1950s, to

Eva Ruiz and Santiago Salazar's efforts with the IIISEO in the 1970s, authorities employed successive generations of Indigenous youth on the basis of their language ability and community membership. This policy would have profound unintended consequences.

In the 1970s these three processes proved explosive throughout the Americas. Indigenous youth and their allies often combined the left-wing politics with invocations of Indigenous history and communal traditions. In Mexico, some could draw material support for their projects through their institutional connections to the SEP or other development agencies. Given that these resurgent politics often arose through the same institutions as that of official multiculturalism, what emerges is an entangled history in which opposing forces centered indigeneity for divergent ends. The reforms won by these activists suggest that concessions went both ways. The institutionalization of bilingual and intercultural education at the end of the century was a product of these intrainstitutional fights and of teacher and community activists who advocated for alternative pedagogies that respected Indigenous languages and cultural knowledge.

Indigenous resurgence was an Americas-wide phenomenon. The combination of development and education reform, articulated in a context of rising antiracism and anticolonialism, provided the coordinates for the emergence of Indigenous rights rhetoric throughout the continent in the 1970s. By the end of the 1980s, one witnessed resurgent politics from the Mapuche of southern Chile to pan-Indigenous coalitions throughout the Andes. Pan-Mayan politics transformed not only Chiapas but also regions north through the Yucatan Peninsula and south through Guatemala.[16] In Chile and Guatemala, these struggles coincided with the return of electoral democracy. Social scientists frequently stressed these movements' rupture with long-standing politics of class and corporatist political systems. Many described the resurgent politics as "new social movements."[17] In this rendering, the movements were largely determined by a neoliberal context that facilitated "identity" claims rather than what was considered a more transformative class politics.

This resurgent politics cannot be understood outside the history of indigenista development. Indeed, the aforementioned 1994 Zapatista rebellion drew strength from decades of Catholic and Maoist organizing in the highlands of Chiapas. The uprising, with bases of support in

Tztozil and Tzetzil Mayan communities, invoked indigeneity to critique neoliberalism's shattering effect on rural agriculture. Zapatista discourse was shaped by postrevolutionary Mexican nationalism: leaders spoke of respecting the constitution and the *patria* but also centered Indigenous peoples, silenced by centuries of marginalization and neglect. Many activists who later formed the cadres of the EZLN had participated in rural development initiatives in prior decades.[18] This continuity of struggle demonstrates how resurgent politics were directly constituted by the experience of development. The Zapatista movement went on to serve as a national lightning rod, coalescing discrete activist initiatives throughout the republic through the creation of the Consejo Nacional Indígena in 1996.[19] The government's response to the EZLN combined military repression with multicultural reform. This does not make multiculturalism inherently authoritarian or neoliberal. Rather, cultural reforms were meaningful for insurgents, but neoliberal governments divorced those reforms from further economic change.

While these movements' discourse reflected a new centering of indigeneity, their political practice and analysis revealed deep connections to New Left politics. Movement leaders often had participated in university and trade union activism, and while they may have foregrounded cultural issues, these "new" movements demanded economic reform as well.[20] Nor was the rupture between class politics and indigeneity as profound as some claimed. It was precisely the commingling of left-wing ideas and political practice in Indigenous communities that shaped a generation of Oaxacan activists. Figures such as Floriberto Díaz, Tomás Cruz Lorenzo, and Jaime Martínez Luna reformulated their radicalism in the context of local communal governing structures and developed the theory of *comunalidad*, communality.[21] Communality is a theory and political practice that embraces the reciprocal relations within Indigenous communities as a model for more equitable relations in society at large. Indigeneity as such remained a productive way of making the past speak to the present. It was neither a "return" nor an "authentic" expression but rather a form of historical thinking, of drawing on histories of exclusion to explain and make visible an unequal present.

The Oaxacan experience of these hemispheric trends also reframes our understanding of twentieth-century Mexico. Scholarship on the subject has long focused on the nature of the postrevolutionary state and the dominant political party, the PRI. Oaxaca's story underscores how local actors wielded tremendous political and social power even while under PRI rule. Municipalities, caciques, and social movements frequently exercised enormous power over government administration.[22] In 2010, the Oaxacan PRI was the last in the republic to lose control of the state government. This long-standing durability of the PRI masked its highly contingent and negotiated relationship with local actors. Local power sometimes took the form of municipal governments, usos y costumbres, and regional organizations, but over the second half of the century it was also expressed through broader claims to Indigenous culture, community, and tradition. What is clear is that the PRI was never a steamroller, and as evidenced in the preceding chapters, it was filled with internal divisions. While Oaxacan politics appeared subdued in comparison to that of its easterly neighbor, Chiapas, that outward stability reflected power from below as often as it reflected effective authoritarian rule.

This reading of Oaxacan history belies the oft-told narrative of Mexican Cold War exceptionalism. Far from being an outlier in the Cold War, Mexico experienced its own forms of political polarization and counterinsurgency.[23] Through this account and others, what comes into view is a history of politicized development policy, student and leftist politics shaping rural struggles, and the emergence of movements of Indigenous resurgence. Mexico's campesino political practice and discourse provided a level of enfranchisement unheard of in its Central American neighbors to the south. And the country's postrevolutionary state and attendant political culture were central to modernization efforts, but they did not make Mexico immune to Cold War dynamics or to its ideological aftermath. Analyzing the history of the Mexico's efforts to modernize regions and peoples marked as Indigenous makes clear that the country shares far more with its Latin American neighbors than commonly presumed.

La Guelaguetza Resurgent

The above requires us to reconsider our initial depiction of the Guelaguetza. Yes, it is a state project and inevitably a state construction of indigeneity. But it is also more than that. Its origins in the postrevolutionary period underscore how regional elites and politicians used the event to unite a fractured state. The first Guelaguetza, then called the Homenaje Racial, took place in 1932. Alfonso Caso was there, and he displayed the recently excavated treasures of Monte Albán's Tomb 7 in an accompanying public exhibit. The festival evolved over the course of the twentieth century. As the language of race fell out of favor, organizers gave the Zapotec word *guelaguetza* more prominence.[24] While *guelaguetza* means "reciprocal exchange," in the context of the festival its meaning evolved to connote "honoring" of the governor and his special guests. This shift reflected the clientelism and patriarchy central to the event. The evolution of the Guelaguetza mirrors the evolution of indigenismo. The event's vocabulary and even organization evolved over the course of the century. Those shifts underscored the persistence of racial thinking and continuity within state invocations of indigeneity. Like indigenismo, which was always contested by its intended subjects, so too was the Guelaguetza.

Like other forms of state pageantry, the Guelaguetza was shaped by its participants. Dancers and musicians, while convoked and confined by festival organizers, at times made the festival their own. While official traditions required them to pay homage to the governor, they also performed for themselves. Many of the dances on display were versions of nineteenth-century waltzes. While one could critique such dances as "inauthentic," this too falls into the trap of essentializing Native cultures. These forms, which may have begun as "playing Indian," often came to serve as expressions of dignity and pride in the face of marginalization. In 1998, Afro-Mexican communities performed for the first time at the festival, scandalizing local newspapers and commentators, many of whom viewed their West African–inspired dances and rhythms with alarm. Afro-Mexican participation suggests the importance of representation in the annual festival, and illustrates that communities struggled for that representation, with full knowledge that it was a government-sponsored event. The inaugural welcome by the Diosa Centéotl too was a moment of possibility, when the traditional deferential remarks to the governor could be interspersed with invocations of ethnic and class pride.

While the form was open to alternative interpretations, context also changed the meaning of the Guelaguetza. In the 1980s, Oaxacans living in Los Angeles, California, staged their own festival. Large numbers of people from the Zapotec town of Tlacolula in Oaxaca's central valleys had migrated to the greater Los Angeles area in previous decades. These migrant-organized festivals had a sharply different meaning, as Tlacolulans living in Los Angeles used the festival to embrace their heritage and strengthen the immigrant community. Similarly, Oaxacans living in Santa

Cruz, California, inaugurated their own Guelaguetza in 2005.[25] In these migrant Guelaguetzas, the original meaning of the word, "reciprocity," began to reappear.

This returns us to 2006, when the initial questions that animate this book first emerged. In the spring of that year, Sección 22 began what had become an annual ritual of strikes and negotiations with the state government. But 2006 was different. After an initial round of negotiations, Governor Ulises Ruiz Ortiz (2004–10) ordered police forces to remove the striking teachers' *plantón* from the Zócalo on June 14. The annual strike quickly grew into much more than the usual fare of pressuring the government for improved salaries and contract negotiations. Sección 22 leaders held a public meeting on June 17, in which what would become the Asamblea Popular de los Pueblos de Oaxaca (APPO) was formed. Comprising not only the teachers' union but broad swaths of Oaxacan civil society, the APPO called for a host of reforms, primary among them the resignation of Governor Ruiz Ortiz. The movement developed a wide array of tactics, including street actions but also the seizure of public television and radio stations, which were then converted to activist programming. The state constitution allowed for the legal removal of the governor only in cases in which the state was proven to be "ungovernable." To this end, movement leadership focused on paralyzing the operations of the state. Their explicit goal was to make Oaxaca "ungovernable." Activists systematically disrupted traffic and physically occupied government offices. The APPO also targeted the government's largest annual public event, the upcoming Guelaguetza. On July 15 the coalition called for a boycott of the festival. That same day, unidentified actors set the dance floor of the Auditorio Guelaguetza on fire. Two days later the governor canceled the festival.

While Sección 22 had successfully liberated itself from PRI control in 1980, the local and national political landscapes changed dramatically over subsequent decades. The mobilized and fiercely democratic trade union culture of the 1980s slowly gave way to a more accommodationist approach, particularly at the level of state politics. During Governor Heladio Ramírez López's administration, Sección 22 reached an agreement with the government that resulted in its increased integration into state structures, specifically through its control over the state education ministry, the Instituto Estatal de Educación Publica de Oaxaca. While this arrangement afforded union members increased benefits and access to resources, it also compromised the union's political independence.[26] Sección

22 had garnered widespread sympathy in the 1980s, but in the early 2000s the union's democratic credentials and close ties to Oaxacan communities began to unravel. By 2006, some sectors of Oaxacan society viewed the annual strikes and negotiations as a nuisance that disrupted work and daily life. Others viewed the union with outright hostility. However, Governor Ruiz Ortiz's violent repression of the movement generated renewed sympathy for teachers. The formation of the APPO confirmed that the movement had quickly outpaced existing union leadership and the sectional demands of Sección 22. Nationally, the July presidential elections resulted in a disputed outcome: the PAN candidate Felipe Calderón claimed a narrow victory over PRD candidate Andrés Manuel López Obrador. López Obrador mounted large-scale demonstrations and *plantones* in Mexico City, challenging the election results. For months Mexico City's downtown was paralyzed by mass action. That national political crisis afforded the movement in Oaxaca space to grow and expand its demands.

The movement did not stop at a mere boycott of the Guelaguetza; it organized its own. Promoting the event as "La Guelaguetza Popular," Sección 22 and its allies planned a festival on the western edge of the city, in the Instituto Tecnológico de Oaxaca's stadium, near the former campus of the IIISEO. Teachers themselves rehearsed and prepared many of the same regional dances featured in the government's festival, such as the Danza de la Piña and the Diablos de la Costa, but in this instance in direct opposition to the governor. On July 24 thousands of spectators and movement allies gathered for the celebration and called for the ouster of the governor. While the form of the festival resembled the official event, the Guelaguetza Popular was part of a resurgent politics. What appeared as folklore in the government's annual celebration was here weaponized against the governor and the state he represented.

Over the summer and early fall of 2006, the movement expanded and elaborated a sophisticated repertoire of strategies to topple the governor and address broader issues of injustice in Oaxacan society. In addition to the Guelaguetza Popular, the APPO mobilized hundreds of thousands in "megamarches," which began on the outskirts of the city and culminated in the Zócalo. In a state with a total population of less than three million people, marches of this size represented not just the mobilized members of the union but large swaths of Oaxacan society. In mid-August, the APPO organized the Foro Construyendo la Gobernabilidad y la Democracia en Oaxaca, held on the campus of the UABJO. There activists debated a series of reforms and proposed a new state constitution. Central to the movement's communication strategy was its control of multiple radio stations, including Radio Plantón, Radio Universidad, and Radio Caracol.[27] Women activists played a key role as radio broadcasters. As the struggle disrupted government functions at all levels, it sparked fierce opposition from the governor, who employed nonuniformed police units to harass and attack presumed activists. In response, the APPO formed its own security details, the Honorable Cuerpo de Topiles and the Policía Magisterial. Government-backed convoys harassed and detained people at night. To protect themselves from the convoys, activists and neighbors erected barricades throughout the city. On August 10 the movement suffered its first casualty when José Jiménez Colmenares was killed. Barricades became sites where people shared information and grievances.[28] They also evolved into grassroots organization. While they began as forms of self-defense, they became mobilized political units that would eventually serve to resist the federal police's siege of the capital later that fall. This level of popular mobilization and organization led many to declare the movement the "Oaxacan commune."

Dubbed "the first insurrection of the twenty-first century," by journalist Diego Enrique Osorno, the 2006 movement revealed the shallowness of democratization in Mexico. While Vicente Fox's 2000 presidential victory was heralded as the end of the PRI, the Oaxacan experience demonstrated the persistence of antidemocratic norms in the Mexican political system. Indeed, many observers pointed to the "Pacto de Huatulco," in which national PRI leaders recognized Felipe Calderón's electoral victory in exchange for the PAN's support of Governor Ruiz Ortiz and the deployment of federal police in the state. That arrangement effectively ended the movement's control of the capital and inaugurated Calderón's *sexenio*. His subsequent declaration of war against drug cartels and deployment of the military throughout the republic inaugurated a period of widespread violence in Mexico that has yet to end. That militarization and violence have their origins in the government's repression of the 2006 Oaxacan social movement.[29]

That movement reflected the double bind of twentieth-century indigenismo. The postrevolutionary state's educational program promised to unite the country but revealed deep divisions based on place, class, gender, ethnicity, and religion. As midcentury policy makers sought to modernize Oaxaca, they invoked narratives of colonial legacies to define their

Indigenous subjects. Nonetheless, regional development projects empowered Indigenous brokers, who at times upended entrenched local power structures and challenged government policy. As the Mexican economy grew and became more interconnected with the economies of the United States and Canada, low-wage Oaxacan workers migrated north, creating an Indigenous diaspora that toiled from the fields of Sinaloa to the farms of British Columbia. In the 1970s Indigenous youth-led struggles raised anew questions of colonialism and challenged an indigenista project accustomed to speaking in the name of Native peoples. In Oaxaca fights over education policy were often about inequality, inclusion, and authoritarian political power. Thus bilingual teachers fueled the struggle against PRI control of Sección 22 in the 1980s.

In 2006, what had become a predictable public ritual of May Day strikes and negotiations proved anything but routine. The state and federal governments' repression of the teachers demonstrated the weakness of the political order and the long-standing illegitimacy of public officials in the eyes of the people. The movement that developed that summer drew on decades of teacher activism and the strength of Oaxacan community ties. The diverse strategies and tactics participants employed reflected the movement's eclectic membership: Catholic lay activists, militants who had come of age in the struggles of the 1970s, heterodox leftists, and urban youth. On many of the cool nights spent at the barricades during the fall of 2006, the flames from the bonfires obscured the view of Monte Albán above. But below, on the city's streets, Oaxacans continued to make history.

Notes

Prologue

1. See Frederick Starr, *In Indian Mexico: A Narrative of Travel and Labor* (Chicago: Forbes, 1908), chap. 11; Frederick Starr, *The Physical Characteristics of the Indians of Southern Mexico* (Chicago: University of Chicago Press, 1902), 53. Starr claimed twenty-five women in total were measured: "Characters of race are better marked in men than in women; women of all tribes are, therefore, more alike than the men; it is more difficult to secure women for measurement than men; when secured, they are less easily measured on account of stubbornness, stupidity, or fear. These are the reason why a less number of female than male subjects was demanded."

2. Starr, *In Indian Mexico*. In the Mixteca Alta town of Santiago Tilantongo a vain priest was reportedly more concerned with getting his own photograph taken, though not his head measured, than attending to the funeral of a local congregant.

3. Starr, *In Indian Mexico*, appendix, 95.

4. Starr, *Indians of Southern Mexico: An Ethnographic Album* (Chicago: Lakeside Press, 1899), 24.

5. For more context and analysis of Starr, see Deborah Poole and Gabriela Zamorano Villarreal, *De frente al perfil: Retratos raciales de Frederick Starr* (Michoacán: El Colegio de Michoacán y el Fideicomiso "Felipe Teixidor y Monserrat Alfau de Teixidor," 2012).

6. Starr, *In Indian Mexico*, conclusion. Jason Ruiz notes Starr dedicated the photographic album to Díaz and his minister of development (*fomento*) Manuel Fernandez Leal. See Jason Ruiz, *Americans in the Treasure House: Travel to Porfirian Mexico and the Cultural Politics of Empire* (Austin: University of Texas Press, 2014), 43.

7. Deborah Poole, "An Image of 'Our Indian': Type Photographs and Racial Sentiments in Oaxaca, 1920–1940," *Hispanic American Historical Review* 84, no. 1 (2004): 39.

8. See, among others, Audra Simpson, "On Ethnographic Refusal: Indigeneity, 'Voice' and Colonial Citizenship," *Junctures: The Journal for Thematic Dialogue* 9 (2007): 67–80.

Introduction

1. Derek Walcott, "The Antilles: Fragments of Epic Memory," Nobel Lecture, December 7, 1992, https://www.nobelprize.org/prizes/literature/1992/walcott/lecture/.

2. See Fernando Benítez, *Los indios de México*, 2 vols. (Mexico City: Biblioteca Era, 1967–68), vol. 1. Henry Ginger, the Mexico City correspondent for the *New York Times* in the late 1960s, engaged in similar tropes regarding Monte Albán: "They show a desire for change but the Mixtec area is still a long way from the modern elegance of the Paseo de la Reforma in Mexico City. Likewise is it distant from the splendor of the pyramids of Monte Alban just outside Oaxaca City, where the two major Oaxacan races of Zapotecs and the Mixtecs once showed their true capabilities." Henry Ginger, "Mexico Pursuing Program of Self-Help for Poverty-Stricken Mixtec Indians," *New York Times*, February 5, 1968.

3. The general concept of the double bind is most associated with the anthropologist Gregory Bateson. Others have also deployed it to explore questions of indigeneity. See Jessica R. Cattelino, "The Double Bind of American Indian Need-Based Sovereignty," *Cultural Anthropology* 25, no. 2 (2010): 235–62.

4. Rick López, *Crafting Mexico: Intellectuals, Artisans, and the State after the Revolution* (Durham, NC: Duke University Press, 2010); Poole, "Image of 'Our Indian'"; Mary Kay Vaughan, *Cultural Politics in Revolution: Teachers, Peasants and Schools in Mexico, 1930–1940* (Tucson: University of Arizona Press, 1997); Helen Delpar, *The Enormous Vogue of Things Mexican: Cultural Relations between the United States and Mexico, 1920–1935* (Tuscaloosa: University of Alabama Press, 1995).

5. See Ann Stoler, "Introduction. 'The Rot Remains': From Ruins to Ruination," in *Imperial Debris: On Ruins and Ruination*, ed. Ann Stoler (Durham, NC: Duke University Press, 2013), 11. For more on cultural patrimony in Mexico, see Christina Bueno, *The Pursuit of Ruins: Archaeology, History, and the Making of Modern Mexico* (Albuquerque: University of New Mexico Press, 2016); Mónica Salas Landa, "(In)Visible Ruins: The Politics of Monumental Reconstruction in Post-revolutionary Mexico," *Hispanic American Historical Review* 98, no. 1 (2018): 43–76.

6. See Paja Faudree, *Singing for the Dead: The Politics of Indigenous Revival in Mexico* (Durham, NC: Duke University Press, 2013).

7. Dress, in particular women's dress, frequently served to signal membership in a particular community. Local foods, such as *tlayudas*, *memelas*, and the famous *mole*, have their roots in Indigenous gastronomy, but the quotidian practices of food consumption can also serve to mark Indigenous difference. In southern Mexico, connection to a community or *municipio* has often been one of the strongest forms of identity. See John Monoghan, introduction to *The Covenants with Earth and Rain: Exchange, Sacrifice, and Revelation in Mixtec Society* (Norman: University of Oklahoma Press, 1995), 3–16; Roger Brubaker and Frederick

Cooper, "Beyond 'Identity,'" *Theory and Society* 29, no. 1 (February 2000): 1–47; Paula López Caballero, "Introduction: Why Beyond Alterity?," with Ariadna Acevedo-Rodrigo, in *Beyond Alterity: Destabilizing the Indigenous Other in Mexico,* ed. Paula López Caballero and Ariadna Acevedo-Rodrigo (Tucson: University of Arizona Press, 2018), 3–30.

8. As Paige Raibmon has described in the case of Kwakwaka'wakw: "They have been involved in the contested and dialogical practice of producing cultural meaning, of making the past and present speak to one another, of using old things in ways that resonate with new needs. Absent such utility, tradition becomes not much more than a burden Aboriginal people must carry." See Paige Raibmon, *Authentic Indians: Episodes of Encounter from the Late-Nineteenth-Century Northwest Coast* (Durham, NC: Duke University Press, 2005), 206.

9. See Rebecca Earle, *The Return of the Native: Indians and Myth-Making in Spanish America, 1810–1930* (Durham, NC: Duke University Press, 2007); David Brading, "Manuel Gamio and Official Indigenismo in Mexico," *Bulletin of Latin American Research* 7, no. 1 (1988): 75–89; Alan Knight, "Racism, Revolution, and *Indigenismo*: Mexico, 1910–1940," in *The Idea of Race in Latin America, 1870–1940,* ed. Richard Graham (Austin: University of Texas Press, 1990), 71–102. Carlos García Mora argues that indigenismo "fue la forma mexicana del racismo en el siglo XX"; see "Los proyectos tarascos, implicaciones actuales," *Diario de Campo: Boletín Interno de los Investigadores del Área de Antropología,* no. 95 (November-December 2008): 100–115.

10. Claudio Lomnitz has offered a succinct definition of the phenomenon as "indigenizing modernity and . . . modernizing the Indians." Claudio Lomnitz-Adler, "Bordering on Anthropology: The Dialectics of a National Tradition in Mexico," *Revue de Synthèse* 121, nos. 3–4 (July-December 2000): 349. On twentieth-century Mexican indigenismo, see Steve Lewis's *Rethinking Mexican Indigenismo: The INI's Coordinating Center in Highland Chiapas and the Fate of a Utopian Project* (Albuquerque: University of New Mexico Press, 2018); María L. O. Muñoz's *Stand Up and Fight: Participatory Indigenismo, Populism, and Mobilization in Mexico, 1970–1984* (Tucson: University of Arizona Press, 2016); Paula López Caballero, "Las políticas indigenistas y la 'fabrica' de su sujeto de intervención en la creación del primer Centro Coordinador del Instituto Nacional Indigenista (1948–1952)," in *Nación y alteridad: Mestizos, indígenas y extranjeros en el proceso de formación nacional,* ed. Daniela Gleizer and Paula López Caballero (Mexico City: Ediciones Educación y Cultura, 2015) , 69–108; Estelle Tarica, *The Inner Life of Mestizo Nationalism* (Minneapolis: University of Minnesota Press, 2008).

11. On the underexplored influence of Mexican indigenista thought on US civil rights history, see Ruben Flores, *Backroads Pragmatists: Mexico's Melting Pot and Civil Rights in the United States* (Philadelphia: University of Pennsylvania Press, 2014).

12. Emiko Saldívar has examined the experience of Indigenous employees of the INI in "Everyday Practices of Indigenismo: An Ethnography of Anthropology and the State in Mexico," *Journal of Latin American and Caribbean Anthropology* 16, no. 1 (2011): 67–89.

13. Alejandro Arauho Pardo and Paula López Caballero, "¿Quién es indígena? El legado insospechado de Alfonso Caso," *Horizontal,* December 9, 2015, http://horizontal.mx/

quien-es-indigena-el-legado-insospechado-de-alfonso-caso/. One could read the history of indigenismo, even its more self-critical post-1968 period, as what Franz Fanon decried as a "strategy of containment." Just as Fanon critiqued moves to decolonize Africa safely within European frameworks, indigenismo sought a state-sanctioned management of cultural difference and empowerment of Native peoples. Nonetheless, just as in processes of decolonization, the daily practice of indigenismo could not always contain insurgent forms of indigeneity, and it at times produced intellectual and political cleavages, which those marked as Indigenous exploited. See Franz Fanon, *The Wretched of the Earth* (1961; repr., New York: Grove Press, 2005), 31.

14. As María Elena Martínez has pointed out, the exceptional nature of Spanish colonialism in the Americas—its "control over some systems of labor, its transformation of large Indigenous populations into tributaries, and its collective incorporation of Native people as Christian vassals of the Crown of Castile"—had long-term consequences for definitions of race and indigeneity in former Spanish colonies. See María de los Ángeles Romero Frizzi, *Economía y vida de los españoles en la Mixteca Alta, 1519–1720* (Mexico City: Instituto Nacional de Antropología e Historia: Gobierno del Estado de Oaxaca, 1990); Kevin Terraciano, *The Mixtecs of Colonial Oaxaca: Ñudzahui History, Sixteenth through Eighteenth Centuries* (Stanford, CA: Stanford University Press, 2001); Yanna Yannakakis, *The Art of Being In-Between: Native Intermediaries, Indian Identity, and Local Rule in Colonial Oaxaca* (Durham, NC: Duke University Press, 2008); María Elena Martínez, *Genealogical Fictions: Limpieza de Sangre, Religion, and Gender in Colonial Mexico* (Palo Alto, CA: Stanford University Press, 2008), 16.

15. During the years of liberal reform and French invasion, Oaxacans played key roles as politicians and generals and provided a disproportionate number of troops to liberal armies. See Peter Guardino, *The Time of Liberty: Popular Political Culture in Oaxaca, 1750–1850* (Durham, NC: Duke University Press, 2005); Francie Chassen-López, *From Liberal to Revolutionary Oaxaca: The View from the South, Mexico 1867–1911* (University Park: Pennsylvania State University Press, 2004).

16. See Ronald Waterbury, "Non-revolutionary Peasants: Oaxaca Compared to Morelos in the Mexican Revolution," *Comparative Studies in Society and History* 17, no. 4 (October 1975): 410–42.

17. Margarita Dalton, *Breve historia de Oaxaca* (Mexico City: El Colegio de México y Fondo de Cultura Económica, 2004), 228.

18. Paul Garner, "Oaxaca: The Rise and Fall of State Sovereignty," in *Provinces of the Revolution: Essays on Regional Mexican History, 1910–1929*, ed. Tomas Benjamin and Mark Wasserman (Albuquerque: University of New Mexico Press, 1990), 163–83. In this regard Garner remains faithful to Alan Knight's concept of "*serrano* revolts"; see Alan Knight, *The Mexican Revolution*, vol. 1 (Cambridge: Cambridge University Press, 1985), 115–17. See Colby Nolan Ristow, *A Revolution Unfinished: The Chegomista Rebellion and the Limits of Revolutionary Democracy in Juchitán, Oaxaca* (Lincoln: University of Nebraska Press, 2018).

19. As José Maria Caballero has observed in the case of the Andes, "What had once been an advantage became a liability." See José Maria Caballero, *Agricultura, reforma agraria, y pobreza campesina* (Lima: Instituto de Estudios Peruanos, 1980), 113.

20. See Gilbert M. Joseph and Daniel Nugent, eds., *Everyday Forms of State Formation: Revolution and the Negotiation of Rule in Modern Mexico* (Durham, NC: Duke University Press, 1994); Vaughan, *Cultural Politics in Revolution*; Gilbert M. Joseph, Anne Rubinstein, and Eric Zolov, eds., *Fragments of a Golden Age: The Politics of Culture in Mexico since 1940* (Durham, NC: Duke University Press, 2001).

21. This has meant much ink has been spilt debating the nature of the postrevolutionary state and the political party that came to dominate Mexico, the PRI, without much discussion of how Mexican history reflected broader trends in the Americas and the world.

22. Paul Gillingham and Benjamin T. Smith, eds., *Dictablanda: Politics, Work and Culture in Mexico, 1938–1968* (Durham, NC: Duke University Press, 2014); Gladys McCormick, "The Last Door: Political Prisoners and the Use of Torture in Mexico's Dirty War," *The Americas* 74, no. 1 (January 2017): 58.

23. Michael Denning, *Culture in the Age of Three Worlds* (London: Verso, 2004); Kevin Young, "Introduction: Revolutionary Actors, Encounters, and Transformations," in *Making the Revolution: Histories of the Latin American Left*, ed. Kevin Young (Cambridge: Cambridge University Press, 2018), 5–6; Alejandra Aquino Moreschi, "La generación de la 'emergencia indígena' y el comunalismo oaxaqueño: Genealogía de un proceso de descolonización," *Cuadernos del Sur* 15, no. 20 (July-December 2010), 7–21; Juan José Rendón, *La comunalidad: Modo de vida en los pueblos indios*, vol. 1 (Mexico City: CONACULTA, 2003).

24. Sarah Babb, *Managing Mexico: Economists from Nationalism to Neoliberalism* (Princeton, NJ: Princeton University Press, 2004); Randal Sheppard, *A Persistent Revolution: History, Nationalism, and Politics in Mexico since 1968* (Albuquerque: University of New Mexico Press, 2016); Louise Walker, *Waking from the Dream: Mexico's Middle Classes after 1968* (Palo Alto, CA: Stanford University Press, 2013).

25. Charles R. Hale, "Neoliberal Multiculturalism: The Remaking of Cultural Rights and Racial Dominance in Central America," *Political and Legal Anthropology Review* 28, no. 1 (2005): 10–28; Nancy Postero, *Now We Are Citizens: Indigenous Politics in Postmulticultural Bolivia* (Palo Alto, CA: Stanford University Press, 2007); Rebecca Overmyer-Velázquez, *Folkloric Poverty: Neoliberal Multiculturalism in Mexico* (University Park: Pennsylvania State University Press, 2010).

26. Bret Gustafson has made a similar point in the case of late twentieth-century and early twenty-first-century Bolivia. See Bret Gustafson, *New Languages of the State: Indigenous Resurgence and the Politics of Knowledge in Bolivia* (Durham, NC: Duke University Press, 2009).

27. As a history of indigenismo, *Oaxaca Resurgent* necessarily privileges a state project. While independent, nonstate voices appear, state actors, discourse, and policy are the central focus of analysis.

28. See Paul Gillingham and Benjamin T. Smith, "Introduction: The Paradoxes of Revolution," in Gillingham and Smith, *Dictablanda*, 8. See also Tanalís Padilla and Louise E. Walker, "In the Archives: History and Politics," *Journal of Iberian and Latin American Reseach* 19, no. 1 (2013): 1–10.

29. Florencia Mallon, "Introduction: Decolonizing Knowledge, Language, and Narrative," in *Decolonizing Native Histories: Collaboration, Knowledge, and Language in the Americas*, ed. Florencia Mallon (Durham, NC: Duke University Press, 2012), 1–20.

Chapter 1

1. Benítez, *Indios de México*, bk. 3 ("En el país de los nubes"), 1:280.
2. James C. Scott, *Seeing Like a State: How Certain Schemes to Improve the Human Condition Have Failed* (New Haven, CT: Yale University Press, 1998), 72.
3. Officials used the vaccinations to prevent yellow fever. DDT was deployed as an delousing agent against various forms of typhus.
4. Rafael Torres Márquez, "Informe presentado a la dirección del Centro Coordinador de las Mixtecas," August 28, 1954, p. 2, Informes del Centro Coordinador de las Mixtecas, 1954, Fondo Documental, Biblioteca Juan Rulfo, Instituto Nacional de los Pueblos Indígenas, Mexico City (hereafter FD-BJR).
5. Torres Márquez, "Informe presentado," p. 2.
6. See Timothy Mitchell, *Rule of Experts: Egypt, Techno-Politics, Modernity* (Berkeley: University of California Press, 2002), chap. 1 ("Can the Mosquito Speak?"), 19–53.
7. The inequalities performed in this moment bring to mind Aníbal Quijano's theorization of the concept of coloniality of power. See Anibal Quijano, "Coloniality of Power, Eurocentrism, and Latin America," *Nepantla: Views from the South* 1, no. 3 (2000): 539.
8. An alternative explanation analyzed the persistence of divergent economic practices within individual countries as uneven and combined development, an archetypal characteristic of capitalist growth, rather than an anomaly.
9. See Julia Tischler, "Cementing Uneven Development: The Central African Federation and the Kariba Dam Scheme," *Journal of Southern African Studies* 40, no. 5 (2014): 1047–64; Tore C. Olsson, *Agrarian Crossings: Reformers and the Remaking of the US and Mexican Countryside* (Princeton, NJ: Princeton University Press, 2017).
10. The 1968 Cuban film *Memorias de subdesarrollo* mocked the ubiquitous deployment of the concept of "underdevelopment" in postcolonial states, drawing attention to how the nominally neutral term often implied a deficit in the national character of postcolonial populations.
11. Scott, *Seeing Like a State*.
12. See Christopher R. Boyer, *Political Landscapes: Forests, Conservation, and Community in Mexico* (Durham, NC: Duke University Press, 2015), chap. 5 ("The Ecology of Development, 1952–1972"), 167–202; Stephen Lewis, "Mexico's National Indigenist Institute and the Negotiation of Applied Anthropology in Highland Chiapas, 1951–1954," *Ethnohistory* 55, no. 4 (Fall 2009): 609–32.
13. Barbara Weinstein, *The Color of Modernity: Sao Paulo and the Making of Race and Nation in Brazil* (Durham, NC: Duke University Press, 2015), 337. As Weinstein notes, "Racialized, classed, and gendered discourses of modernity have been constitutive elements in the production and reproduction of inequalities—material, political, and cultural—

naturalized through association with a particular geographic space denominated as a region."

14. Nicholas Rosenthal, *Reimagining Indian Country: Native American Migration and Identity in Twentieth-Century Los Angeles* (Chapel Hill: University of North Carolina Press, 2014).

15. For the etymology of the word *Mixtec*, see Terraciano, *Mixtecs of Colonial Oaxaca*, 318–19. *Mixtec* and *Mixteca* are Nahuatl terms referring to the people of the clouds, used first by the Aztec Empire and then appropriated by the Spanish. In their own language, the people of the Mixteca often refer to themselves by some version of *tay ñudzahui*, or the people of the rain.

16. See Romero Frizzi, *Economía y vida*.

17. See Jeremy Baskes, *Indians, Merchants, and Markets: A Reinterpretation of the Repartimiento and Spanish-Indian Economic Relations in Colonial Oaxaca, 1750–1821* (Stanford, CA: Stanford University Press, 2000), 185.

18. Ronald Spores, *Ñuu Ñudzahui: La mixteca de Oaxaca. La evolución de la cultura mixteca desde los primeros pueblos hasta la Independencia* (Oaxaca: Fondo Editorial, IEEPO, 2007). A counterexample is the experience of the Inca and the Andes; see Karen Spalding, *Huarochirí: An Andean Society under Inca and Spanish Rule* (Stanford, CA: Stanford University Press, 1984); Steve Stern, *Peru's Indian Peoples and the Challenge of Spanish Conquest: Huamanga to 1640* (Madison: University of Wisconsin Press, 1982).

19. For a detailed description of how liberal reform shaped Mixtec municipal politics, see Timo Schaefer, "Citizen-Breadwinners and Vagabond-Soldiers: Military Recruitment in Early Republican Southern Mexico," *Journal of Social History* 46, no. 4 (June 2013): 953–70.

20. Leticia Reina, *Las rebeliones campesinas en México (1819–1906)*, 2nd ed. (Mexico City: Siglo Veintiuno Editores, 1984), 235–37. See also Chassen-López, *From Liberal to Revolutionary Oaxaca*, 302.

21. Alejandro Marroquín, *La ciudad mercado (Tlaxiaco)* (Mexico City: UNAM, 1957), 23.

22. Alejandro Méndez Aquino, *Historia de Tlaxiaco (Mixteca)* (Oaxaca: Instituto Oaxaqueño de las Culturas / Fondo Estatal para la Cultura y las Artes, 1985), 323; Garner, "Oaxaca"; Francisco José Ruiz Cervantes, "El movimiento de la soberanía en Oaxaca (1915–1920)," in *La revolución en Oaxaca (1900–1930)*, ed. Víctor Raúl Martínez Vásquez (Mexico City: Consejo Nacional para la Cultura y las Artes, 1993), 277–381.

23. Víctor Raúl Martínez Vásquez, *Historia de la educación en Oaxaca, 1825–1940* (Oaxaca: Instituto de Investigaciones Sociológicas UABJO, 1994), 124.

24. Méndez Aquino, *Historia de Tlaxiaco*, 366.

25. Alexander S. Dawson, *Indian and Nation in Revolutionary Mexico* (Tucson: University of Arizona Press, 2004), 51.

26. Méndez Aquino, *Historia de Tlaxiaco*, 356. See also Benjamin T. Smith, *The Roots of Conservatism in Mexico: Catholicism, Society, and Politics in the Mixteca Baja, 1750–1962* (Albuquerque: University of New Mexico Press, 2012), chap. 5.

27. Marroquín, *Ciudad mercado*, 102–3. The Compañía Minera de la Mixteca, S.A., received both US and Mexican financing and controlled mines in Tejocotes along with lead and zinc mines in the barrio of Séptimo (Guadalupe Hidalgo). The company extracted antimony through an open-pit method and at its height employed over eight hundred male workers; see Moisés T. de la Peña, *Problemas sociales y económicos de las Mixtecas* (Mexico City: Instituto Nacional Indigenista, 1950), 94.

28. Tlaxiaqueños residing in Mexico City collaborated with state and municipal governments to acquire a used 150-horsepower generator for the town, which began operating in mid-1951. Marroquín claimed the generator was purchased from a yacht previously owned by US president Franklin Delano Roosevelt; Marroquín, *Ciudad mercado*, 138.

29. Marroquín, *Ciudad mercado*, 96, 98. See also Benjamin Smith, *Pistoleros and Popular Movements: The Politics of State Formation in Postrevolutionary Oaxaca* (Lincoln: University of Nebraska Press, 2009), 307.

30. Marroquín, *Ciudad mercado*, 55, 63. Only 9 percent of land was classified as ejidal in 1950. To demonstrate this concentration of land, Marroquín presented data for 1950 in which 92 percent of the region's private property was held in parcels of five hectares or less. These smallholders he described as *minifundio*. Parcels of more than five but less than fifty hectares, which he termed *parvifundio*, constituted 4 percent of private property. He considered the 0.5 percent of private property held in lots of fifty hectares or more *cuasi-latifundio*.

31. Marroquín, *Ciudad mercado*, 67. Marroquín characterized this as a mutually beneficial relationship between friends, not an exploitative form of sharecropping.

32. Francisco López Bárcenas, *Muertes sin fin: Crónicas de represión en la región Mixteca Oaxaqueña* (Mexico City: Centro de Estudios Antropológicos, Científicos, Artísticos, Tradicionales y Lingüísticos, 2002), 12.

33. Monaghan, *Covenants with Earth and Rain*, 268–69.

34. Pablo Velásquez Gallardo and Carlos Incháustegui, untitled report, Centro Coordinador Indigenista de la Mixteca Alta (hereafter CCIMA), 1954, p. 7, Informes del Centro Coordinador de las Mixtecas, 1954, FD-BJR.

35. Lucio Mendieta y Nuñez, ed., *Los zapotecos: Monografía histórica, etnográfica y económica* (Mexico City: Imprenta Universitaria, 1949), and, for the speech, *Valor económico y social de las razas indígenas de México* (Mexico City: DAPP, 1938).

36. Elsie Clews Parsons was another early anthropologist interested in Oaxaca. See *Mitla, Town of the Souls: And Other Zapoteco-Speaking Pueblos of Oaxaca, México* (Chicago: University of Chicago Press, 1936).

37. Bronislaw Malinowski and Julio de la Fuente, *La economía de un sistema de mercados en México: Un ensayo de etnografía contemporánea y cambio social en un valle mexicano* (Mexico City: Escuela Nacional de Antropologia e Historia, Sociedad de Alumnos, 1957).

38. The distinction between these two traditions should not be overstated, as both shared certain development assumptions dating to the early twentieth century. See Christy

Thornton, *Revolution in Development: Mexico and the Governance of the Global Economy* (Oakland: University of California Press, 2021).

39. Lewis, "Mexico's National Indigenist Institute"; Diana Schwartz, "Transforming the Tropics: Development, Displacement, and Anthropology in the Papaloapan, Mexico, 1940s–1970s" (PhD diss., University of Chicago, 2016).

40. Jason Pribilsky, "Development and the 'Indian Problem' in the Cold War Andes: *Indigenismo*, Science, and Modernization in the Making of the Cornell-Peru Project at Vicos," *Diplomatic History* 33, no. 3 (2009): 405–26.

41. Enrique Ochoa, "Lic. Moisés de la Peña: The Economist on Horseback," in *The Human Tradition in Mexico*, ed. Jeffrey Pilcher (Lanham, MD: Rowman and Littlefield, 2003), 176.

42. While the study was not published until 1957, it became available in mimeographed form in 1954. Carlos García Mora, "Alejandro Marroquín: Tianguis y capitalismo," *Nexos* 1 (August 1978), https://www.nexos.com.mx/?p=3187.

43. Gonzalo Aguirre Beltrán, "El problema humano de las Mixtecas," introductory essay to Marroquín, *Ciudad mercado*, 7–29.

44. de la Peña, *Problemas sociales*, 47.

45. Marroquín, *Ciudad mercado*, 240.

46. de la Peña, *Problemas sociales*, 95.

47. The team's work focused almost exclusively on the Oaxacan portions of the Mixteca.

48. de la Peña, *Problemas sociales*, 124.

49. Benítez, *Indios de México*, 1:280.

50. de la Peña, *Problemas sociales*, 124–25.

51. See Christopher R. Boyer, *Becoming Campesinos: Politics, Identity, and Agrarian Struggle in Postrevolutionary Michoacán, 1920–1935* (Stanford, CA: Stanford University Press, 2003).

52. de la Peña, *Problemas sociales*, 144.

53. Torres Márquez, "Informe presentado," p. 7.

54. Gonzalo Aguirre Beltrán, "El problema humano de las Mixtecas," introduction to Marroquín, *Ciudad mercado*.

55. Benítez, *Indios de México*, 1:364.

56. On the INI's development and public health efforts in Jamiltepec, see Stephanie L. Baker, "*Salud Colectiva*: The Role of Public Health Campaigns in Building a Modern Mexican Nation, 1940s–1960s" (PhD diss., University of Illinois at Chicago, 2012), 134–70.

57. Lewis, *Rethinking Mexican Indigenismo*, 60. On the Tlaxiaco experience, see Ramón Hernández López, interview by author, San Agustín Tlacotepec, August 27, 2010.

58. Carlos García Mora, "Un antropólogo purépecha: Entre el estudio del y por el pueblo mexicano y la mexicanística estadounidense," in *Ciencia en los márgenes: Ensayos de historia de las ciencias en México*, ed. Mechthild Rutsch and Carlos Serrano (Mexico City: UNAM, 1997), 57.

59. Alvin Gordon and Darley Gordon, *Our Son Pablo* (New York: McGraw-Hill, 1946).

60. García Mora, "Antropólogo purépecha."

61. CCIMA, "Tercer informe del Centro Coordinador de las Mixtecas," 1954, pp. 2–4, Informes del Centro Coordinador de las Mixtecas, 1954, FD-BJR.
62. CCIMA, "Informe del Centro Coordinador de las Mixtecas," April 15, 1954, p. 6.
63. Aguirre Beltrán, "Problema humano," 12.
64. de la Peña, *Problemas sociales*, 47, 131–32.
65. Pablo Velásquez Gallardo to Alfonso Caso, October 29, 1954, Informes del Centro Coordinador de las Mixtecas, 1954, FD-BJR.
66. Velásquez Gallardo and Incháustegui, untitled report, CCIMA, 1954, p. 15.
67. López Bárcenas, *Muertes sin fin*, 12.
68. Velásquez Gallardo and Incháustegui, untitled report, CCIMA, 1954, pp. 11–12, FD-BJR.
69. CCIMA, "Tercer informe," p. 8.
70. Barbara Weinstein, "Developing Inequality," *American Historical Review* 113, no. 1 (February 2008): 1–18.
71. Between 1954 and 1957 Aguirre Beltrán rarely advocated for preservation of Native languages. In the mid-1960s, he began to speak in favor of the issue publicly.
72. Gustafson, *New Languages of the State*, 121. Gustafson has described *castellanización* efforts among the Guaraní in Bolivia as "the violent shedding of other modes of being."
73. Lewis, "Mexico's National Indigenista Institute."
74. Scott, *Seeing Like a State*; James Ferguson, *The Anti-politics Machine: Development, Depoliticization, and Bureaucratic Power in Lesotho* (Minneapolis: University of Minnesota Press, 1994).
75. Boyer, *Political Landscapes*, 201.

Chapter 2

1. "Identidad de la radiofusora (ca. 1963)," caja 9, Serie Escuelas Radiofónicas, Educación, Archivo Histórico del Centro Coordinador Indigenista de la Mixteca Alta, Tlaxiaco (hereafter AH-CCIMA).
2. Elena Albarrán Jackson, *Seen and Heard in Mexico: Children and Revolutionary Cultural Nationalism* (Lincoln: University of Nebraska Press, 2015); J. Justin Castro, *Radio in Revolution: Wireless Technology and State Power in Mexico, 1897–1938* (Lincoln: University of Nebraska Press, 2016); Sonia Robles, *Mexican Waves: Radio Broadcasting along Mexico's Northern Border, 1930–1950* (Tucson: University of Arizona Press, 2019).
3. Isaías Sánchez López, interview by author, Tlaxiaco, September 9, 2010.
4. For more on López Mateos and Mexico's foreign relations during this period, see Eric Zolov, *The Last Good Neighbor: Mexico in the Global Sixties* (Durham, NC: Duke University Press, 2020).
5. Renata Keller, *Mexico's Cold War: Cuba, the United States, and the Legacy of the Mexican Revolution* (Cambridge: Cambridge University Press, 2015); Tanalís Padilla, *Rural Resistance in the Land of Zapata: The Jaramillista Movement and the Myth of the Pax Priísta*,

1940–1962 (Durham, NC: Duke University Press, 2008); Gladys McCormick, *The Logic of Compromise in Mexico: How the Countryside Was Key to the Emergence of Authoritarianism* (Chapel Hill: University of North Carolina Press, 2016).

6. Vaughan, *Cultural Politics in Revolution*, 33–36.

7. Smith, *Roots of Conservatism*, chap. 6 ("En el nombre de Dios, adelante").

8. This dynamic is true for other regions of southern Mexico. See Smith, *Roots of Conservatism*; Paul Gillingham, "Ambiguous Missionaries: Rural Teachers and State Facades in Guerrero, 1930–1950," *Mexican Studies / Estudios Mexicanos* 22, no. 2 (Summer 2006): 331–60; Lewis, *Rethinking Mexican Indigenismo*.

9. Muñoz, *Stand Up and Fight*, 40.

10. See Flores, *Backroads Pragmatists*.

11. Vaughan, *Cultural Politics in Revolution*, chap. 3.

12. Joy Elizabeth Hayes, *Radio Nation: Communication, Popular Culture, and Nationalism in Mexico, 1920–1950* (Tucson: University of Arizona Press, 2000), 60.

13. Todd Hartch, *Missionaries of the State: The Summer Institute of Linguistics, State Formation, and Indigenous Mexico, 1935–1985* (Tuscaloosa: University of Alabama Press, 2006), 57; Dawson, *Indian and Nation*, 79.

14. Dawson, *Indian and Nation*, 57–59; Lorena Ojeda Dávila and Marco Antonio Calderón Mólgora, "Cardenismo e indigenismo en Michoacán," *Mexican Studies / Estudios Mexicanos* 32, no. 1 (February 2016)): 83–110; García Mora, "Proyectos tarascos."

15. Brooke Larson, "Warisata: A Historical Footnote," *ReVista: Harvard Review on Latin America*, October 2011, https://revista.drclas.harvard.edu/book/warisata; Gustafson, *New Languages of the State*, 52.

16. Elsie Rockwell, *Hacer escuela, hacer estado: La educación posrevolucionaria vista desde Tlaxcala* (Zamora: El Colegio de Michoacán, 2007), 157.

17. Stephen E. Lewis, "Modernizing Message, Mystical Messenger: The Teatro Petul in the Chiapas Highlands, 1954–1974," *The Americas* 67, no. 3 (2011): 375–97; Schwartz, "Transforming the Tropics."

18. Romain Robinet, "'Hermanos de raza . . .': La Confederación Nacional de Jóvenes Indígenas, entre el indigenismo y la política (1940–1960)," in *La condición juvenil en Latinoamérica*, ed. Ivonne Meza Huacuja and Sergio Moreno Juárez (Mexico City: UNAM/IISUE, 2019), 275–99.

19. "Escuela Cañada de Galicia, Yosondúa, 1928–1969" and "San Pedro Siniyuvi, Putla, 1929–1978," caja 14, Dirección General de Educación Primaria en los Estados y Territorios, Archivo Histórico de la Secretaría de Educación Pública.

20. Sánchez López, interview: "At that time, secondary education was considered to be a lot."

21. Ramón Hernández López, "Educación," report on work done in 1954, p. 3, Informes del Centro Coordinador de las Mixtecas, 1954, CCIMA, FD-BJR.

22. Marcos Abraham Cruz Bautista, interview by author, San Miguel el Grande, Ranchería Vicente Guerrero, November 11, 2009.

23. Hernández López, "Educación," 7.

24. Edward Wright-Rios, *Revolutions in Mexican Catholicism: Reform and Revelation in Oaxaca, 1887–1934* (Durham, NC: Duke University Press, 2009), 277.

25. Smith, *Roots of Conservatism*, 257.

26. Benjamin T. Smith, "Anticlericalism and Resistance: The Diocese of Huajuapam de León, 1930–1940," *Journal of Latin American Studies* 37, no. 3 (August 2005): 469–505.

27. Smith, *Roots of Conservatism*, chap. 2.

28. "Escuelas radiofónicas," March 22, 1958, AH-CCIMA.

29. Ramón Hernández López, interview by author, San Agustín Tlacotepec, August 27, 2010. Hernández claimed a SEP official had visited Colombia and witnessed the program.

30. Mary Roldán, "Popular Cultural Action, Catholic Transnationalism, and Development in Colombia before Vatican II," in *Local Church, Global Church: Catholic Activism in the Americas before Vatican II*, ed. Stephen J. C. Andes and Julia C. Young (Washington, DC: Catholic University of America Press, 2016): 245–74; Radio Sutatenza: Una revolución cultural en el campo colombiano, online archive, http://proyectos.banrepcultural.org/radio-sutatenza/es.

31. Hernández López, interview.

32. "Informe mensual," Ramón Hernández López to Alberto Jimenez Rodriguez, July 10, 1957, AH-CCIMA.

33. Each agency contributed a third of the financing. The Comité Nacional de Comunicaciones Vecinales was a dependency of the Secretaria de Obras Públicas.

34. Betsy Konefal, *For Every Indio Who Falls: A History of Maya Activism in Guatemala, 1960–1990* (Albuquerque: University of New Mexico Press, 2015); Alfonso Gumucio-Dagron, "Miners' Radio Stations: A Unique Communication Experience from Bolivia," in *Media and Glocal Change Rethinking Communication for Development*, ed. Oscar Herner and Thomas Tufte (Buenos Aires: CLASCO; Göteborg: Nordon, 2005), 317–23; Josh Davis, "The Intertribal Drum of Radio: The Indians for Indians Hour and Native American Media, 1941–1951," *Western Historical Quarterly* 49 (Autumn 2018): 249–73.

35. Philip J. Deloria, *Indians in Unexpected Places* (Lawrence: University of Kansas Press, 2004).

36. Benítez, *Indios de México*, 1:365.

37. "Instrucciones de Manejo, Phillips," caja 3, Serie Escuelas Radiofónicas, Educación, AH-CCIMA.

38. "Escuelas radiofónicas," p. 5, AH-CCIMA.

39. "Radio Transmission Schedule," March 22, 1960, AH-CCIMA.

40. , "Guion numero 106," October 1, 1962, caja 7, Serie Escuelas Radiofónicas, Educación, AH-CCIMA .

41. Antolín Osorio Nicolás, interview by author, Oaxaca City, February 22, 2010.

42. Osorio Nicolás, interview, February 22, 2010; Sánchez López, interview.

43. "Escuelas radiofónicas," p. 5.

44. See Francisco López Bárcenas, *San Juan Copala: Dominación política y resistencia popular. De las rebeliones de Hilarión a la formación del municipio autónomo* (Mexico City: Universidad Autónoma Metropolitana, Unidad Xochimilco, 2009).

45. Sánchez López, interview.
46. CCIMA, "Informe de labores del CCI Mixteca Alta, 1963," CCI Tlaxiaco Informes, 1963–1968, FD-BJR. Government authorities believed the Triqui region shared mutually intelligible language variants.
47. Osorio Nicolás, interview by author, Oaxaca City, April 21, 2010.
48. Hernández López, interview.
49. José Sánchez García to Prof. Ramón Hernández López, March 4, 1964, caja 9, Serie Escuelas Radiofónicas, Educación, AH-CCIMA.
50. Macedonio Alcalá wrote the score for "Dios nunca muere" in 1868.
51. Gobierno, Correspondencia Emitida, 1961–63, Correspondencia, expediente 3, Archivo Histórico Municipal de la Heroica Ciudad de Tlaxiaco.
52. Hernández's remarks were published in "Oaxaca: El 'comunismo' en Tlaxiaco," *Política* (Mexico), December 1, 1961, 30.
53. Hernández López, interview.
54. Smith, *Roots of Conservativism*, 266.
55. Smith, *Roots of Conservativism*, 289–90.
56. Gema Santamaría, "Lynching, Religion and Politics in Twentieth-Century Puebla," in *Global Lynching and Collective Violence*, vol. 2, *The Americas and Europe*, ed. Michael J. Pfeifer (Champaign: University of Illinois Press, 2017), 85–114.
57. See Ben Fallaw, *Religion and State Formation in Postrevolutionary Mexico* (Durham, NC: Duke University Press. 2013).
58. Sánchez López, interview.
59. On the history of the PPS, see Rosendo Bolívar Meza, "La mesa redonda de los marxistas mexicanos: El Partido Popular y el Partido Popular Socialista," *Estudios de Historia Moderna y Contemporánea de México* 16 (2006): 193–213; Xicohtencatl Gerardo Luna Ruiz, "Un estudio de caso de colonización dirigida desde la Mixteca Alta hacia la costa Oaxaqueña: Indigenismo, contacto comercial, conflicto agrario y reorganización comunitaria" (master's thesis, Centro de Investigaciones y Estudios Superiores en Antropología Social, 2010), 94n64.
60. CCIMA, "Informe de labores del CCI Mixteca Alta, 1963," p. 13.
61. Benítez, *Indios de México*, 1:426.
62. CCIMA, "Informe de labores del CCI Mixteca Alta, 1963–1965," p. 6.
63. Sánchez López, interview. See also "Se comunica de un micrófono," February 15, 1966, caja 8, Serie Escuelas Radiofónicas, Educación, AH-CCIMA.
64. Antoni Castells i Talens, "'Todo se puede decir sabiéndolo decir': Maleabilidad en políticas de medios indigenistas," *Revista Mexicana de Sociología* 73, no. 2 (April-June 2011): 297–328.
65. For Morelos, see Salvador Salinas, "Untangling Mexico's Noodle: El Tallarín and the Revival of Zapatismo in Morelos, 1934–1938," *Journal of Latin American Studies* 46 (2014): 471–99; for Chiapas, see Lewis, "Mexico's National Indigenist Institute"; and for Guerrero, see Gillingham, "Ambiguous Missionaries."

Chapter 3

1. Nicolás Morales Hernández, a relocated Mixtec campesino, is quoted in Luna Ruiz, "Estudio de caso," 124.
2. Mitchell, *Rule of Experts*, 7.
3. See Robert Stone, *Prime Green: Remembering the Sixties* (New York: Harper Collins, 2007); Rebecca Schreiber, *Cold War Exiles in Mexico: U.S. Dissidents and the Culture of Critical Resistance* (Minneapolis: University of Minnesota Press, 2008); Theodore W. Cohen, *Finding Afro-Mexico: Race and Nation after the Revolution* (Cambridge: Cambridge University Press, 2020).
4. de la Peña, *Problemas sociales*, 123.
5. Paula López Caballero, "Domesticating Social Taxonomies: Local and National Identifications as Seen through Susan Drucker's Anthropological Fieldwork in Jamiltepec, Oaxaca, Mexico, 1957–1963," *Hispanic American Historical Review* 100, no. 2 (2020): 285–321; John Radley Milstead, "Afro-Mexicans and the Making of Modern Mexico: Citizenship, Race, and Capitalism in Jamiltepec, Oaxaca (1821–1910)" (PhD diss., Michigan State University, 2019).
6. Ramón Hernández López, "Antecedentes sobre el pueblo de reacomodo de La Tuza, municipio de Jamiltepec," May 8, 1968, Jamiltepec, caja 86, expedientes 924–9/10 and 924–10/10, Acervo Alfonso Caso, Museo del ex Convento de Santo Domingo en Yanhuitlán, Yanhuitlan, Oaxaca (hereafter AAC).
7. Handwritten declaration, Jamiltepec, caja 86, expedientes 924–9/10; 924–10/10, AAC.
8. Francisco Javier Alvarez, "A los CC vecinos de La Tuza 21," September 1968, Jamiltepec, caja 86, expedientes 924–9/10 and 924–10/10, AAC.
9. de la Peña, *Problemas sociales*, 24.
10. Torcuato di Tella and Gino Germani, working in Argentina, developed a number of interrelated theses on populism. Another generation of scholars, including Stanly Stein, Héctor Aguilar Camín, and Nora Hamilton, influenced by dependency theory, argued that this type of hierarchal populist project was tied to dependent capitalist development.
11. Luna Ruiz, "Estudio de caso," 102.
12. The scholarship on Mixtec migration and the Mixtec diaspora is vast. See Abigail Andrews, "Departures and Returns: Migration, Gender, and the Politics of Transnational Mexican Communities" (PhD diss., University of California, Berkeley, 2014); Felipe H. López and David Runsten, "Mixtecs and Zapotecs Working in California: Rural and Urban Experiences," in *Indigenous Mexican Migrants in the United States*, ed. Jonathan Fox and Gaspar Rivera-Salgado (Center for U.S.-Mexican Studies, University of California San Diego, 2004), 249–78; Lynn Stephen, "The Creation and Re-creation of Ethnicity: Lessons from the Zapotec and Mixtec of Oaxaca," *Latin American Perspectives* 23, no. 2 (1996): 17–37; Michael Kearney, "Mixtec Political Consciousness: From Passive to Active Resistance," in *Rural Revolt in Mexico: U.S. Intervention and the Domain of Subaltern Politics*, ed. Daniel Nugent (Durham, NC: Duke University Press, 1998), 134–46; Carmen Martínez

Novo, *Who Defines Indigenous? Identities, Development, Intellectuals, and the State in Northern Mexico* (New Brunswick, NJ: Rutgers University Press, 2006); Gaspar Rivera-Salgado, "Mixtec Activism in Oaxacalifornia: Transborder Grassroots Political Strategies," *American Behavioral Scientist* 42, no. 9 (June 1999): 1439–58.

13. A full reckoning with the relationship between indigeneity and Blackness on the Costa Chica is beyond the scope of this chapter. I plan to pursue the topic in a future project focused on the region, its people, and midcentury development initiatives.

14. T. Cohen, *Finding Afro-Mexico*.

15. See de la Peña, *Problemas sociales*, on poverty; also Marroquín, *Ciudad mercado*.

16. Mitchell, *Rule of Experts*, 321. On overpopulation as a concept, see chap. 7 ("The Object of Development"). As Mitchell points out, in the case of Egypt, once problems were defined as "natural rather than political, questions of social inequality and powerlessness disappeared into the background."

17. Quoted in Jürgen Buchenau and Gilbert M. Joseph, *The Once and Future Revolution: Social Upheaval and the Negotiation of Rule during Mexico's Long Twentieth Century* (Durham, NC: Duke University Press, 2013), 159.

18. See Scott, *Seeing Like a State*, Part III ("The Social Engineering of Rural Settlement and Production"), 181–306. Scott qualifies his diagnosis of failure by noting that Soviet authorities achieved their goal of seizure of grain, yet failed in their high modernist aims of achieving rational, efficient production in the countryside (217).

19. Schwartz, "Transforming the Tropics."

20. For a counterexample, see Sarah Hines, "The Power and Ethics of Vernacular Modernism: The Misicuni Dam Project in Cochabamba, Bolivia, 1944–2017," *Hispanic American Historical Review* 98, no. 2 (2018): 223–56.

21. Douglas K. Miller, *Indians on the Move: Native American Mobility and Urbanization in the Twentieth Century* (Chapel Hill: University of North Carolina Press, 2019); Rosenthal, *Reimagining Indian Country*, 70.

22. Héctor Martínez, *Las migraciones internas en el Perú: Ensayo* (Caracas: Monte Ávila, 1970), and *Las migraciones altiplánicas y la colonización del Tambopata* (Lima: Centro de Estudios de Población y Desarollo, 1969). For Bolivia's March to the East, see Ben Nobbs-Thiessen, *Landscape of Migration: Mobility and Environmental Change on Bolivia's Tropical Frontier, 1952 to the Present* (Chapel Hill: University of North Carolina Press, 2020).

23. López Caballero, "Domesticating Social Taxonomies," 306–8.

24. Sebastián Bautista Mariscal, untitled document, June 14, 1962, Tlaxiaco, caja 103, expediente 1503, AAC.

25. Ramón Hernández López, "Atenta Circular," September 30, 1961, Tlaxiaco, caja 103, expediente 1503, AAC.

26. Comisariado de Bienes Comunales, "Asunto: Solicitamos información sobre distribución de tierras," Tlaxiaco, caja 103, expediente 1503, AAC.

27. Among those who voiced interest in the project, many failed to fill out the requisite census data and forms and were chastised by INI officials.

28. Multiple reports, Tlaxiaco, caja 102, expediente 1492, AAC.

29. Martha W. Rees et al., "City and Crisis: The Case of Oaxaca, Mexico," *Urban Anthropology and Studies of Cultural Systems and World Economic Development* 20, no. 1 (Spring 1991): 15–29.

30. For a discussion of the way that debt acquired through land leasing drove migration patterns, see Abigail L. Andrews, "Legacies of Inequity: How Hometown Political Participation and Land Distribution Shape Migrants' Paths into Wage Labor," *World Development* 87 (2016): 318–32. De la Pena's 1949 regional study confirms many of Andrews's arguments.

31. Henry Ginger, "Mexico Pursuing Program of Self-Help for Poverty-Stricken Mixtec Indians," *New York Times*, February 5, 1968.

32. Carlos Incháustegui, "Magdalena Peñasco," 1968, 20/019, FD-BJR.

33. Incháustegui, "Magdalena Peñasco," pp. 98, 72.

34. Lynn Stephen, *Transborder Lives: Indigenous Oaxacans in Mexico, California, and Oregon* (Durham, NC: Duke University Press, 2007), 48.

35. Incháustegui, "Magdalena Peñasco," 35–38.

36. Joseph Cotter, *Troubled Harvest: Agronomy and Revolution in Mexico, 1880–2002* (Westport, CT: Praeger, 2003), chap. 6 ("The Mexican Revolution and the Green Revolution, 1950–1970"), 233–79; Angus Wright, *The Death of Ramón González: The Modern Agricultural Dilemma* (Austin: University of Texas Press, 2005).

37. Steve Velásquez, "Vincente Ramirez," Item #482, accessed June 14, 2018, Bracero History Archive, http://braceroarchive.org/items/show/482.

38. Antonio Santiago León, "La contratación de braceros en la ciudad de Oaxaca en 1944" (master's thesis, El Colegio de San Luis, A.C., 2015).

39. Deborah Cohen, *Braceros: Migrant Citizens and Transnational Subjects in the Postwar United States and Mexico* (Chapel Hill: University of North Carolina Press, 2013); Mireya Loza, *Defiant Braceros: How Migrant Workers Fought for Racial, Sexual, and Political Freedom* (Chapel Hill: University of North Carolina Press, 2016), 26, 33–35.

40. Loza, *Defiant Braceros*, 32.

41. Contemporary federal statistics classify much of the Mixteca Alta as communities of "high expulsion."

42. Ana Elizabeth Rosas, *Abrazando el Espíritu: Bracero Families Confront the US-Mexico Border* (Oakland: University of California Press, 2014).

43. Ramón Hernández López to Governor Brena Torres, 1963, Tlaxiaco, caja 103, expediente 1505, AAC.

44. Nuyoó Municipal Authorities to Manuel Hernández Hernández, 1963, Tlaxiaco, caja 103, expediente 1502, AAC.

45. Tlaxiaco, caja 102, expediente 1492, AAC.

46. Multiple *informes*, Jamiltepec, caja 85, expediente 911, AAC.

47. Gonzalo Aguirre Beltrán, *Cuijla: Esbozo etnográfico de un pueblo negro* (Mexico City: Fondo de Cultura Económica, 1958); Guiterre Tibón, *Pinotepa Nacional: Mixtecos, negros y triques* (Mexico City: Universidad Autónoma de México, 1961).

48. T. Cohen, *Finding Afro-Mexico*, chap. 7.

49. Manuel Mejido, *México amargo* (Mexico City: Siglo Veintiuno Editores, 1973), 370.
50. Antonio Salas Ortega to Reynaldo Salvatierra, May 7, 1963, Tlaxiaco, caja 102, expediente 1492, AAC.
51. Luna Ruiz, "Estudio de caso," 108–9.
52. Luna Ruiz, "Estudio de caso," 108, n91.
53. Andrews has emphasized debt as the prime driver, rejecting "cultural or ethnic" explanations of migratory strategies. See Andrews, "Legacies of Inequity," 328.
54. See Colleen O'Neill, *Working the Navajo Way: Labor and Culture in the Twentieth Century* (Lawrence: University Press of Kansas, 2005), 159. As O'Neill states regarding Diné participation in mine labor, "They were clearing modern pathways with traditional tools and in the process redefining both." See also M. Bianet Castellanos, *A Return to Servitude: Maya Migration and the Tourist Trade in Cancún* (Minneapolis: University of Minnesota Press, 2010).
55. This is the classic critique of high modernism, its inability to account for or incorporate "metis," local knowledge, in such initiatives. See Scott, *Seeing Like a State*.
56. Kearney, "Mixtec Political Consciousness."
57. Michael S. Danielson, *Emigrants Get Political: Mexican Migrants Engage Their Home Towns* (New York: Oxford University Press, 2018).
58. Frederick Cooper, "Writing the History of Development," *Journal of Modern European History* 8, no. 1 (2010): 5–23. As Cooper aptly summarizes: "Development as a state affair entails relations of power; it demands and rewards expertise; it presumes inequality and hierarchy, even if it claims to be promoting a leveling upward of all people's living standards" (11).
59. Ramón Hernández López, interview by author, San Agustín Tlacotepec, August 27, 2010.
60. Véronique Flanet, *Viviré, si Dios quiere: Un estudio de la violencia en la Mixteca de la Costa* (Mexico City: Instituto Nacional Indigenista, 1977).
61. Many twentieth-century descriptions of African-descended peoples on the Costa Chica echoed colonial tropes of Black violence.

Chapter 4

1. Alejandro D. Marroquín, "Economía indígena y desarrollo, trabajo presentado al VI Congreso Indigenista Interamericano," *América Indígena* 28, no. 4 (October 1968): 936–37.
2. The city's hosting of the first congress in 1940 and its designation as the site for the Proyecto Tarasco and the subsequent 1975 Congreso Nacional de los Pueblos Indígenas (CNPI) all testify to its symbolic importance in indigenista politics. On the history of twentieth-century Pátzcuaro, see Jennifer Jolly, *Creating Pátzcuaro, Creating Mexico: Art, Tourism, and Nation Building under Lázaro Cárdenas* (Austin: University of Texas Press, 2018).
3. Alejandro Ortíz Reza, "Un polvorín en Centroamérica: Millones de indígenas en condiciones insoportables," *Excélsior* (Mexico), April 19, 1968.

4. Elena Poniatowska, *Massacre in Mexico* (Columbia: University of Missouri Press, 1991).

5. Jeffery L. Gould, "Solidarity under Siege: The Latin American Left, 1968," *American Historical Review* 114, no. 2 (April 2009): 348–75.

6. See, among others, Carole Fink, Philipp Gassert, and Detlef Junker, eds., *1968: The World Transformed* (Cambridge: Cambridge University Press, 1998); and Pedro Monaville, "June 4th 1969: Violence, Political Imagination, and the Student Movement in Kinshasa," in *The Third World in the Global Sixties*, ed. Samantha Christiansen and Zachary Scarlett (New York: Berghahn Books, 2012), 159–70.

7. For the reception of international events in Mexico, see Jorge Volpi, *La imaginación y el poder: Una historia intelectual de 1968* (Mexico City: Ediciones Era, 1998); and Jaime Pensado, *Rebel Mexico: Student Unrest and Authoritarian Political Culture during the Long Sixties* (Stanford, CA: Stanford University Press, 2013). For contemporary coverage, see the dissident Mexico City magazine *Por Qué?* edited by Mario Menéndez.

8. Scholars are now analyzing 1968 less as a detonator of change than as emblematic of changes that had come into play during the preceding thirty years. For Mexico, see Mary Kay Vaughan, *Portrait of a Young Painter: Pepe Zúñiga and Mexico City's Rebel Generation* (Durham, NC: Duke University Press, 2014); Walker, *Waking from the Dream*, 12; Jaime Pensado and Enrique Ochoa, eds., *México beyond 1968: Revolutionaries, Radicals, and Repression during the Global Sixties and Subversive Seventies* (Tucson: University of Arizona Press, 2018). In addition, see Greg Grandin, "Living in Revolutionary Time: Coming to Terms with the Violence of Latin America's Long Cold War," in *Century of Revolution: Insurgent and Counterinsurgent Violence during Latin America's Long Cold War*, ed. Greg Grandin and Gilbert M. Joseph (Durham, NC: Duke University Press, 2010), 29; and Victoria Langland, *Speaking of Flowers: Student Movements and the Making and Remembering of 1968 in Military Brazil* (Durham, NC: Duke University Press, 2013), 12.

9. Vijay Prashad, *The Darker Nations: A People's History of the Third World* (New York: New Press, 2008); Christopher Lee, *Making a World after Empire: The Bandung Moment and Its Political Afterlives* (Athens: Ohio University Press, 2010).

10. Zolov, *Last Good Neighbor*, chap. 7.

11. For historical treatments of Echeverría's New International Economic Order, see Thornton, *Revolution in Development*; Vanessa Ogle, "State Rights against Private Capital: The 'New International Economic Order' and the Struggle over Aid, Trade, and Foreign Investment, 1962–1981," *Humanity* 5, no. 2 (Summer 2014): 211–34. Also see the special issue of *Humanity* (vol. 6, no. 1 [Spring 2015]), particularly the introductory essay, Nils Gilman, "The New International Economic Order: A Reintroduction," *Humanity: An International Journal of Human Rights, Humanitarianism, and Development* 6, no. 1 (Spring 2015): 1–16.

12. Samuel Moyn, *Not Enough: Human Rights in an Unequal World* (Cambridge, MA: Harvard University Press, 2018); Thornton, *Revolution in Development*, chap. 8.

13. Joe Foweraker, *Popular Mobilization in Mexico: The Teachers' Movement, 1977–1987* (Cambridge: Cambridge University Press, 1993), 22.

14. See Lynn Stephen, *Zapata Lives! Histories and Cultural Politics in Southern Mexico* (Berkeley: University of California Press, 2002).

15. Alan Knight, "Cárdenas and Echeverría: Two 'Populist' Presidents Compared," in *Populism in Twentieth-Century Mexico: The Presidencies of Lázaro Cárdenas and Luis Echeverría*, ed. Amelia Kiddle and Maria L. O. Muñoz (Tucson: University of Arizona Press, 2010), 28.

16. Gilbert M. Joseph and Jürgen Buchenau report that in the 1970s the population grew at more than 3.5 percent annually. See Joseph and Buchenau, *Mexico's Once and Future Revolution*, 173.

17. While historians have developed a complex view of how power operated in midcentury Mexico, understandings of the post-1968 era have only recently begun to shift from what is best described as *memoria* to *historia*. Eric Zolov, "Introduction: Latin America in the Global Sixties," *The Americas* 70, no. 3 (January 2014): 349. Some scholars have embraced an analysis of the democratic opening as part of a broader tradition of populism in Latin America. In this vein, Kiddle and Muñoz emphasize Echeverría's political style and response to a perceived crisis as fundamentally populist in nature, whereas Joseph and Buchenau describe Echeverría's *sexenio* as a "neopopulist revival." Amelia Kiddle and Maria L. O. Muñoz, introduction to Kiddle and Muñoz, *Populism in Twentieth-Century Mexico*, 1–14; Joseph and Buchenau, *Mexico's Once and Future Revolution*, 168; Walker, *Waking from the Dream*, 21.

18. Gerardo Cruz Majluf, "Reformas a la educación rural?" in *Reforma educativa y "apertura democrática,"* ed. Fernando Carmona (Mexico City: Editorial Nuestro Tiempo, 1972), 125–51.

19. Víctor Raúl Martínez Vásquez, "El movimiento de 1968 en Oaxaca," *Cuadernos del Sur* 14, no. 27 (April 2009): 89–100.

20. See Víctor Raúl Martínez Vásquez, *Movimiento popular y política en Oaxaca (1968–1986)* (Mexico City: CONACULTA, 1990).

21. Santiago Salazar, interview by author, Oaxaca City, Oaxaca, April 19, 2010.

22. Report, February 28, 1974, caja 963, expediente 2, Archivo General de la Nación, Dirección General de Investigaciones Políticas y Sociales (hereafter AGN IPS).

23. See Howard Campbell, *Zapotec Renaissance: Ethnic Politics and Cultural Revivalism in Southern Mexico* (Albuquerque: University of New Mexico Press, 1994); and Jeffrey W. Rubin, *Decentering the Regime: Ethnicity, Radicalism, and Democracy in Juchitán, Mexico* (Durham, NC: Duke University Press, 1997).

24. Rubin, *Decentering the Regime*, 42–43; Jan Rus, "The 'Comunidad Revolucionaria Institucional': The Subversion of Native Government in Highland *Chiapas*, 1936–1968," in Joseph and Nugent, *Everyday Forms of State Formation*, 265–300.

25. David Recondo, *La política del gatopardo: Multiculturalismo y democracia en Oaxaca* (Mexico City: Centro de Investigaciones y Estudios Superiores en Antropología Social / Centro de Estudios Mexicanos y Centroamericanos, 2007), 79–80.

26. For a contrasting example in El Salvador, see Joaquín M. Chávez, "Catholic Action, the Second Vatican Council, and the Emergence of the New Left in El Salvador (1950–1975)," *The Americas* 70, no. 3 (January 2014): 459–87.

27. On the conservative Catholic context in Oaxaca, see Heiko Kiser, "Mit der Jungfrau gegen die Hochmoderne: Religion als Ressource der indigenen Bevölkerung gegen staatliche Modernisierungsprojekte in Oaxaca, Mexiko, 1950 bis heute," *Archiv für Sozialgeschichte* 51 (2011): 445–86.

28. Carrasco Briseño was a close collaborator of Archbishop Samuel Ruiz in Chiapas.

29. Xóchitl Leyva Solano, "Regional, Communal, and Organizational Transformations in Las Cañadas," in *Mayan Lives, Mayan Utopias: The Indigenous Peoples of Chiapas and the Zapatista Rebellion*, ed. Jan Rus, Rosalva Aída Hernández Castillo, and Shannan L. Mattiace (Lanham, MD: Rowman and Littlefield, 2003), 164.

30. See Neil Harvey, *The Chiapas Rebellion: The Struggle for Land and Democracy* (Durham, NC: Duke University Press, 1998); and Adela Cedillo and Fernando Herrera Calderón, eds., *Challenging Authoritarianism in Mexico: Revolutionary Struggles and the Dirty War, 1964–1982* (New York: Routledge, 2012).

31. Alan Knight has explained this phenomenon as the outcome of Echeverría's feeling "obliged to extend an olive branch to the left, especially the student left," in the wake of the repression of youth protest. See Knight, "Cárdenas and Echeverría," 22.

32. For the shifting Cold War context in Latin America, see Tanya Harmer, *Allende's Chile and the Inter-American Cold War* (Chapel Hill: University of North Carolina Press, 2011). The contradictions of Mexico's foreign and domestic policy were rife. Mexico provided asylum to various Latin American guerillas and dissidents, including Brazilian political prisoners released in 1969 in exchange for the kidnapped US ambassador to Brazil, Charles Burke Elbrick. At the same time, Mexico pursued its own dirty war. See Alexander Aviña, *Specters of Revolution: Peasant Guerrillas in the Cold War Mexican Countryside* (Oxford: Oxford University Press, 2014); Alberto Ulloa Bornemann, *Surviving Mexico's Dirty War: A Political Prisoner's Memoir*, ed. Arthur Schmidt and Aurora Camacho de Schmidt (Philadelphia: Temple University Press, 2007).

33. Eric Zolov, *Refried Elvis: The Rise of the Mexican Counterculture* (Oakland: University of California Press, 1999), 191.

34. Velasco oversaw unprecedented agrarian reform and instituted bilingual education in Quechua, one of Peru's major languages. See Miguel La Serna, *Corner of the Living: Ayacucho on the Eve of the Shining Path Insurgency* (Chapel Hill: University of North Carolina Press, 20112), 105–8.

35. See Walker, *Waking from the Dream*, chap. 2; José Agustín, *Tragicomedia mexicana*, vol. 2, *La vida México de 1970–1988* (Mexico City: Editorial Planeta Mexicana, 1998).

36. The bombs were placed in the Palacio Municipal, the offices of the newspaper *Oaxaca Gráfico*, and a military garrison. See "Atentados dinamiteros contra tres locales en Oaxaca; un muerto," *Excelsior* (Mexico), July 23, 1972.

37. The youths' demands were articulated a year earlier, and a tentative agreement was established between the promotores, the state government, and the IIISEO administration. However, it was not respected in the period that followed. See "Pliego Petitorio," *Carteles del Sur* (Oaxaca), April 4, 1974; "Convenio que se celebra entre la Dirección General del IIISEO y la Coalición de Promotores," April 23, 1974, personal papers of Santiago Salazar.

38. "Regresan las mejoradoras a sus comunidades a enseñar," *Carteles del Sur* (Oaxaca), May 3, 1969.

39. *Periódico Oficial*, Gobierno Constitucional del Estado Libre y Soberano de Oaxaca, August 2, 1969, vol. 51, no. 31, decree no. 68, concertación, costal IIISEO Archivo General del Poder Ejecutivo del Estado de Oaxaca (hereafter AGPEEO); "Castellanización e integración es la meta de las mejoradoras y promotores sociales," *Carteles del Sur*, March 23, 1969; "Plan de castellanización," *Carteles del Sur*, March 24, 1969. For a brief description of the IIISEO's origins, see Salvador Sigüenza, *Héroes y escuelas: La educación en la Sierra Norte de Oaxaca, 1927–1972* (Mexico City: INAH; IEEPO, 2007), 251–53; and María Luisa Acevedo Conde, interview by author, Oaxaca City, May 12, 2010.

40. See Gloria Ruiz de Bravo Ahuja, *La enseñanza del español a los indígenas mexicanos* (Mexico City: Colegio de México, 1977), 292–326. Here she outlines the linguistic foundation for what she termed the "audiovisual" method.

41. The INI did engage in research throughout its existence. However, in the 1970s its expansion meant it often focused primarily on the administration of government resources.

42. Over the decade that the IIISEO operated, it graduated a number of people with bachelor's degrees and a handful of master's degrees, but never produced a PhD.

43. Elsie Rockwell, interview by author, Mexico City, April 5, 2010.

44. See A. S. Dillingham, "Indigenismo and Its Discontents: Bilingual Teachers and the Democratic Opening in Oaxaca, Mexico, 1954–1982" (PhD diss., University of Maryland, College Park, 2012), 82–114.

45. Arturo Warman et al., *De eso que llaman antropología mexicana* (Mexico City: Editorial Nuestro Tiempo, 1970), 58. Some of the same figures were involved in a short-lived project begun in 1971 in Chiapas, the Escuela de Desarrollo Regional. See Lewis, *Rethinking Mexican Indigenismo*, chap. 11.

46. Warman et al., *De eso*, 80.

47. Karin Alejandra Rosemblatt, "Other Americas: Transnationalism, Scholarship, and the Culture of Poverty in Mexico and the United States," *Hispanic American Historical Review* 89, no. 4 (November 2009), 639; Todd Shepard, "Algeria, France, Mexico, UNESCO: A Transnational History of Anti-racism and Decolonization, 1932–1962," *Journal of Global History* 6, no. 2 (July 2011): 273–97.

48. Fernando Cardoso and Enzo Faletto, *Dependency and Development in Latin America* (Berkeley: University of California Press, 1979).

49. For his most representative work, see Ivan Illich, *Deschooling Society* (New York: Harper and Row, 1971).

50. See the influential work of Louis-Jean Calvet, *Linguistique et colonialisme: Petit traité de glottophaige* (Paris: Editions Payot, 1974).

51. IIISEO, ca. April 1974, María Luisa Acevedo Conde, personal papers, Oaxaca City. In addition, Evangelina Arana de Swadesh, a linguist from the ENAH and wife of US linguist Morris Swadesh, along with SIL researchers, collaborated with the IIISEO in its initial years.

52. IIISEO, ca. April 1974, María Luisa Acevedo Conde, personal papers, Oaxaca City, p. 3. "For the first time, this group is offered real access to higher levels of education without necessarily ceasing to be Indigenous."

53. The entrance exam was framed along the lines of a Spearman factor G exam. The institute chose the Spearman model because of its alleged ability to test general aptitude and intellectual capacity regardless of one's language abilities.

54. Bases del IIISEO, Victor Bravo Ahuja and Ramón Bonfíl, ca. 1972, p. 8, caja 9188, folio 38, Secretaría de Educación Pública, Dirección General de Educación Extraescolar en el Medio Indígena (hereafter SEP DGEEMI). See also Gloria Ruiz de Bravo Ahuja and Beatriz Garza Cuarón, *Problemas de integración* (Mexico City: IIISEO, 1970), 14.

55. María Luisa Acevedo Conde's personal papers, Oaxaca City. In this way the institution drew directly from Gonzalo Aguirre Beltrán's "regions of refuge" thesis. See Gonzalo Aguirre Beltrán, *Regiones de refugio: El desarrollo de la comunidad y el proceso dominical en mestizo América* (Mexico City: Instituto Indigenista Interamericano, 1967).

56. Felipe Feria, interview by author, Santa Rosa, Oaxaca City, April 28, 2010.

57. "Los promotores del IIISEO," ca. April 1974, personal papers of María Luisa Acevedo Conde, Oaxaca City.

58. Eleazar García Ortega, interview by Alverino López López, Oaxaca City, August 2, 2007.

59. Servando Vérulo Aparicio López, interview by author, San Lucas Yosonicaje, Oaxaca, September 8, 2010.

60. One conflict involving a local cacique took place in San Pedro Amuzgos (Putla) and involved the promotores Melchor Camerino López and Filegonio Moreno Olmedo. See the report of January 23, 1976, caja 1770C, expediente 12, AGN IPS.

61. Victor Bravo Ahuja and Ramón Bonfíl, "Bases del IIISEO," ca. 1972, p. 9, caja 9188, folio 98, SEP DGEEMI.

62. Acevedo Conde, interview.

63. México, Dirección General de Estadística, *IX Censo general de población, January 28, 1970, Estado de Oaxaca*, vol. 1 (Mexico City: Secretaria de Industria y Comercio, Dirección General de Estadística, 1971), 3.

64. The 1971 documentary film *México: La revolución congelada*, by Argentine director Raymundo Gleyzer, depicts the crisis facing parts of rural Mexico. In 1972 the INI commissioned a documentary on the Mixteca Alta's regional market, entitled *Iño savi* and directed by Olivia Carrión, Epigmenio Ibarra, and Gonzálo Infante. It too portrays material deprivation in the countryside.

65. For long-standing disputes, see Smith, *Pistoleros and Popular Movements*. For examples of land seizures, see Cuauhtémoc González Pacheco, "La lucha de clases en Oaxaca: 1960–1970 (primera parte)," in *Oaxaca: Una lucha reciente: 1960–1978*, ed. René V. Bustamente (Mexico City: Ediciones Nueva Sociología, 1978), 29.

66. Flanet, *Viviré, si Dios quiere*; Francisco José Ruiz Cervantes, "La lucha de clases en Oaxaca: 1971–1977 (segunda parte)," in Bustamente, *Oaxaca*, 49.

67. Rubin, *Decentering the Regime*, 131.

68. Jaime Bailón Corres, "Los avatares de la democracia (1970–2008)," in *Oaxaca: Historia breve* (Mexico City: Colegio de México / Fondo de Cultura Económica, 2010), 254.

69. This lack of support led Santiago Salazar, an eventual leader of the promotores' movement, to describe his generation as *soldados sin fusil* (soldiers without arms). Santiago Salazar, interview by author, Oaxaca City, December 15, 2009.

70. Report, April 30, 1975, caja 1544-A, expediente 2, AGN IPS.

71. Salazar, interview, December 15, 2009.

72. Ricardo López has offered a parallel argument for youth employed in Alliance for Progress initiatives in Colombia. See Ricardo López, "From Middle Class to Petit Bourgeoisie: Cold War Politics and Classed Radicalization in Bogotá, 1958–1972," *Estudios Interdisciplinarios de América Latina y el Caribe* 25, no. 2 (2014): 99–130.

73. García Ortega, interview by López López.

74. Ibid.

75. La Serna, *Corner of the Living*, 64.

76. Salazar, interview, April 19, 2010.

77. IIISEO rosters, ca. April 1974, María Luisa Acevedo Conde's personal papers, Oaxaca City*f*.

78. Feria, interview. For a discussion of postrevolutionary athletic reforms, see Vaughan, *Cultural Politics in Revolution*, 94.

79. Acevedo Conde, interview.

80. "Convenio que se celebra entra la Dirección General del IIISEO y la Coalición de Promotores," April 23, 1974, personal papers of Santiago Salazar. The Coalition was officially founded on April 2, 1974.

81. For a comparable experience in the state of Michoacán, see María Eugenia Vargas, *Educación e ideología: Constitución de una categoría de intermediarios en la comunicación interétnica. El caso de los maestros bilingües tarascos (1964–1982)* (Mexico City: CIESAS, 1994), 140.

82. Report, November 30, 1974, caja 1544-A, expediente 2, AGN IPS.

83. Ibid.

84. Report, July 31, 1975, file: Zarate Aquino, caja 148, parte 1/4, AGN DFS.

85. Many federal agents ended their reports with the phrase "hasta el momento no se han suscitado incidentes violentos" (So far, no violent incidents have occurred).

86. The director of the Tlaxiaco center, José Martínez Fortiz, cabled INI offices in Mexico City, on April 7, stating, "Allow me to inform you that a group of IIISEO promotores are causing problems at this office." Radiogram, April 7, 1975, costal 1975, Radiogramas, AH-CCIMA.

87. Report, April 8, 1975, caja 1544-A, expediente 2, AGN IPS.

88. Salazar, interview, December 15, 2009.

89. Francisco Abardía Moros, interview by author, San Cristóbal de las Casas, Chiapas, March 11, 2014.

90. Report, April 30, 1975, caja 1544-A, expediente 2, AGN IPS.

91. Rubin, *Decentering the Regime*, 131.

92. See the report of February 10, 1976, caja 1770C, expediente 12, AGN IPS.

93. Eva Ruiz Ruiz, interview by author, Santa Lucia del Camino, Oaxaca, December 11, 2009.

94. "Convenio que se celebra por una parte la Secretaría de Educación Pública y por la otra los representantes de los promotores bilingües egresados del Instituto de Investigación y Integración Social del Estado de Oaxaca," May 3, 1975, expediente S.P.-5.12/9/75-IIISEOAGPEEO, Concentración, costal IIISEO.

95. Estado de Oaxaca (306), undated report, ca. April 1975, caja 147, primera parte, AGN DFS. The report states that it "became known that a commission of the promotores, led by members of the Coalición Obrero-Campesina-Estudiantil, would meet with the president of the republic on May 2, in Tuxtepec, Oaxaca, and that they would make known to him their problems."

96. Paco Ignacio Taibo II, "Experimento en Oaxaca (1): 'En esta barranca se enseña castellano.' El trabajo de los promotores en pueblos perdidos," *El Universal* (Mexico), December 27, 1976.

97. The IIISEO campus was converted into the Instituto Tecnológico de Oaxaca.

98. Jeffrey W. Rubin, "Contextualizing the Regime: What 1938–1968 Tells Us about Mexico, Power, and the Twentieth Century," in Gillingham and Smith, *Dictablanda*, 390.

99. Jeffry Rubin has urged scholars to examine "practices or spaces that are alternative enough to enable people to live and compromise somewhat differently or even nudge the path of history in unexpected directions." Rubin, "Contextualizing the Regime," 390.

100. Acevedo Conde, interview.

101. Aparicio López, interview.

102. See Christopher R. W. Dietrick, "Oil Power and Economic Theologies: The United States and the Third World in the Wake of the Energy Crisis," *Diplomatic History* 40, no. 3 (2016): 550–29.

103. See Adam David Morton, *Revolution and State in Modern Mexico: The Political Economy of Uneven Development* (Lanham, MD: Rowman and Littlefield, 2013), 114.

104. Ramón Cota Meza articulates an argument regarding developmentalism's unintended consequences in his article "Indigenismo y autonomía indígena," *Letras Libres* (Mexico) 3, no. 32 (August 2001): 47–50.

Chapter 5

1. Jaime Martínez Luna is a Oaxacan intellectual, activist, and songwriter. He pioneered, along with others, the theory of *comunalidad*, communality. Martínez Luna engaged in activism and songwriting alongside the Oaxacan dissident teachers' movement, performing his songs at protests and public gatherings.

2. Mary Coffey, "'All Mexico on a Wall': Diego Rivera's Murals at the Ministry of Public Education," in *Mexican Muralism, A Critical History*, ed. Alejandro Anreus, Leonard Folgarait, and Robin Adele Greeley (Berkeley: University of California Press, 2012), 56–74.

3. "Invadió la Coalición de Promotores Indígenas del Estado de Oaxaca los patios de la SEP," *El Universal*, November 23, 1978.

4. "Acuerdo al que llegan la secretaria de educación pública, representada por el director general de educación indígena y la coalición de promotores indígenas (IIISEO de Oaxaca) con la presencia del C. delegado de la secretaria de educación publica en el estado de Oaxaca." November 25, 1979, personal papers of Santiago Salazar.

5. Maria Lorena Cook, *Organizing Dissent: Unions, the State, and the Democratic Teachers' Movement in Mexico* (University Park: Pennsylvania State University Press, 1996); Foweraker, *Popular Mobilization in Mexico*; Dan La Botz, *Mask of Democracy: Labor Suppression in Mexico Today* (Boston: South End Press, 1992).

6. My definition of neoliberalism is one of a state and regulatory apparatus that facilitates capital's movement and market development, not necessarily a shrinking of the state. For an elaboration of this argument, see Quinn Slobodian, *Globalists: The End of Empire and the Birth of Neoliberalism* (Cambridge, MA: Harvard University Press, 2018).

7. David Harvey, *A Brief History of Neoliberalism* (Oxford: Oxford University Press, 2005), 98.

8. Greg Grandin, "The Empire's Amnesia," *Jacobin* 25 (Spring 2017), https://www.jacobinmag.com/2017/05/the-empires-amnesia; Thomas Skidmore, *The Politics of Military Rule in Brazil, 1964–85* (New York: Oxford University Press, 1988); Alejandro Velasco, *Barrio Rising: Urban Popular Politics and the Making of Modern Venezuela* (Oakland: University of California Press, 2015).

9. Enrique Ochoa, *Feeding Mexico: The Political Uses of Food since 1910* (Lanham, MD: Rowman and Littlefield, 2001).

10. In contrast to migrants from western states of Jalisco or Michoacán, who had longer-established networks in the United States, Oaxacan migrants frequently worked the lowest-paying and most dangerous jobs, on either side of the border. August Wright eloquently drew attention to these issues in his exposé *The Death of Ramón González*. The life of González, who, as Wright notes, was "born in one of these neglected traditional regions and died in a frontier of profitable agribusiness," underscores the direct connection between Indigenous labor and modern global markets. Wright, *Death of Ramón González*, 8–9.

11. Martínez Vásquez, *Movimiento popular y política*.

12. Ruiz Cervantes, "Lucha de clases."

13. Reports of March 2, 1977, at 22:20 hours and 23:15 hours, caja 1770C, expediente 15, AGN IPS.

14. Aviña, *Specters of Revolution*.

15. Isidoro Yescas Martínez and Gloria Zafra, *La insurgencia magisterial en Oaxaca, 1980* (Oaxaca: Fondo Editorial IEEPO IISUABJO, 1985), 78.

16. Cook, *Organizing Dissent*, 61.

17. Foweraker, *Popular Mobilization in Mexico*.

18. César Carrizales Retamoza, "El SNTE ante la política educativa del régimen," in *Las luchas magisteriales, 1979–1981: Documentos*, vol. 1, ed. Luis Hernández (Mexico City: Editorial Macehual, 1981), 27–39; Cook, *Organizing Dissent*, 71.

19. See A. S. Dillingham, "Mexico's Turn toward the Third World: Rural Development under President Luis Echeverría," in Pensado and Ochoa, *México beyond 1968*, 113–33; Muñoz, *Stand Up and Fight*.

20. Cook, *Organizing Dissent*, 111, 75.

21. The CIA at the time described Muñoz Ledo as a "recognized leftist." See Central Intelligence Agency, "Latin America: Regional and Political Analysis," August 4, 1977, pp. 4–7, https://www.cia.gov/library/readingroom/docs/CIA-RDP79T00912A000700010005-7.pdf.

22. Carlos B. Gil, ed. *Hope and Frustration: Interviews with Leaders of Mexico's Political Opposition* (Wilmington, DE: Scholarly Resources, 1992), 180–81.

23. Gil, *Hope and Frustration*.

24. Cook, *Organizing Dissent*, 82.

25. Untitled report beginning "Oaxaca, de Juárez, Oax. A 29 de junio de 1977," caja 1506A, expediente 1, AGN IPS.

26. "Inquietud política se observa en la Sección 22 del SNTE, de Oaxaca," July 1, 1977, caja 1506A, expediente 1, AGN IPS.

27. Yescas Martínez and Zafra, *Insurgencia magisterial en Oaxaca*, 42, 58.

28. Michael Snodgrass, "'New Rules for the Unions': Mexico's Steelworkers Confront Privatization and the Neoliberal Challenge," *Labor: Studies in Working-Class History of the Americas* 4, no. 3 (2007): 83.

29. "El maestro es educación al pueblo y para el pueblo!," report, January 11, 1980, caja 1506B, expediente 10, "Informacion de Huajuapan de Leon," AGN IPS.

30. Cook, *Organizing Dissent*, 118.

31. Yescas Martínez and Zafra, *Insurgencia magisterial en Oaxaca*, 27.

32. Vaughan, *Cultural Politics in Revolution*; Stephen Lewis, *The Ambivalent Revolution: Forging State and Nation in Chiapas, 1910–1945* (Tucson: University of New Mexico Press, 2005).

33. Alexander Dawson, *Indian and Nation in Revolutionary Mexico* (Tucson: University of Arizona Press, 2004).

34. For more on rural normal schools, see Tanalís Padilla, "Memories of Justice: Rural *Normales* and the Cardenista Legacy," *Mexican Studies / Estudios Mexicanos* 32, no. 1 (February 1, 2016): 111–43.

35. IPS caja 1506 B, expediente 10. For Tuxtepec, see the report "Información de Tuxtepec," October 16, 1978. For Tlaxiaco, see the report "Información de Tlaxiaco," December 1, 1979.

36. Ramos M. Aurelio, "Oprime o pasa hambre el maestro en Oaxaca," *Excélsior*, December 3, 1978.

37. "Perfil politico del estado de Oaxaca con respeto a la suspension indefinida de labores escolares en la entidad planteada por la Seccion xxii del SNTE," report, April 27, 1980, caja 1506B, expediente 10, AGN IPS.

38. Untitled report beginning "Estado de Oaxaca, Información de Oaxaca," May 1, 1980, caja 1506B, expediente 10, AGN IPS. See also Víctor Raúl Martínez Vásquez, *No que no, sí que sí: Testimonios y crónicas del movimiento magisterial oaxaqueño* (SNTE, Sección 22, 2005), 6.

39. Foweraker, *Popular Mobilization in Mexico*, 56.

40. Ignacio Santiago Pérez, interview, August 9–10, 2010, Oaxaca City and San Pedro Tidaá. This is corroborated by other teachers and in the secondary literature; see Sánchez López, interview; Cook, *Organizing Dissent*, 233.
41. Santiago Pérez, interview.
42. Michael Snodgrass, "'New Rules for the Unions': Mexico's Steelworkers Confront Privatization and the Neoliberal Challenge," *Labor: Studies in Working-Class History of the Americas* 4, no. 3 (2007): 86.
43. Santiago Salazar Marcial, "Reflexiones de 10 años de lucha, 1974–1984," Coalición de Maestros y Promotores Indígenas de Oaxaca, p. 9, personal papers of Santiago Salazar.
44. "Actuamos en suma, a la manera muy similar de nuestros pueblos indios, y esta situación es la característica principal de la coalición." Santiago Salazar, "Reflexiones," p. 10.
45. Donald C. Hodges and Ross Gandy, *Mexico, the End of the Revolution* (Westport, CT: Praeger, 2002), 125.
46. Hodges and Gandy, *Mexico*, 129.
47. Jill Freidberg, *Granito de arena* (Corrugated Films, 2005).
48. Sánchez López, interview, p. 28.
49. Martínez Vásquez, *No que no*, 32.
50. Rubin, *Decentering the Regime*.
51. Martínez Vásquez, *No que no*, 87.
52. Sánchez López, interview, p. 29.
53. Antolín Osorio Nicolás, interview, April 21, 2010, Oaxaca City.
54. Untitled report beginning "Estado de Oaxaca, Información de Huajuapan de Leon." May 29, 1979, caja 1544B, expediente 6, AGN IPS.
55. Untitled report beginning "Estado de Oaxaca, Información de Huajuapan." April 22, 1980, caja 1506B, expediente 10, AGN IPS; Osorio Nicolas, interview, April 21, 2010.
56. Martínez Vásquez, *No que no*, 110, 115.
57. Diane E. Davis, *Urban Leviathan: Mexico City in the Twentieth Century* (Philadelphia: Temple University Press, 1994), 281; Walker, *Waking from the Dream*, chap. 6.
58. On the 1988 election fraud, see Julia Preston and Samuel Dillon, *Opening Mexico: The Making of a Democracy* (New York: Farrar, Straus and Giroux, 2005), 149–80; Daniel Levy and Kathleen Bruhn, *Mexico: The Struggle for Democratic Development*, 2nd ed. (Berkeley: University of California Press, 2006).
59. Snodgrass, "'New Rules for the Unions,'" 100, 94.
60. Homero Campa, "En Los Pinos y gobernación el SNTE cambió con todo y líderes," *Proceso*, May 1, 1989, 14–18.
61. Cook, *Organizing Dissent*. While Cook's research emphasizes the democratic nature of the struggle, she concedes the persistence of nondemocratic practices among dissident activists.
62. Sánchez López, interview.
63. CMPIO, *Movimiento pedagógico* (pamphlet), personal papers of Santiago Salazar.

64. Víctor Raúl Martínez Vásquez, *La educación en Oaxaca* (Oaxaca: IIS-UABJO, 2004), 26–27.

65. Walker makes a similar point, underscoring the "messiness" and the series of discrete decisions made by presidents de la Madrid and Salinas that contributed to the shift toward a neoliberal order (*Waking from the Dream*, 148–49).

66. Roger Bartra, "El reto de la izquierda," *Nexos* 59 (November 1982): 15–20.

67. Coffey, "'All Mexico on a Wall.'"

Chapter 6

1. On human rights, see Moyn, *Not Enough*; Patrick William Kelly, *Sovereign Emergencies: Latin America and the Making of Global Human Rights Politics* (New York: Cambridge University Press, 2018). On the rise of cultural rights frameworks, see Charles Hale, *Más que un Indio: More Than an Indian: Racial Ambivalence and Neoliberal Multiculturalism in Guatemala* (Santa Fe, NM: School of American Research Press, 2006).

2. Nicholas Matthew Copeland, "Bitter Earth: Counterinsurgency Strategy and the Roots of Mayan Neo-authoritarianism in Guatemala" (PhD diss., University of Texas at Austin, 2007).

3. Moyn, *Not Enough*, 120.

4. Margarita Dalton, "Encierro intelectual: Entrevista con Salomón Nahmad," *Desacatos*, no. 9 (Spring-Summer 2002): 163–76.

5. After Nahmad's jailing, President de la Madrid appointed Miguel Limón Rojas to serve as INI director for the remainder of his term (1983–88).

6. Indeed, historians continue to debate the turn toward "cultural rights" frameworks, with the lines of debate not very different from those of the 1980s.

7. Daniel Cazés, "Zapotecas rebeldes rechazan ser indios profesionales," *unomásuno* (Mexico), June 29, 1980.

8. Cruz Bautista, interview.

9. Mutsuo Nakamura, "Programa de Formación Profesional de Etnolinguistas (Primera Generación 1979–1982)" (master's thesis, Centro de Investigaciones y Estudios Superiores en Antropología Social, Mexico City, 2000).

10. Nakamura, "Programa de Formación Profesional," 29. Fifty-four of the students who entered completed the program.

11. Dirección General de Educación Indígena, Centro de Información y Documentación de Educación Indígena, Mexico City (hereafter DGEI-CIDEI), *Programa de educación para todos: Programa de castellanización, Informe anual 78–79* (Mexico City: SEP/INI, 1979), 22. The INI provided financial support to the program, while the Dirección General de Educación Indígena, Secretaria de Educación Publica (hereafter DGEI-SEP) and the Centro de Investigaciones Superiores del Instituto Nacional de Antropología e Historia provided instructors.

12. Nakamura, "Programa de Formación Profesional," appendix 3.

13. Course descriptions are from Nakamura, "Programa de Formación Profesional," 41–51.

14. Nakamura, "Programa de Formación Profesional," 249–65.
15. See, for example, Juan Julián Caballero, *El papel del maestro en el etnocidio en San Antonio Huitepec, Oaxaca*, Etnolingüística 20, Cuadernos de Información y Divulgación para Maestros Bilingües (Mexico City: SEP/INI, 1982).
16. Todd Hartch, *Missionaries of the State: The Summer Institute of Linguistics, State Formation and Indigenous Mexico, 1935–1985* (Tuscaloosa: University of Alabama Press, 2006), 157. For a detailed discussion of the break, see chap. 10 ("Denounced! Anthropology Turns against the SIL").
17. Mark Twain, "Story of the Wycliffe Translators Pacifying the Last Frontiers," *NACLA's Latin America and Empire Report* 7, no. 10 (1973): 15–23; "Wycliffe Is a Global Corporation," *NACLA's Latin America and Empire Report* 7, no. 10 (1973): 24–31.
18. Hartch, *Missionaries of the State*, 149. For the 1975 congress, see Muñoz, *Stand Up and Fight*.
19. "The Declaration of Barbados: For the Liberation of the Indians," *Current Anthropology* 14, no. 3 (June 1973): 267–70.
20. Hartch, *Missionaries of the State*, 152. Also see Agence Latinoamericana d'information, "El Instituto Lingüístico de Verano, instrumento del imperialismo," *Nueva Antropología, Revista de Ciencias Sociales*, no. 9 (October 1978): 116–42.
21. Hartch, *Missionaries of the State*, 157. The group would eventually operate in Mexico again, though under a different relationship with Mexican authorities.
22. Cruz Bautista, interview.
23. Juan Julián Caballero, interview by author, Oaxaca City, January 29, 2010. See also anonymous profiles in Nakamura, "Programa de Formación Profesional."
24. Julián Caballero, interview, p. 11.
25. Daniel Cazés, "Zapotecas rebeldes."
26. Nakamura, "Programa de Formación Profesional," 141–74; Juan Julian Caballero, "La Academia de la Lengua Mixteca: Espacios de reflexión compartida," *Cuadernos del Sur* 5, no. 14 (May 1999): 129–39.
27. See DGEI, *Diario oficial*, Articulo 19, Corresponde a la Dirección General de Educación Indígena, September 11, 1978.
28. Hernández López, interview.
29. The National Service of Bilingual Promoters began in 1964 and expanded exponentially over the subsequent decade. For more on the INI's role in pioneering bilingual methods, see Lewis, *Rethinking Mexican Indigenismo*.
30. DGEI-CIDEI, *Programa de educación*, 25–26, 40.
31. DGEI-CIDEI, *Programa de educación*, 6: "personal de origen indígena (bilingüe) con nivel de Secundaria en promedio; y que hablan el idioma de los niños con quienes cumplen su tarea."
32. For the latter, see Bravo Ahuja, *Enseñanza del español*.
33. DGEI-CIDEI, *Programa de educación*, 7.
34. Elisa Ramírez Castañeda, *La educación indígena en México* (Mexico City: UNAM, 2006), 171.

35. For a comparative discussion of the *albergues*, see Alexander Dawson, "Histories and Memories of the Indian Boarding Schools in Mexico, Canada, and the United States," *Latin American Perspectives* 39, no. 5 (2012): 80–99.

36. The SEP managed hostel schools with financing from the INI. With the creation of the DGEI, teacher training and evaluation of the albergues came under its control. DGEI-CID, *Programa de educación*, 8. The albergue system had 46,900 students in attendance nationally.

37. Dalton, "Encierro intelectual."

38. DGEI-CIDEI, *Programa de educación*; Gabina Reyes Bautista and Pauala Fería Barrios, *Manuel para la enseñanza de lecto-escritura en lengua mixteca: Libro del maestro, primer grado, Tlaxiaco Este, Oaxaca* (Mexico City: SEP, 1985).

39. Reyes Bautista and Fería Barrios, *Manuel para la enseñanza*, 8.

40. "30 Aniversario 1974–2004," Coalición de Maestros y Promotores Indígenas de Oaxaca, March 31, 2003, p. 5, personal papers of Santiago Salazar.

41. See Greg Grandin, introduction to *The Last Colonial Massacre: Latin America in the Cold War* (Chicago: University of Chicago Press, 2004), 1–18.

42. Jorge Hernández Díaz, "Condiciones de vida y diferenciación social en la población indígena oaxaqueña," *Cuadernos del Sur* 5 (November 1998), 107–18.

43. Hernández Díaz is careful with his use of statistics and avoids equating poverty and indigeneity. However, to chart indigeneity within official statistics, he uses language practices, an inherently partial measure of Indigenous difference.

44. Stefano Varese, ed., *Indígenas y educación en México* (Mexico City: CEE, 1983), 124 (contributors listed but not linked to specific book sections).

45. Varese, *Indígenas y educación*, 27.

46. The CMPIO operates as three structures: a union delegation within Sección 22, a school district, and a civic association.

47. Alverino López López, interview by author, Nochixtlán, Oaxaca, November 20, 2009.

48. On rural normal schools, see Tanalís Padilla, "Rural Education, Political Radicalism, and *Normalista* Identity in Mexico after 1940," in Gillingham and Smith, *Dictablanda*, 341–59.

49. López López, interview.

50. Aparicio López, interview.

51. Abardía Moros, interview.

52. Abardía Moros, interview.

53. Here I draw on Alexander Dawson's insights, see Alexander S. Dawson, *The Peyote Effect: From the Inquisition to the War on Drugs* (Oakland: University of California Press, 2018), chap. 7 ("1957: The Holy Thursday Experiment").

54. Abardía Moros, interview.

55. Aquino Moreschi, "Generación de la 'emergencia indígena.'"

56. Jorge Hernández-Díaz, *Reclamos de la identidad: La formación de las organizaciones indígenas en Oaxaca, México* (Mexico City: UABJO-Miguel Angel Porrúa, Grupo Editorial,

2001); López Bárcenas, *San Juan Copala*; Miguel Bartolomé, *Gente de costumbre y gente de razón: Las identidades étnicas en Mexico* (Mexico City: Siglo XXI, 1997), 178; Kristin Norget, "The Politics of 'Liberation': The Popular Church, Indigenous Theology and Grassroots Mobilization in Oaxaca, Mexico," *Latin American Perspectives* 24, no. 5 (1997): 96–127; Maria de los Angeles Romero Frizzi, *Escribir para dos mundos: Testimonios y experiencias de los escritores mixtecos* (Oaxaca: Fondo Editorial, Instituto Estatal de Educacion Publica de Oaxaca, 2003); Julian Caballero, "Academia de la Lengua Mixteca"; Faudree, *Singing for the Dead*.

57. Paja Faudree has made a similar observation regarding this period: "Left-leaning intellectuals were espousing new models of nationhood in which indigenous peoples would participate directly in formulating policies that affected them." Faudree, *Singing for the Dead*, 204.

Conclusion

1. Biblioteca de Investigación Juan de Córdova, "Mesa redonda sobre la Guelaguetza y los pueblos indígenas: Un acercamiento crítico," July 24, 2013, https://www.youtube.com/watch?v=YaHSNdum6_E; Poole, "Image of 'Our Indian.'"

2. President Salinas was the first Mexican head of state to attend the Gueglaguetza. Menchú arrived in Mexico in the fall of 1992 after Guatemalan authorities had forced her into exile once again.

3. Lyrics from Los Fabulosos Cadillacs, "Quinto centenario" (1992).

4. Gustafson: *New Languages of the State*, 64; Hale, *Más que un Indio*; Kay Warren, *Indigenous Movements and Their Critics: Pan-Maya Activism in Guatemala* (Princeton, NJ: Princeton University Press, 1998); Glen Sean Coulthard, *Red Skin, White Masks: Rejecting the Colonial Politics of Recognition* (Minneapolis: University of Minnesota Press, 2014), 2; Charles Taylor, *Multiculturalism: Examining the Politics of Recognition*, ed. Amy Gutman (Princeton, NJ: Princeton University Press, 1994).

5. Guillermo Bonfil Batalla, *México profundo: Una civilización negada* (Mexico City: Random House Mondadori, 2005), 102. Claudio Lomnitz has offered a thoughtful critique of Bonfil Batalla's framework; see Claudio Lomnitz, *Deep Mexico, Silent Mexico: An Anthropology of Nationalism* (Minneapolis: University of Minnesota Press, 2001).

6. Ramírez Castañeda, *Educación indígena en México*, 172–74. Following that, in 2003 the Ley General de Derechos Lingüísticos de los Pueblos Indígenas was passed, which led to the creation of the Instituto Nacional de Lenguas Indígenas.

7. Paula López Caballero, *Indígenas de la nación: Etnografía histórica de la alteridad en México (Milpa Alta, siglos XVII-XXI)* (Mexico City: Fondo de Cultura Económica, 2017), 273.

8. David Recondo, "Usos y costumbres, procesos electorales y autonomía indígena en Oaxaca," in *Costumbres, leyes y movimiento indio en Oaxaca y Chiapas*, ed. Lourdes de León Pasquel (Mexico City: CIESAS; Miguel Angel Porrua, 2001), 91–92; Recondo, *Política del gatopardo*.

9. Hale, "Neoliberal Multiculturalism," 16. Eric D. Larson has applied this line of argument to the Oaxacan experience. See Eric D. Larson, "Tradition and Transition: Neoliberal Multiculturalism and the Containment of Indigenous Insurgency in Southern Mexico in the 1990s," *Latin American and Caribbean Ethnic Studies* 13, no. 1 (2018): 22–46.

10. Hale is one of the earliest and most insightful critics of the phenomenon. It is perhaps telling that he notes "the gloomy sense of entrapment in my argument" ("Neoliberal Multiculturalism," 14).

11. Taylor, *Multiculturalism*, 58.

12. Coulthard, *Red Skin, White Masks*, 15. Coulthard argues that colonial relations are reproduced "through the asymmetrical exchange of mediated forms of state recognition and accommodation."

13. Coulthard, *Red Skin, White Masks*, 32.

14. Antonio Escobar, *Encountering Development: The Making and Unmaking of the Third World* (Princeton, NJ: Princeton University Press, 2011); María Josefina Saldaña-Portillo, *The Revolutionary Imagination in the Americas and the Age of Development* (Durham, NC: Duke University Press, 2003); Frederick Cooper, "Writing the History of Development," *Journal of Modern European History* 8, no. 1 (2010): 5–23.

15. Coulthard, *Red Skin, White Masks*, 6; "Declaration of Barbados"; Rosenthal, *Reimaging Indian Country*.

16. Florencia Mallon, *Courage Tastes of Blood: The Mapuche Community of Nicolás Ailío and the Chilean State, 1906–2001* (Durham, NC: Duke University Press, 2005); Warren, *Indigenous Movements*; Marc Becker, *Indians and Leftists in the Making of Ecuador's Modern Indigenous Movements* (Durham, NC: Duke University Press, 2008); Xavier Albo, "El retorno del indio," *Revista Andina* 9, no. 2 (December 1991): 299–366; Postero, *Now We Are Citizens*.

17. Deborah Yashar, "Democracy, Indigenous Movements, and the Postliberal Challenge in Latin America," *World Politics* 52, no. 1 (1999): 76–104; Donna Van Cott, *The Friendly Liquidation of the Past: The Politics of Diversity in Latin America* (Pittsburgh, PA: University of Pittsburgh Press, 2000); Alison Brysk, *From Tribal Village to Global Village: Indian Rights and International Relations in Latin America* (Stanford, CA: Stanford University Press, 2000); Overmyer-Velázquez, *Folkloric Poverty*.

18. Juan Pedro Viqueira, *Encrucijadas chiapanecas: Economía, religión e identidades* (Mexico City: Tusquets Editores / El Colegio de México, 2002); N. Harvey, *Chiapas Rebellion*.

19. Among others, the Consejo Guerréense 500 Años de Resistencia Indígena marched to Mexico City in April 1994 to support EZLN. Bartolomé, *Gente de costumbre*, 179. See also Overmyer-Velázquez, *Folkloric Poverty*.

20. In the case of Ecuador, Marc Becker, citing Fernando Guerrero Cazar and Pablo Ospina Peralta (*El poder de la comunidad. Ajuste estructural y movimiento indígena en los Andes ecuatorianos* [Buenos Aires: CLACSO, 2003], 26–27), identifies the Communist Party, developmentalist policies of the 1960s, and progressive Catholic groups as the main contributors to Indigenous resurgence; see *Indians and Leftists*, 12.

21. Aquino Moreschi, "Generacion de la 'emergencia indígena.'"

22. Smith, *Pistoleros and Popular Movements*.

23. Aviña, *Specters of Revolution*; McCormick, "Last Door"; Pensado and Ochoa, *México beyond 1968*.

24. Poole, "Image of 'Our Indian'"; Deborah Poole, "Mestizaje, Distinction, and Cultural Presence: The View from Oaxaca," in *Histories of Race and Racism: The Andes and Mesoamerica from Colonial Times to the Present*, ed. Laura Gotkowitz (Durham, NC: Duke University Press, 2011), 179–203; Jesus Lizama Quijano, *La Guelaguetza en Oaxaca: Fiesta, relaciones interétnicas y procesos deconstrucción simbólica en el contexto urbano* (Mexico City: CIESAS, 2006), 103–4.

25. Eventually Mexican federal authorities sponsored migrant festivals in the United States.

26. In effect, the arrangement constituted a partial reconstitution of the PRI's authoritarian control.

27. Fernando Lobo, *La insurrección transmitida: Oaxaca 2006* (Mexico City: Pepitas, 2018); Víctor Raúl Martínez Vásquez, *Autoritarismo, movimiento popular y crisis política: Oaxaca 2006* (Oaxaca: UABJO, 2007).

28. Lynn Stephen, *We Are the Face of Oaxaca: Testimony and Social Movements* (Durham, NC: Duke University Press, 2013), 86.

29. Diego Enrique Osorno, *Oaxaca sitiada: La primera insurrección del siglo xxi* (Mexico City: Grijalbo, 2007); José Sotelo Marbán, *Oaxaca: Insurgencia civil y terrorismo de estado* (Mexico City: Ediciones Era, 2008). On drug war violence under Calderón, see Anabel Hernández, *Narcoland: The Mexican Drug Lords and their Godfathers* (New York: Verso Press, 2014); Francisco Quijano, "El crimen más grande," *Revista Común*, July 22, 2020, https://www.revistacomun.com/blog/el-crimen-mas-grande.

Bibliography

Archival Sources

Acervo Alfonso Caso, Museo del ex Convento de Santo Domingo en Yanhuitlán, Yanhuitlán, Oaxaca
Archivo General de la Nación, Mexico City
Archivo General del Poder Ejecutivo del Estado de Oaxaca, Oaxaca City
Archivo Histórico de la Secretaría de Educación Pública, Mexico City
Archivo Histórico del Centro Coordinador Indigenista de la Mixteca Alta, Tlaxiaco, Oaxaca
Archivo Histórico Municipal de la Heroica Ciudad de Tlaxiaco, Tlaxiaco, Oaxaca
Dirección General de Educación Indígena, Centro de Información y Documentación de Educación Indígena, Mexico City
Fondo Documental, Biblioteca Juan Rulfo, Instituto Nacional de los Pueblos Indígenas, Mexico City

Interviews

Interview by Alverino López López:
García Ortega, Eleazar. Oaxaca City, August 2, 2007.
Interviews by author:
Abardía Moros, Francisco. San Cristóbal de las Casas, Chiapas, March 11, 2014.
Acevedo Conde, María Luisa. Oaxaca City, May 12, 2010 (conducted with Salvador Sigüenza Orozco).
Aparicio López, Servando Vérulo. San Lucas Yosonicaje, September 8, 2010.
Cruz Bautista, Marcos Abraham. San Miguel el Grande, Rancheria Vicente Guerrero, November 11, 2009.
Feria, Felipe. Santa Rosa, Oaxaca City, April 28, 2010.
Hernández López, Ramón. San Agustín Tlacotepec, August 27, 2010.

Julián Caballero, Juan. CIESAS Sur, Oaxaca City, January 29, 2010.
López López, Alverino. Nochixtlán, November 20, 2009.
Martínez Vásquez, Víctor Raúl. Oaxaca City, November 9, 2009.
Osorio Nicolás, Antolín. Oaxaca City, February 22 and April 21, 2010.
Rockwell, Elsie. Mexico City, April 5, 2010.
Ruiz Ruiz, Eva. Oaxaca City, Santa Lucia del Camino, December 11, 2009.
Salazar, Santiago. Oaxaca City, December 15, 2009, and April 19, 2010.
Sánchez Bautista, Felipe. San Agustín Tlacotepec, November 11, 2009.
Sánchez López, Isaías. Tlaxiaco, September 9, 2010.
Santiago Pérez, Ignacio. Oaxaca City and San Pedro Tidaá, August 9–10, 2010.

Periodicals

Carteles del Sur, Oaxaca City
Excélsior, Mexico City
New York Times
Política, Mexico City
Por qué?, Mexico City
Proceso, Mexico City
Sol de México, Mexico City
El Universal, Mexico City
Unomásuno, Mexico City

Primary and Secondary Sources

Agence Latino-americaine d'information. "El Instituto Lingüístico de Verano, instrumento del imperialismo." *Nueva Antropología, Revista de Ciencias Sociales*, no. 9 (October 1978): 116–42.
Aguirre Beltrán, Gonzalo. *Cuijla: Esbozo etnográfico de un pueblo negro*. Mexico City: Fondo de Cultura Económica, 1958.
Aguirre Beltrán, Gonzalo. "El problema humano de las Mixtecas." Introduction to *La ciudad mercado (Tlaxiaco)*, by Alejandro D. Marroquín. Mexico City: UNAM, 1957.
Aguirre Beltrán, Gonzalo. *Regiones de refugio: El desarrollo de la comunidad y el proceso dominical en mestizo América*. Mexico City: Instituto Indigenista Interamericano, 1967.
Agustín, José. *Tragicomedia mexicana*. Vol. 2, *La vida México de 1970–1988*. Mexico City: Editorial Planeta Mexicana, 1998.
Albarrán Jackson, Elena. *Seen and Heard in Mexico: Children and Revolutionary Cultural Nationalism*. Lincoln: University of Nebraska Press, 2015.
Albo, Xavier. "El retorno del indio." *Revista Andina* 9, no. 2 (December 1991): 299–366.
Andrews, Abigail L. "Departures and Returns: Migration, Gender, and the Politics of Transnational Mexican Communities." PhD diss., University of California, Berkeley, 2014.

Andrews, Abigail L. "Legacies of Inequity: How Hometown Political Participation and Land Distribution Shape Migrants' Paths into Wage Labor." *World Development* 87 (2016): 318–32.

Aquino Moreschi, Alejandra. "La generación de la 'emergencia indígena' y el comunalismo oaxaqueño: Genealogía de un proceso de descolonización." *Cuadernos del Sur* 15, no. 20 (July-December 2010): 7–21.

Arauho Pardo, Alejandro, and Paula López Caballero. "¿Quién es indígena? El legado insospechado de Alfonso Caso." *Horizontal*, December 9, 2015. http://horizontal.mx/quien-es-indigena-el-legado-insospechado-de-alfonso-caso/.

Aviña, Alexander. *Specters of Revolution: Peasant Guerrillas in the Cold War Mexican Countryside*. Oxford: Oxford University Press, 2014.

Babb, Sarah. *Managing Mexico: Economists from Nationalism to Neoliberalism*. Princeton, NJ: Princeton University Press, 2004.

Bailón Corres, Jaime. "Los avatares de la democracia (1970–2008)." In *Oaxaca: Historia breve*, edited by Maria de los Ángeles Romero Frizzi. Mexico City: Colegio de México / Fondo de Cultura Económica, 2010.

Baker, Stephanie L. "*Salud Colectiva*: The Role of Public Health Campaigns in Building a Modern Mexican Nation, 1940s–1960s." PhD. diss., University of Illinois at Chicago, 2012.

Bartolomé, Miguel. *Gente de costumbre y gente de razón: Las identidades étnicas en Mexico*. Mexico City: Siglo XXI, 1997.

Bartra, Roger. "El reto de la izquierda." *Nexos* 59 (November 1982): 15–20.

Baskes, Jeremy. *Indians, Merchants, and Markets: A Reinterpretation of the Repartimiento and Spanish-Indian Economic Relations in Colonial Oaxaca, 1750–1821*. Palo Alto, CA: Stanford University Press, 2000.

Becker, Marc. *Indians and Leftists in the Making of Ecuador's Modern Indigenous Movement*. Durham, NC: Duke University Press, 2008.

Benítez, Fernando. *Los indios de México*. 2 vols. Mexico City: Biblioteca Era, 1967–68.

Bentley, Derek Andrew. "Democratic Openings: Organized Business, Conservative Protest, and Political-Economic Transformation in Mexico, 1970-1986." PhD diss., University of Georgia, 2017.

Bolívar Meza, Rosendo. "La mesa redonda de los marxistas mexicanos: El Partido Popular y el Partido Popular Socialista." *Estudios de Historia Moderna y Contemporánea de México* 16 (2006): 193–213.

Bonfil Batalla, Guillermo. *México profundo: Una civilización negada*. Mexico City: Random House Mondadori, 2005.

Boyer, Christopher R. *Becoming Campesinos: Politics, Identity, and Agrarian Struggle in Postrevolutionary Michoacán, 1920–1935*. Stanford, CA: Stanford University Press, 2003.

Boyer, Christopher R. *Political Landscapes: Forests, Conservation, and Community in Mexico*. Durham, NC: Duke University Press, 2015.

Brading, David. "Manuel Gamio and Official Indigenismo in Mexico." *Bulletin of Latin American Research* 7, no. 1 (1988): 75–89.

Brubaker, Roger, and Frederick Cooper. "Beyond 'Identity.'" *Theory and Society* 29, no. 1 (February 2000): 1–47.
Brysk, Alison. *From Tribal Village to Global Village: Indian Rights and International Relations in Latin America*. Stanford, CA: Stanford University Press, 2000.
Buchenau, Jürgen, and Gilbert M. Joseph. *The Once and Future Revolution: Social Upheaval and the Negotiation of Rule during Mexico's Long Twentieth Century*. Durham, NC: Duke University Press, 2013.
Bueno, Christina. *The Pursuit of Ruins: Archaeology, History, and the Making of Modern Mexico*. Albuquerque: University of New Mexico Press, 2016.
Bustamante, René V., ed. *Oaxaca: Una lucha reciente, 1960–1978*. Mexico City: Ediciones Nueva Sociología, 1978.
Caballero, José Maria. *Agricultura, reforma agraria, y pobreza campesina*. Lima: Instituto de Estudios Peruanos, 1980.
Calvet, Louis-Jean. *Linguistique et colonialisme: Petit traité de glottophaige*. Paris: Editions Payot, 1974.
Campbell, Howard. *Zapotec Renaissance: Ethnic Politics and Cultural Revivalism in Southern Mexico*. Albuquerque: University of New Mexico Press, 1994.
Cardoso, Fernando, and Enzo Faletto. *Dependency and Development in Latin America*. Berkeley: University of California Press, 1979.
Carrizales Retamoza, César. "El SNTE ante la política educativa del régimen." In *Las luchas magisteriales, 19791981: Documentos*, vol. 1, edited by Luis Hernández, 27–39. Mexico City: Editorial Macehual, 1981.
Castellanos, M. Bianet. *A Return to Servitude: Maya Migration and the Tourist Trade in Cancún*. Minneapolis: University of Minnesota Press, 2010.
Castells i Talens, Antoni. "'Todo se puede decir sabiéndolo decir': Maleabilidad en políticas de medios indigenistas." *Revista Mexicana de Sociología* 73, no. 2 (April-June 2011): 297–328.
Castro, J. Justin. *Radio in Revolution: Wireless Technology and State Power in Mexico, 1897–1938*. Lincoln: University of Nebraska Press, 2016.
Cattelino, Jessica R. "The Double Bind of American Indian Need-Based Sovereignty." *Cultural Anthropology* 25, no. 2 (2010): 235–62.
Cedillo, Adela, and Fernando Herrera Calderón, eds. *Challenging Authoritarianism in Mexico: Revolutionary Struggles and the Dirty War, 1964–1982*. New York: Routledge, 2012.
Central Intelligence Agency. "Latin America: Regional and Political Analysis." August 4, 1977. https://www.cia.gov/library/readingroom/docs/CIA-RDP79T00912A000700010005-7.pdf.
Chassen-López, Francie. *From Liberal to Revolutionary Oaxaca: The View from the South, Mexico 1867–1911*. University Park: Pennsylvania State University Press, 2004.
Chávez, Joaquín M. "Catholic Action, the Second Vatican Council, and the Emergence of the New Left in El Salvador (1950–1975)." *The Americas* 70, no. 3 (January 2014): 459–87.

Christiansen, Samantha, and Zachary Scarlett, eds. *The Third World in the Global Sixties*. New York: Berghahn Books, 2012.
Coffey, Mary. "'All Mexico on a Wall': Diego Rivera's Murals at the Ministry of Public Education." In *Mexican Muralism: A Critical History*, edited by Alejandro Anreus, Leonard Folgarait, and Robin Adele Greeley, 56–74. Berkeley: University of California Press, 2012.
Cohen, Deborah. *Braceros: Migrant Citizens and Transnational Subjects in the Postwar United States and Mexico*. Chapel Hill: University of North Carolina Press, 2013.
Cohen, Theodore W. *Finding Afro-Mexico: Race and Nation after the Revolution*. Cambridge: Cambridge University Press, 2020.
Cook, Maria Lorena. *Organizing Dissent: Unions, the State, and the Democratic Teachers' Movement in Mexico*. University Park: Pennsylvania State University Press, 1996.
Cooper, Frederick. "Writing the History of Development." *Journal of Modern European History* 8, no. 1 (2010): 5–23.
Copeland, Nicholas Matthew. "Bitter Earth: Counterinsurgency Strategy and the Roots of Mayan Neo-authoritarianism in Guatemala." PhD diss., University of Texas at Austin, 2007.
Cota Meza, Ramón. "Indigenismo y autonomía indígena." *Letras Libres* 3, no. 32 (August 2001): 47–50.
Cotter, Joseph. *Troubled Harvest: Agronomy and Revolution in Mexico, 1880–2002*. Westport, CT: Praeger, 2003.
Coulthard, Glen Sean. *Red Skin, White Masks: Rejecting the Colonial Politics of Recognition*. Minneapolis: University of Minnesota Press, 2014.
Cruz Majluf, Gerardo. "Reformas a la educación rural?" In *Reforma educativa y "apertura democrática,"* edited by Fernando Carmona, 125–51. Mexico City: Editorial Nuestro Tiempo, 1972.
Dalton, Margarita. *Breve historia de Oaxaca*. Mexico City: El Colegio de México y Fondo de Cultura Económica, 2004.
Dalton, Margarita. "Encierro intelectual: Entrevista con Salomón Nahmad." *Desacatos*, no. 9 (Spring-Summer 2002): 163–76.
Danielson, Michael S. *Emigrants Get Political: Mexican Migrants Engage Their Home Towns*. New York: Oxford University Press, 2018.
Davis, Diane E. *Urban Leviathan: Mexico City in the Twentieth Century*. Philadelphia: Temple University Press, 1994.
Dawson, Alexander S. "Histories and Memories of the Indian Boarding Schools in Mexico, Canada, and the United States." *Latin American Perspectives* 39, no. 5 (2012): 80–99.
Dawson, Alexander S. *Indian and Nation in Revolutionary Mexico*. Tucson: University of Arizona Press, 2004.
Dawson, Alexander S. *The Peyote Effect: From the Inquisition to the War on Drugs*. Oakland: University of California Press, 2018.
"The Declaration of Barbados: For the Liberation of the Indians." *Current Anthropology* 14, no. 3 (June 1973): 267–70.

de la Fuente, Julio. *Educación, antropología, y desarrollo de la comunidad.* Mexico City: INI, 1964.

de la Peña, Moisés T. *Problemas sociales y económicos de las mixtecas.* Mexico City: Instituto Nacional Indigenista, 1950.

Deloria, Philip J. *Indians in Unexpected Places.* Lawrence: University of Kansas Press, 2004.

Delpar, Helen. *The Enormous Vogue of Things Mexican: Cultural Relations between the United States and Mexico, 1920–1935.* Tuscaloosa: University of Alabama Press, 1995.

Denham, Diana, and CASA Collective. *Teaching Rebellion: Stories from the Grassroots Mobilization in Oaxaca.* Oakland, CA: P.M. Press, 2008.

Denning, Michael. *Culture in the Age of Three Worlds.* London: Verso, 2004.

Dietrick, Christopher R. W. "Oil Power and Economic Theologies: The United States and the Third World in the Wake of the Energy Crisis." *Diplomatic History* 40, no. 3 (2016): 500–529.

Dillingham, A. S. "Indigenismo and Its Discontents: Bilingual Teachers and the Democratic Opening in Oaxaca, Mexico, 1954–1982." PhD diss., University of Maryland, College Park, 2012.

Dillingham, A. S. "Mexico's Turn toward the Third World: Rural Development under President Luis Echeverría." In *México beyond 1968: Revolutionaries, Radicals, and Repression during the Global Sixties and Subversive Seventies,* edited by Jaime Pensado and Enrique Ochoa, 113–33. Tucson: University of Arizona Press, 2018.

Earle, Rebecca. *The Return of the Native: Indians and Myth-Making in Spanish America, 1810–1930.* Durham, NC: Duke University Press, 2007.

Eiss, Paul. *In the Name of El Pueblo: Place, Community, and the Politics of History in Yucatán.* Durham, NC: Duke University Press, 2010.

Escobar, Antonio. *Encountering Development: The Making and Unmaking of the Third World.* Princeton, NJ: Princeton University Press, 2011.

Fallaw, Ben. *Religion and State Formation in Postrevolutionary Mexico.* Durham, NC: Duke University Press. 2013.

Fanon, Franz. *The Wretched of the Earth.* 1961. Reprint, New York: Grove Press, 2005.

Faudree, Paja. *Singing for the Dead: The Politics of Indigenous Revival in Mexico.* Durham, NC: Duke University Press, 2013.

Ferguson, James. *The Anti-politics Machine: Development, Depoliticization, and Bureaucratic Power in Lesotho.* Minneapolis: University of Minnesota Press, 1994.

Fink, Carole, Philipp Gassert, and Detlef Junker, eds. *1968: The World Transformed.* Cambridge: Cambridge University Press, 1998.

Flanet, Véronique. *Viviré, si Dios quiere: Un estudio de la violencia en la Mixteca de la Costa.* Mexico City: Instituto Nacional Indigenista, 1977.

Flores, Ruben. *Backroads Pragmatists: Mexico's Melting Pot and Civil Rights in the United States.* Philadelphia: University of Pennsylvania Press, 2014.

Foweraker, Joe. *Popular Mobilization in Mexico: The Teachers' Movement, 1977–1987.* Cambridge: Cambridge University Press, 1993.

Freije, Vanessa. "Speaking of Sterilization: Rumors, the Urban Poor, and the Public Sphere in Greater Mexico City." *Hispanic American Historical Review* 99, no. 2 (2019): 303–36.
García Mora, Carlos. "Alejandro Marroquín: Tianguis y capitalismo." *Nexos*, August 1, 1978. https://www.nexos.com.mx/?p=3187.
García Mora, Carlos. "Un antropólogo purépecha: Entre el estudio del y por el pueblo mexicano y la mexicanística estadounidense." In *Ciencia en los márgenes: Ensayos de historia de las ciencias en México*, edited by Mechthild Rutsch and Carlos Serrano, 51–78. Mexico City: UNAM, 1997.
García Mora, Carlos. "Los proyectos tarascos, implicaciones actuales." *Diario de Campo: Boletín Interno de los Investigadores del Área de Antropología*, no. 95 (November-December 2008): 100–115.
Garner, Paul. "Oaxaca: The Rise and Fall of State Sovereignty." In *Provinces of the Revolution: Essays on Regional Mexican History, 1910–1929*, edited by Tomas Benjamin and Mark Wasserman, 163–83. Albuquerque: University of New Mexico Press, 1990.
Garrett-Davis, Josh. "The Intertribal Drum of Radio: The Indians for Indians Hour and Native American Media, 1941–1951." *Western Historical Quarterly* 49 (Autumn 2018): 249–73.
Gil, Carlos B., ed. *Hope and Frustration: Interviews with Leaders of Mexico's Political Opposition*. Wilmington, DE: Scholarly Resources, 1992.
Gillingham, Paul. "Ambiguous Missionaries: Rural Teachers and State Facades in Guerrero, 1930–1950." *Mexican Studies / Estudios Mexicanos* 22, no. 2 (2006): 331–60.
Gillingham, Paul, and Benjamin T. Smith, eds. *Dictablanda: Politics, Work and Culture in Mexico, 1938–1968*. Durham, NC: Duke University Press, 2014.
Gillingham, Paul, and Benjamin T. Smith. "Introduction: The Paradoxes of Revolution." In *Dictablanda: Politics, Work and Culture in Mexico, 1938–1968*, edited by Paul Gillingham and Benjamin T. Smith, 1–44. Durham, NC: Duke University Press, 2014.
Gilman, Nils. "The New International Economic Order: A Reintroduction." *Humanity: An International Journal of Human Rights, Humanitarianism, and Development* 6, no. 1 (Spring 2015): 1–16.
Giraudo, Laura, and Juan Martín-Sánchez, eds. *La ambivalente historia del indigenismo: Campo interamericano y trayectorias nacionales, 1940–1970*. Lima: Instituto de Estudios Peruanos, 2011.
Gleizer, Daniela, and Paula López Caballero, eds. *Nación y alteridad: Mestizos, indígenas y extranjeros en el proceso de formación nacional*. Mexico City: Ediciones Educación y Cultura, 2015.
González Pacheco, Cuauhtémoc. "La lucha de clases en Oaxaca: 1960–1970 (primera parte)." In *Oaxaca: Una lucha reciente: 1960–1978*, edited by René V. Bustamente. Mexico City: Ediciones Nueva Sociología, 1978.
Gordon, Alvin, and Darley Gordon. *Our Son Pablo*. New York: McGraw-Hill, 1946.
Gould, Jeffery L. "Solidarity under Siege: The Latin American Left, 1968." *American Historical Review* 114, no. 2 (April 2009): 348–75.

Grandin, Greg. "The Empire's Amnesia." *Jacobin* 25 (Spring 2017). https://jacobinmag.com/2017/05/the-empires-amnesia.

Grandin, Greg. *The Last Colonial Massacre: Latin America in the Cold War*. Chicago: University of Chicago Press, 2004.

Grandin, Greg. "Living in Revolutionary Time: Coming to Terms with the Violence of Latin America's Long Cold War." In *A Century of Revolution: Insurgent and Counterinsurgent Violence during Latin America's Long Cold War*, edited by Greg Grandin and Gilbert M. Joseph, 3–44. Durham, NC: Duke University Press, 2010.

Grandin, Greg, and Gilbert M. Joseph, eds. *Century of Revolution: Insurgent and Counterinsurgent Violence during Latin America's Long Cold War*. Durham, NC: Duke University Press, 2010.

Guardino, Peter. *The Time of Liberty: Popular Political Culture in Oaxaca, 1750–1850*. Durham, NC: Duke University Press, 2005.

Guerrero Cazar, Fernando, and Pablo Ospina Peralta. *El poder de la comunidad: Ajuste estructural y movimiento indígena en los Andes ecuatorianos*. Argentina: CLACSO, 2003.

Gumucio-Dagron, Alfonso. "Miners' Radio Stations: A Unique Communication Experience from Bolivia." In *Media and Glocal Change: Rethinking Communication for Development*, edited by Oscar Herner and Thomas Tufte, 317–23. Buenos Aires: CLASCO; Göteborg: Nordicom, 2005.

Gustafson, Bret. *New Languages of the State: Indigenous Resurgence and the Politics of Knowledge in Bolivia*. Durham, NC: Duke University Press, 2009.

Hale, Charles R. *Más que un Indio: More Than an Indian: Racial Ambivalence and Neoliberal Multiculturalism in Guatemala*. Santa Fe, NM: School of American Research Press, 2006.

Hale, Charles R. "Neoliberal Multiculturalism: The Remaking of Cultural Rights and Racial Dominance in Central America." *Political and Legal Anthropology Review* 28, no. 1 (2005): 10–28.

Harmer, Tanya. *Allende's Chile and the Inter-American Cold War*. Chapel Hill: University of North Carolina Press, 2011.

Hartch, Todd. *Missionaries of the State: The Summer Institute of Linguistics, State Formation, and Indigenous Mexico, 1935–1985*. Tuscaloosa: University of Alabama Press, 2006.

Harvey, David. *A Brief History of Neoliberalism*. Oxford: Oxford University Press, 2005.

Harvey, Neil. *The Chiapas Rebellion: The Struggle for Land and Democracy*. Durham, NC: Duke University Press, 1998.

Hayes, Joy Elizabeth. *Radio Nation: Communication, Popular Culture, and Nationalism in Mexico, 1920–1950*. Tucson: University of Arizona Press, 2000.

Hernández, Anabel. *Narcoland: The Mexican Drug Lords and Their Godfathers*. New York: Verso Press, 2014.

Hernández Díaz, Jorge. "Condiciones de vida y diferenciación social en la población indígena oaxaqueña." *Cuadernos del Sur* 5 (November 1998): 107–18.

Hernández-Díaz, Jorge. *Reclamos de la identidad: La formación de las organizaciones indígenas en Oaxaca, México*. Mexico City: UABJO-Miguel Angel Porrúa, Grupo Editorial, 2001.

Hines, Sarah. "The Power and Ethics of Vernacular Modernism: The Misicuni Dam Project in Cochabamba, Bolivia, 1944–2017." *Hispanic American Historical Review* 98, no. 2 (2018): 223–56.

Hodges, Donald C., and Ross Gandy. *Mexico, the End of the Revolution*. Westport, CT: Praeger, 2002.

Illich, Ivan. *Deschooling Society*. New York: Harper and Row, 1971.

Immerwahr, Daniel. *Thinking Small: The United States and the Lure of Community Development*. Cambridge, MA: Harvard University Press, 2015.

Jolly, Jennifer. *Creating Pátzcuaro, Creating Mexico: Art, Tourism, and Nation Building under Lázaro Cárdenas*. Austin: University of Texas Press, 2018.

Joseph, Gilbert M., and Daniel Nugent, eds. *Everyday Forms of State Formation: Revolution and the Negotiation of Rule in Modern Mexico*. Durham, NC: Duke University Press, 1994.

Joseph, Gilbert M., Anne Rubinstein, and Eric Zolov, eds. *Fragments of a Golden Age: The Politics of Culture in Mexico since 1940*. Durham, NC: Duke University Press, 2001.

Julián Caballero, Juan. "La Academia de la Lengua Mixteca: Espacios de reflexión compartida," *Cuadernos del Sur* 5, no. 14 (May 1999): 129–39.

Julián Caballero, Juan. *El papel del maestro en el etnocidio en San Antonio Huitepec, Oaxaca*. Etnolingüística 20, Cuadernos de Información y Divulgación para Maestros Bilingües. Mexico City: SEP/INI, 1982.

Kearney, Michael. "Mixtec Political Consciousness: From Passive to Active Resistance." In *Rural Revolt in Mexico: U.S. Intervention and the Domain of Subaltern Politics*, edited by Daniel Nugent, 134–46. Durham, NC: Duke University Press, 1998.

Keller, Renata. *Mexico's Cold War: Cuba, the United States, and the Legacy of the Mexican Revolution*. Cambridge: Cambridge University Press, 2015.

Kelly, Patrick William. *Sovereign Emergencies: Latin America and the Making of Global Human Rights Politics*. New York: Cambridge University Press, 2018.

Kiddle, Amelia, and Marie L. O. Muñoz. Introduction to *Populism in Twentieth-Century Mexico: The Presidencies of Lázaro Cárdenas and Luis Echeverría*, edited by Amelia Kiddle and Maria L. O. Muñoz, 1–14. Tucson: University of Arizona Press, 2010.

Kiddle, Amelia, and Maria L. O. Muñoz, eds. *Populism in Twentieth-Century Mexico: The Presidencies of Lázaro Cárdenas and Luis Echeverría*. Tucson: University of Arizona Press, 2010.

Kiser, Heiko. "Mit der Jungfrau gegen die Hochmoderne: Religion als Ressource der indigenen Bevölkerung gegen staatliche Modernisierungsprojekte in Oaxaca, Mexiko, 1950 bis heute." *Archiv für Sozialgeschichte* 51 (2011): 445–86.

Knight, Alan. "Cárdenas and Echeverría: Two 'Populist' Presidents Compared." In *Populism in Twentieth-Century Mexico: The Presidencies of Lázaro Cárdenas and Luis Echeverría*, edited by Amelia Kiddle and Maria L. O. Muñoz, 15–37. Tucson: University of Arizona Press, 2010.

Knight, Alan. *The Mexican Revolution*. Vol. 1. Cambridge: Cambridge University Press, 1985.

Knight, Alan. "Racism, Revolution, and *Indigenismo*: Mexico, 1910–1940." In *The Idea of Race in Latin America, 1870–1940*, edited by Richard Graham, 71–102. Austin: University of Texas Press, 1990.

Konefal, Betsy. *For Every Indio Who Falls: A History of Maya Activism in Guatemala, 1960–1990*. Albuquerque: University of New Mexico Press, 2015.

La Botz, Dan. *Mask of Democracy: Labor Suppression in Mexico Today*. Boston: South End Press, 1992.

Langland, Victoria. *Speaking of Flowers: Student Movements and the Making and Remembering of 1968 in Military Brazil*. Durham, NC: Duke University Press, 2013.

Larson, Brooke. "Warisata: A Historical Footnote." *ReVista: Harvard Review on Latin America*, October 2011. https://revista.drclas.harvard.edu/book/warisata.

Larson, Eric D. "Tradition and Transition: Neoliberal Multiculturalism and the Containment of Indigenous Insurgency in Southern Mexico in the 1990s." *Latin American and Caribbean Ethnic Studies* 13, no. 1 (2018): 22–46.

La Serna, Miguel. *Corner of the Living: Ayacucho on the Eve of the Shining Path Insurgency*. Durham, NC: University of North Carolina Press, 2012.

Lee, Christopher. *Making a World after Empire: The Bandung Moment and Its Political Afterlives*. Athens: Ohio University Press, 2010.

León Pasquel, Lourdes, ed. *Costumbres, leyes y movimiento indio en Oaxaca y Chiapas*. Mexico City: CIESAS / Miguel Ángel Porrúa, 2001.

Levy, Daniel, and Kathleen Bruhn. *Mexico: The Struggle for Democratic Development*. 2nd ed. Berkeley: University of California Press, 2006.

Lewis, Stephen E. *The Ambivalent Revolution: Forging State and Nation in Chiapas, 1910–1945*. Tucson: University of New Mexico Press, 2005.

Lewis, Stephen E. "Mexico's National Indigenist Institute and the Negotiation of Applied Anthropology in Highland Chiapas, 1951–1954." *Ethnohistory* 55, no. 4 (Fall 2009): 609–32.

Lewis, Stephen E. "Modernizing Message, Mystical Messenger: The Teatro Petul in the Chiapas Highlands, 1954–1974." *The Americas* 67, no. 3 (2011): 375–97.

Lewis, Stephen E. *Rethinking Mexican Indigenismo: The INI's Coordinating Center in Highland Chiapas and the Fate of a Utopian Project*. Albuquerque: University of New Mexico Press, 2018.

Lizama Quijano, Jesus. *La Guelaguetza en Oaxaca: Fiesta, relaciones interétnicas y procesos de construcción simbólica en el contexto urbano*. Mexico City: CIESAS, 2006.

Lobo, Fernando. *La insurrección transmitida: Oaxaca 2006*. Mexico City: Pepitas, 2018.

Lomnitz, Claudio. *Deep Mexico, Silent Mexico: An Anthropology of Nationalism*. Minneapolis: University of Minnesota Press, 2001.

Lomnitz-Adler, Claudio. "Bordering on Anthropology: The Dialectics of a National Tradition in Mexico." *Revue de Synthèse* 121, nos. 3–4 (July-December 2000): 349–79.

López, Felipe H., and David Runsten. "Mixtecs and Zapotecs Working in California: Rural and Urban Experiences." In *Indigenous Mexican Migrants in the United States*, edited by Jonathan Fox and Gaspar Rivera-Salgado, 249–78. San Diego: Center for U.S.-Mexican Studies, University of California San Diego, 2004.

López, Ricardo. "From Middle Class to Petit Bourgeoisie: Cold War Politics and Classed Radicalization in Bogotá, 1958–1972." *Estudios Interdisciplinarios de América Latina y el Caribe* 25, no. 2 (2014): 99–130.

López, Rick. *Crafting Mexico: Intellectuals, Artisans, and the State after the Revolution.* Durham, NC: Duke University Press, 2010.

López Bárcenas, Francisco. *Muertes sin fin: Crónicas de represión en la región mixteca oaxaqueña.* Mexico City: Centro de Estudios Antropológicos, Científicos, Artísticos, Tradicionales y Lingüísticos, 2002.

López Bárcenas, Francisco. *San Juan Copala: Dominación política y resistencia popular. De las rebeliones de Hilarión a la formación del municipio autónomo.* Mexico City: Universidad Autónoma Metropolitana, Unidad Xochimilco, 2009.

López Caballero, Paula. "Domesticating Social Taxonomies: Local and National Identifications as Seen through Susan Drucker's Anthropological Fieldwork in Jamiltepec, Oaxaca, Mexico, 1957–1963." *Hispanic American Historical Review* 100, no. 2 (2020): 285–321.

López Caballero, Paula. *Indígenas de la nación: Etnografía histórica de la alteridad en México (Milpa Alta, siglos XVII–XXI).* Mexico City: Fondo de Cultura Económica, 2017.

López Caballero, Paula. "Introduction: Why Beyond Alterity?" With Ariadna Acevedo-Rodrigo. In *Beyond Alterity: Destabilizing the Indigenous Other in Mexico*, edited by Paula López Caballero and Ariadna Acevedo-Rodrigo, 3–30. Tucson: University of Arizona Press, 2018.

López Caballero, Paula. "Las políticas indigenistas y la 'fabrica' de su sujeto de intervención en la creación del primer Centro Coordinador del Instituto Nacional Indigenista (1948–1952)." In *Nación y alteridad: Mestizos, indígenas y extranjeros en el proceso de formación nacional*, edited by Daniela Gleizer and Paula López Caballero, 69–108. Mexico City: Ediciones Educación y Cultura, 2015.

Loza, Mireya. *Defiant Braceros: How Migrant Workers Fought for Racial, Sexual, and Political Freedom.* Chapel Hill: University of North Carolina Press, 2016.

Luna Ruiz, Xicohtencatl Gerardo. "Un estudio de caso de colonización dirigida desde La Mixteca Alta hacia la costa oaxaqueña: Indigenismo, contacto comercial, conflicto agrario y reorganización comunitaria." Master's thesis, Centro de Investigaciones y Estudios Superiores en Antropología Social, Pacífico Sur, 2010.

Malinowski, Bronislaw, and Julio de la Fuente. *La economía de un sistema de mercados en México: Un ensayo de etnografía contemporánea y cambio social en un valle mexicano.* Mexico City: Escuela Nacional de Antropologia e Historia, Sociedad de Alumnos, 1957.

Mallon, Florencia. *Courage Tastes of Blood: The Mapuche Community of Nicolás Ailío and the Chilean State, 1906–2001.* Durham, NC: Duke University Press, 2005.

Mallon, Florencia. "Introduction: Decolonizing Knowledge, Language, and Narrative." In *Decolonizing Native Histories: Collaboration, Knowledge, and Language in the Americas*, 1–20. Durham, NC: Duke University Press, 2012.

Marroquín, Alejandro D. *La ciudad mercado (Tlaxiaco).* Mexico City: UNAM, 1957.

Marroquín, Alejandro D. "Economía indígena y desarrollo, trabajo presentado al VI Congreso Indigenista Interamericano." *América Indígena* 28, no. 4 (October 1968): 936–37.

Martínez, Héctor. *Las migraciones altiplánicas y la colonización del Tambopata*. Lima: Centro de Estudios de Población y Desarollo, 1969.

Martínez, Héctor. *Las migraciones internas en el Perú: Ensayo*. Caracas: Monte Ávila, 1970.

Martínez, María Elena. "The Black Blood of New Spain: Limpieza de Sangre, Racial Violence, and Gendered Power in Early Colonial Mexico." *William and Mary Quarterly*, 3rd ser., 61, no. 3 (July 2004): 479–520.

Martínez, María Elena. *Genealogical Fictions: Limpieza de Sangre, Religion, and Gender in Colonial Mexico*. Palo Alto, CA: Stanford University Press, 2008.

Martínez Novo, Carmen. *Who Defines Indigenous? Identities, Development, Intellectuals, and the State in Northern Mexico*. New Brunswick, NJ: Rutgers University Press, 2006.

Martínez Vásquez, Víctor Raúl. *Autoritarismo, movimiento popular y crisis política: Oaxaca 2006*. Oaxaca: UABJO, 2007.

Martínez Vásquez, Víctor Raúl. *La educación en Oaxaca*. Oaxaca: Instituto de Investigaciones Sociológicas, UABJO, 2004.

Martínez Vásquez, Víctor Raúl. *Historia de la educación en Oaxaca, 1825–1940*. Oaxaca: Instituto de Investigaciones Sociológicas UABJO, 1994.

Martínez Vásquez, Víctor Raúl. "El movimiento de 1968 en Oaxaca." *Cuadernos del Sur* 14, no. 27 (April 2009): 89–100.

Martínez Vásquez, Víctor Raúl. *Movimiento popular y política en Oaxaca (1968–1986)*. Mexico City: CONACULTA, 1990.

Martínez Vásquez, Víctor Raúl. *No que no, sí que sí: Testimonios y crónicas del movimiento magisterial oaxaqueño*. Oaxaca: SNTE, 2005.

McCormick, Gladys. "The Last Door: Political Prisoners and the Use of Torture in Mexico's Dirty War." *The Americas*, 74, no. 1 (January 2017): 57–81.

McCormick, Gladys. *The Logic of Compromise in Mexico: How the Countryside Was Key to the Emergence of Authoritarianism*. Chapel Hill: University of North Carolina Press, 2016.

McIntyre, Kathleen M. *Protestantism and State Formation in Postrevolutionary Oaxaca*. Albuquerque: University of New Mexico Press, 2019.

Mejido, Manuel. *México amargo*. Mexico City: Siglo Veintiuno Editores, 1973.

Méndez Aquino, Alejandro. *Historia de Tlaxiaco (Mixteca)*. Mexico: Instituto Oaxaqueño de las Culturas/Fondo Estatal para la Cultura y las Artes, 1985.

Mendieta y Nuñez, Lucio, ed. *Valor económico y social de las razas indígenas de México*. Mexico City: DAPP, 1938.

Mendieta y Nuñez, Lucio, ed. *Los zapotecos: Monografía histórica, etnográfica y económica*. Mexico City: Imprenta Universitaria, 1949.

México. Dirección General de Estadística. *IX Censo general de población, January 28, 1970, Estado de Oaxaca*. Vol. 1. Mexico City: Secretaria de Industria y Comercio, Dirección General de Estadística, 1971.

Miller, Douglas K. *Indians on the Move: Native American Mobility and Urbanization in the Twentieth Century*. Chapel Hill: University of North Carolina Press, 2019.

Mills, Kenneth R., William B. Taylor, and Sandra Lauderdale Graham, eds. *Colonial Latin America: A Documentary History*. Lanham, MD: Rowman and Littlefield, 2002.

Milstead, John Radley. "Afro-Mexicans and the Making of Modern Mexico: Citizenship, Race, and Capitalism in Jamiltepec, Oaxaca (1821–1910)." PhD diss., Michigan State University, 2019.

Mitchell, Timothy. *Rule of Experts: Egypt, Techno-Politics, Modernity*. Berkeley: University of California Press, 2002.

Monaville, Pedro. "June 4th 1969: Violence, Political Imagination, and the Student Movement in Kinshasa." In *The Third World in the Global Sixties*, edited by Samantha Christiansen and Zachary Scarlett, 159–70. New York: Berghahn Books, 2012.

Monoghan, John. *The Covenants with Earth and Rain: Exchange, Sacrifice, and Revelation in Mixtec Society*. Norman: University of Oklahoma Press, 1995.

Morton, Adam David. *Revolution and State in Modern Mexico: The Political Economy of Uneven Development*. Lanham, MD: Rowman and Littlefield, 2013.

Moyn, Samuel. *Not Enough: Human Rights in an Unequal World*. Cambridge, MA: Harvard University Press, 2018.

Muñoz, María L. O. *Stand Up and Fight: Participatory Indigenismo, Populism, and Mobilization in Mexico, 1970–1984*. Tucson: University of Arizona Press, 2016.

Nakamura, Mutsuo. "Programa de formación profesional de etnolinguistas (primera generación 1979–1982)." Master's thesis, Centro de Investigaciones y Estudios Superiores en Antropología Social, Mexico City, 2000.

Navarrete, Federico. *México racista: Una denuncia*. Mexico: Grijalba, 2016.

Nobbs-Thiessen, Ben. *Landscape of Migration: Mobility and Environmental Change on Bolivia's Tropical Frontier, 1952 to the Present*. Chapel Hill: University of North Carolina Press, 2020.

Norget, Kristin. "The Politics of Liberation: The Popular Church, Indigenous Theology and Grassroots Mobilization in Oaxaca, Mexico." *Latin American Perspectives* 24, no. 5 (1997): 96–127.

Ochoa, Enrique. *Feeding Mexico: The Political Uses of Food since 1910*. Lanham, MD: Rowman and Littlefield, 2001.

Ochoa, Enrique. "Lic. Moisés de la Peña: The Economist on Horseback." In *The Human Tradition in Mexico*, edited by Jeffrey Pilcher, 165–79. Lanham, MD: Rowman and Littlefield, 2003.

Offner, Amy. *Sorting Out the Mixed Economy: The Rise and Fall of Welfare and Developmental States in the Americas*. Princeton, NJ: Princeton University Press.

Ogle, Vanessa. "State Rights against Private Capital: The "New International Economic Order" and the Struggle over Aid, Trade, and Foreign Investment, 1962–1981." *Humanity* 5, no. 2 (Summer 2014): 211–34.

Ojeda Dávila, Lorena, and Marco Antonio Calderón Mólgora. "Cardenismo e indigenismo en Michoacán." *Mexican Studies / Estudios Mexicanos* 32, no. 1 (February 2016): 83–110.

Olsson, Tore C. *Agrarian Crossings: Reformers and the Remaking of the US and Mexican Countryside*. Princeton, NJ: Princeton University Press, 2017.

O'Neill, Colleen. *Working the Navajo Way: Labor and Culture in the Twentieth Century*. Lawrence: University Press of Kansas, 2005.

Osorno, Diego Enrique. *Oaxaca sitiada: La primera insurrección del siglo XXI.* Mexico City: Grijalbo, 2007.

Overmyer-Velázquez, Rebecca. *Folkloric Poverty: Neoliberal Multiculturalism in Mexico.* University Park: Pennsylvania State University Press, 2010.

Padilla, Tanalís. "Memories of Justice: Rural *Normales* and the Cardenista Legacy." *Mexican Studies / Estudios Mexicanos* 32, no. 1 (February 2016): 111–43.

Padilla, Tanalís. "Rural Education, Political Radicalism, and *Normalista* Identity in Mexico after 1940." In *La Dictablanda: Soft Authoritarianism in Mexico, 1938–1968,* edited by Paul Gillingham and Ben Smith, 379–96. Durham, NC: Duke University Press, 2014.

Padilla, Tanalís. *Rural Resistance in the Land of Zapata: The Jaramillista Movement and the Myth of the Pax Priísta, 1940–1962.* Durham, NC: Duke University Press, 2008.

Padilla, Tanalís, and Louise E. Walker. "In the Archives: History and Politics." *Journal of Iberian and Latin American Research* 19, no. 1 (2013): 1–10.

Parsons, Elsie Clews. *Mitla, Town of the Souls: And Other Zapoteco-Speaking Pueblos of Oaxaca, México.* Chicago: University of Chicago Press, 1936.

Pensado, Jaime. *Rebel Mexico: Student Unrest and Authoritarian Political Culture during the Long Sixties.* Stanford, CA: Stanford University Press, 2013.

Pensado, Jaime, and Enrique Ochoa, eds. *México beyond 1968: Revolutionaries, Radicals, and Repression during the Global Sixties and Subversive Seventies.* Tucson: University of Arizona Press, 2018.

Poniatowska, Elena. *Massacre in Mexico.* Columbia: University of Missouri Press, 1991.

Poole, Deborah. "An Image of 'Our Indian': Type Photographs and Racial Sentiments in Oaxaca, 1920–1940." *Hispanic American Historical Review* 84, no. 1 (2004): 37–82.

Poole, Deborah. "Mestizaje, Distinction, and Cultural Presence: The View from Oaxaca." In *Histories of Race and Racism: The Andes and Mesoamerica from Colonial Times to the Present,* edited by Laura Gotkowitz, 179–203. Durham, NC: Duke University Press, 2011.

Poole, Deborah. *Vision, Race, and Modernity: A Visual Economy of the Andean Image World.* Princeton, NJ: Princeton University Press, 1997.

Poole, Deborah, and Gabriela Zamorano Villarreal. *De frente al perfil: Retratos raciales de Frederick Starr.* Michoacán: El Colegio de Michoacán y el Fideicomiso "Felipe Teixidor y Monserrat Alfau de Teixidor," 2012.

Postero, Nancy. *Now We Are Citizens: Indigenous Politics in Postmulticultural Bolivia.* Palo Alto, CA: Stanford University Press, 2007.

Prashad, Vijay. *The Darker Nations: A People's History of the Third World.* New York: New Press, 2008.

Preston, Julia, and Samuel Dillon. *Opening Mexico: The Making of a Democracy.* New York: Farrar, Straus and Giroux, 2005.

Pribilsky, Jason. "Development and the 'Indian Problem' in the Cold War Andes: *Indigenismo,* Science, and Modernization in the Making of the Cornell-Peru Project at Vicos." *Diplomatic History* 33, no. 3 (2009): 405–26.

Quijano, Anibal. "Coloniality of Power, Eurocentrism, and Latin America." *Nepantla: Views from the South* 1, no. 3 (2000): 533–80.

Quijano, Francisco. "El crimen más grande." *Revista Común*, July 22, 2020. https://www.revistacomun.com/blog/el-crimen-mas-grande.
Raibmon, Paige. *Authentic Indians: Episodes of Encounter from the Late-Nineteenth-Century Northwest Coast*. Durham, NC: Duke University Press, 2005.
Ramírez Castañeda, Elisa. *La educación indígena en México*. Mexico City: UNAM, 2006.
Rappaport, Joanne. *The Politics of Memory: Native Historical Interpretation in the Colombian Andes*. Cambridge: Cambridge University Press, 1998.
Recondo, David. *La política del gatopardo: Multiculturalismo y democracia en Oaxaca*. Mexico City: Centro de Investigaciones y Estudios Superiores en Antropología Social / Centro de Estudios Mexicanos y Centroamericanos, 2007.
Recondo, David. "Usos y costumbres, procesos electorales y autonomía indígena en Oaxaca." In *Costumbres, leyes y movimiento indio en Oaxaca y Chiapas*, edited by Lourdes de León Pasquel, 91–113. Mexico City: CIESAS; Miguel Angel Porrua, 2001.
Rees, Martha W., Arthur D. Murphy, Earl W. Morris, and Mary Winter. "City and Crisis: The Case of Oaxaca, Mexico." *Urban Anthropology and Studies of Cultural Systems and World Economic Development* 20, no. 1 (Spring 1991): 15–29.
Reina, Leticia. *Las rebeliones campesinas en México (1819–1906)*. Mexico City: Siglo Veintiuno Editores, 1984.
Rendón, Juan José. *La comunalidad: Modo de vida en los pueblos indios*. Vol. 1. Mexico City: CONACULTA, 2003.
Reyes Bautista, Gabina, and Pauala Fería Barrios. *Manuel para la enseñanza de lecto-escritura en lengua mixteca: Libro del maestro, primer grado, Tlaxiaco Este, Oaxaca*. Mexico City: SEP, 1985.
Ristow, Colby Nolan. *A Revolution Unfinished: The Chegomista Rebellion and the Limits of Revolutionary Democracy in Juchitán, Oaxaca*. Lincoln: University of Nebraska Press, 2018.
Rivera Cusicanqui, Silvia. *Oprimidos pero no vencidos: Luchas del campesinado aymara y qhechwa de Bolivia, 1900–1980*. Geneva: Instituto de Investigaciones de las Naciones Unidas para el Desarrollo Social, 1986.
Rivera-Salgado, Gaspar. "Mixtec Activism in Oaxacalifornia: Transborder Grassroots Political Strategies." *American Behavioral Scientist* 42, no. 9 (June 1999): 1439–58.
Robinet, Romain. "'Hermanos de raza . . .': La Confederación Nacional de Jóvenes Indígenas, entre el indigenismo y la política (1940–1960)." In *La condición juvenil en Latinoamérica*, edited by Ivonne Meza Huacuja y Sergio Moreno Juárez, 275–99. Mexico City: UNAM/IISUE, 2019.
Robles, Sonia. *Mexican Waves: Radio Broadcasting along Mexico's Northern Border, 1930–1950*. Tucson: University of Arizona Press, 2019.
Rockwell, Elsie. *Hacer escuela, hacer estado: La educación posrevolucionaria vista desde Tlaxcala*. Zamora: El Colegio de Michoacán, 2007.
Roldán, Mary. "Popular Cultural Action, Catholic Transnationalism, and Development in Colombia before Vatican II." In *Local Church, Global Church: Catholic Activism in the Americas before Vatican II*, edited by Stephen J. C. Andes and Julia C. Young, 245–74. Washington, DC: Catholic University of America Press, 2016.

Romero Frizzi, María de los Ángeles. *Economía y vida de los españoles en la Mixteca Alta, 1519–1720*. Mexico City: Instituto Nacional de Antropología e Historia: Gobierno del Estado de Oaxaca, 1990.

Romero Frizzi, Maria de los Ángeles. *Escribir para dos mundos: Testimonios y experiencias de los escritores mixtecos*. Oaxaca: Fondo Editorial, Instituto Estatal de Educacion Publica de Oaxaca, 2003.

Rosas, Ana Elizabeth. *Abrazando el Espíritu: Bracero Families Confront the US-Mexico Border*. Oakland: University of California Press, 2014.

Rosemblatt, Karin Alejandra. "Other Americas: Transnationalism, Scholarship, and the Culture of Poverty in Mexico and the United States." *Hispanic American Historical Review* 89, no. 4 (November 2009): 603–41.

Rosemblatt, Karin Alejandra. *The Science and Politics of Race in Mexico and the United States, 1910–1950*. Chapel Hill: University of North Carolina Press, 2018.

Rosenthal, Nicholas. *Reimagining Indian Country: Native American Migration and Identity in Twentieth-Century Los Angeles*. Chapel Hill: University of North Carolina Press, 2014.

Rubin, Jeffrey W. "Contextualizing the Regime: What 1938–1968 Tells Us about Mexico, Power, and the Twentieth Century." In *La Dictablanda: Soft Authoritarianism in Mexico, 1938–1968*, edited by Paul Gillingham and Ben Smith, 379–96. Durham, NC: Duke University Press, 2014.

Rubin, Jeffrey W. *Decentering the Regime: Ethnicity, Radicalism, and Democracy in Juchitán, Mexico*. Durham, NC: Duke University Press, 1997.

Ruiz, Jason. *Americans in the Treasure House: Travel to Porfirian Mexico and the Cultural Politics of Empire*. Austin: University of Texas Press, 2014.

Ruiz Cervantes, Francisco José. "La lucha de clases en Oaxaca: 1971–1977 (segunda parte)." In *Oaxaca: Una lucha reciente: 1960–1978*, edited by René V. Bustamante, 43–69. Mexico City: Ediciones Nueva Sociología, 1978.

Ruiz Cervantes, Francisco José. "El movimiento de la soberanía en Oaxaca (1915–1920)." In *La revolución en Oaxaca (1900–1930)*, edited by Víctor Raúl Martínez Vásquez, 277–381. Mexico City: Consejo Nacional para la Cultura y las Artes, 1993.

Ruiz de Bravo Ahuja, Gloria. *La enseñanza del español a los indígenas mexicanos*. Mexico City: Colegio de México, 1977.

Ruiz de Bravo Ahuja, Gloria, and Beatriz Garza Cuarón. *Problemas de integración*. Mexico City: IIISEO, 1970.

Rus, Jan. "The 'Comunidad Revolucionaria Institucional': The Subversion of Native Government in Highland Chiapas, 1936–1968." In *Everyday Forms of State Formation: Revolution and the Negotiation of Rule in Modern Mexico*, edited by Gilbert M. Joseph and Daniel Nugent, 265–300. Durham, NC: Duke University Press, 1994.

Salas Landa, Mónica. "(In)Visible Ruins: The Politics of Monumental Reconstruction in Post-revolutionary Mexico." *Hispanic American Historical Review* 98, no. 1 (2018): 43–76.

Saldaña-Portillo, María Josefina. *Indian Given: Racial Geographies across Mexico and the United States*. Durham, NC: Duke University Press, 2016.

Saldaña-Portillo, María Josefina. *The Revolutionary Imagination in the Americas and the Age of Development*. Durham, NC: Duke University Press, 2003.

Saldívar, Emiko. "Everyday Practices of Indigenismo: An Ethnography of Anthropology and the State in Mexico." *Journal of Latin American and Caribbean Anthropology* 16, no. 1 (2011): 67–89.

Salinas, Salvador. "Untangling Mexico's Noodle: El Tallarín and the Revival of Zapatismo in Morelos, 1934–1938." *Journal of Latin American Studies* 46 (2014): 471–99.

Santamaría, Gema. "Lynching, Religion and Politics in Twentieth-Century Puebla." In *Global Lynching and Collective Violence*, vol. 2, *The Americas and Europe*, edited by Michael J. Pfeifer, 85–114. Champaign: University of Illinois Press, 2017.

Santiago León, Antonio. "La contratación de braceros en la ciudad de Oaxaca en 1944." Master's thesis, El Colegio de San Luis, A.C., 2015.

Schaefer, Timo. "Citizen-Breadwinners and Vagabond-Soldiers: Military Recruitment in Early Republican Southern Mexico." *Journal of Social History* 46, no. 4 (Summer 2013): 953–70.

Schreiber, Rebecca. *Cold War Exiles in Mexico: U.S. Dissidents and the Culture of Critical Resistance*. Minneapolis: University of Minnesota Press, 2008.

Schwartz, Diana. "Transforming the Tropics: Development, Displacement, and Anthropology in the Papaloapan, Mexico, 1940s–1970s." PhD diss., University of Chicago, 2016.

Scott, James C. *Seeing Like a State: How Certain Schemes to Improve the Human Condition Have Failed*. New Haven, CT: Yale University Press, 1998.

Shepard, Todd. "Algeria, France, Mexico, UNESCO: A Transnational History of Antiracism and Decolonization, 1932–1962." *Journal of Global History* 6, no. 2 (July 2011): 273–97.

Sheppard, Randal. *A Persistent Revolution: History, Nationalism, and Politics in Mexico since 1968*. Albuquerque: University of New Mexico Press, 2016.

Sigüenza Orozco, Salvador. *Héroes y escuelas: La educación en la Sierra Norte de Oaxaca, 1927–1972*. Mexico City: INAH; Oaxaca: IEEPO, 2007.

Simpson, Audra. "On Ethnographic Refusal: Indigeneity, 'Voice' and Colonial Citizenship." *Junctures: The Journal for Thematic Dialogue* 9 (2007): 67–80.

Skidmore, Thomas. *The Politics of Military Rule in Brazil, 1964–85*. New York: Oxford University Press, 1988.

Slobodian, Quinn. *Globalists: The End of Empire and the Birth of Neoliberalism*. Cambridge, MA: Harvard University Press, 2018.

Smith, Benjamin T. "Anticlericalism and Resistance: The Diocese of Huajuapam de León, 1930–1940." *Journal of Latin American Studies* 37, no. 3 (August 2005): 469–505.

Smith, Benjamin T. *The Mexican Press and Civil Society, 1940–1976: Stories from the Newsroom, Stories from the Street*. Chapel Hill: University of North Carolina Press, 2018.

Smith, Benjamin T. *Pistoleros and Popular Movements: The Politics of State Formation in Postrevolutionary Oaxaca*. Lincoln: University of Nebraska Press, 2009.

Smith, Benjamin T. *The Roots of Conservatism in Mexico: Catholicism, Society, and Politics in the Mixteca Baja, 1750–1962*. Albuquerque: University of New Mexico Press, 2012.

Snodgrass, Michael. "New Rules for the Unions: Mexico's Steelworkers Confront Privatization and the Neoliberal Challenge." *Labor: Studies in Working-Class History of the Americas* 4, no. 3 (2007): 81–103.

Sotelo Marbán, José. *Oaxaca: Insurgencia civil y terrorismo de estado*. Mexico City: Ediciones Era, 2008.

Spalding, Karen. *Huarochirí: An Andean Society under Inca and Spanish Rule*. Stanford, CA: Stanford University Press, 1984.

Spores, Ronald. *Ñuu Ñudzahui: La mixteca de Oaxaca. La evolución de la cultura mixteca desde los primeros pueblos hasta la Independencia*. Mexico City: Fondo Editorial, IEEPO, 2007.

Starr, Frederick. *Indians of Southern Mexico: An Ethnographic Album*. Chicago: Lakeside Press, 1899.

Starr, Frederick. *In Indian Mexico: A Narrative of Travel and Labor*. Chicago: Forbes, 1908.

Starr, Frederick. *The Physical Characteristics of the Indians of Southern Mexico*. Chicago: University of Chicago Press, 1902.

Stephen, Lynn. "The Creation and Re-creation of Ethnicity: Lessons from the Zapotec and Mixtec of Oaxaca." *Latin American Perspectives* 23, no. 2 (1996): 17–37.

Stephen, Lynn. *Transborder Lives: Indigenous Oaxacans in Mexico, California, and Oregon*. Durham, NC: Duke University Press, 2007.

Stephen, Lynn. *We Are the Face of Oaxaca: Testimony and Social Movements*. Durham, NC: Duke University Press, 2013.

Stephen, Lynn. *Zapata Lives! Histories and Cultural Politics in Southern Mexico*. Oakland: University of California Press, 2002.

Stern, Steve. *Peru's Indian Peoples and the Challenge of Spanish Conquest: Huamanga to 1640*. Madison: University of Wisconsin Press, 1982.

Stoler, Ann. "Introduction. 'The Rot Remains': From Ruins to Ruination." In *Imperial Debris: On Ruins and Ruination*, edited by Ann Stoler, 1–38. Durham, NC: Duke University Press, 2013.

Stone, Robert. *Prime Green: Remembering the Sixties*. New York: Harper Collins, 2007.

Tarica, Estelle. *The Inner Life of Mestizo Nationalism*. Minneapolis: University of Minnesota Press, 2008.

Taylor, Charles. *Multiculturalism: Examining the Politics of Recognition*. Edited by Amy Gutman. Princeton, NJ: Princeton University Press, 1994.

Terraciano, Kevin. *The Mixtecs of Colonial Oaxaca: Ñudzahui History, Sixteenth through Eighteenth Centuries*. Palo Alto, CA: Stanford University Press, 2001.

Thornton, Christy. *Revolution in Development: Mexico and the Governance of the Global Economy*. Oakland: University of California Press, 2021.

Tibón, Guiterre. *Pinotepa Nacional: Mixtecos, negros y triques*. Mexico City: Universidad Autónoma de México, 1961.

Tischler, Julia. "Cementing Uneven Development: The Central African Federation and the Kariba Dam Scheme." *Journal of Southern African Studies* 40, no. 5 (2014): 1047–64.

Twain, Mark. "Story of the Wycliffe Translators Pacifying the Last Frontiers." *NACLA's Latin America and Empire Report* 7, no. 10 (1973): 15–23.

Ulloa Bornemann, Alberto. *Surviving Mexico's Dirty War: A Political Prisoner's Memoir.* Edited by Arthur Schmidt and Aurora Camacho de Schmidt. Philadelphia: Temple University Press, 2007.

Van Cott, Donna. *The Friendly Liquidation of the Past: The Politics of Diversity in Latin America.* Pittsburgh, PA: University of Pittsburgh Press, 2000.

Varese, Stefano, ed. *Indígenas y educación en México.* Mexico City: CEE, 1983.

Vargas, María Eugenia. *Educación e ideología: Constitución de una categoría de intermediarios en la comunicación interétnica. El caso de los maestros bilingües tarascos (1964–1982).* Mexico City: CIESAS, 1994.

Vaughan, Mary Kay. *Cultural Politics in Revolution: Teachers, Peasants and Schools in Mexico, 1930–1940.* Tucson: University of Arizona Press, 1997.

Vaughan, Mary Kay. *Portrait of a Young Painter: Pepe Zúñiga and Mexico City's Rebel Generation.* Durham, NC: Duke University Press, 2014.

Velasco, Alejandro. *Barrio Rising: Urban Popular Politics and the Making of Modern Venezuela.* Oakland: University of California Press, 2015.

Villoro, Luis. *Los grandes momentos del indigenismo en México.* 2nd ed. Mexico City: Fondo de Cultura Económica, 2014.

Viqueira, Juan Pedro. *Encrucijadas chiapanecas: Economía, religión e identidades.* Mexico City: Tusquets Editores / El Colegio de México, 2002.

Volpi, Jorge. *La imaginación y el poder: Una historia intelectual de 1968.* Mexico City: Ediciones Era, 1998.

Walker, Louise. *Waking from the Dream: Mexico's Middle Classes after 1968.* Palo Alto, CA: Stanford University Press, 2013.

Warman, Arturo, Margarita Nolasco, Guillermo Bonfil Batalla, Mercedes Olivera, and Enrique Valencia. *De eso que llaman antropología mexicana.* Mexico City: Editorial Nuestro Tiempo, 1970.

Warren, Kay. *Indigenous Movements and Their Critics: Pan-Maya Activism in Guatemala.* Princeton, NJ: Princeton University Press, 1998.

Waterbury, Ronald. "Non-revolutionary Peasants: Oaxaca Compared to Morelos in the Mexican Revolution." *Comparative Studies in Society and History* 17, no. 4 (October 1975): 410–42.

Weinstein, Barbara. *The Color of Modernity: Sao Paulo and the Making of Race and Nation in Brazil.* Durham, NC: Duke University Press, 2015.

Weinstein, Barbara. "Developing Inequality." *American Historical Review* 113, no. 1 (February 2008): 1–18.

Whitener, Brian. *Crisis Cultures: The Rise of Finance in Mexico and Brazil.* Pittsburgh, PA: University of Pittsburgh Press, 2019.

Wright, Angus. *The Death of Ramón González: The Modern Agricultural Dilemma.* Austin: University of Texas Press, 2005.

Wright-Rios, Edward. *Revolutions in Mexican Catholicism: Reform and Revelation in Oaxaca, 1887–1934.* Durham, NC: Duke University Press, 2009.

"Wycliffe Is a Global Corporation." *NACLA's Latin America and Empire Report* 7, no. 10 (1973): 24–31.

Yannakakis, Yanna. *The Art of Being In-Between: Native Intermediaries, Indian Identity, and Local Rule in Colonial Oaxaca*. Durham, NC: Duke University Press, 2008.

Yashar, Deborah. "Democracy, Indigenous Movements, and the Postliberal Challenge in Latin America." *World Politics* 52, no. 1 (1999): 76–104.

Yescas Martínez, Isidoro, and Gloria Zafra. *La insurgencia magisterial en Oaxaca, 1980*. Mexico City: Fondo Editorial IEEPO IISUABJO, 1985.

Young, Kevin. "Introduction: Revolutionary Actors, Encounters, and Transformations." In *Making the Revolution: Histories of the Latin American Left*, edited by Kevin Young, 1–18. Cambridge: Cambridge University Press, 2018.

Zolov, Eric. "Introduction: Latin America in the Global Sixties." *The Americas* 70, no. 3 (January 2014): 349–62.

Zolov, Eric. *The Last Good Neighbor: Mexico in the Global Sixties*. Durham, NC: Duke University Press, 2020.

Zolov, Eric. *Refried Elvis: The Rise of the Mexican Counterculture*. Oakland: University of California Press, 1999.

Index

Page numbers in italic type indicate maps or photographs.

Abardía Moros, Francisco, 114, 168–69
Acapulco, 72
Acción Cultural Popular (ACPO), 57, 67
Acevedo Conde, María Luisa, 117
ACPO. *See* Acción Cultural Popular
Africa, state-directed development in, 78
African-descended peoples: in Costa Chica, 72–73, 87; government neglect of, 76, 88; at Guelaguetza, 183; influences of, 42; in Mixteca, 27, 41; population of, 87
agriculture: coastal plains as site for development of, 44, 72, 74–77, 80; crisis in (1970s), 125, 161–62; development/modernization and, 13, 24–25, 72, 74–78, 80; Indigenous practice of, 28, 32, 42, 80–83, 109; of Mixteca Alta, 32, 42; seasonal migration related to, 13, 33, 42, 81, 83–86, 165. *See also* land and land tenure
Aguilar, Hilario, 107
Aguilar Flores, Ernesto, 130
Aguilera Dorantes, Mario, 59, 64
Aguirre Beltrán, Gonzalo, 4, 36, 39, 86–88, 97, *149*, 156, 198n71
albergues, 156, 158
Alejandra, María, *3*, 3–5
Alemán, Miguel, 24, 74, 77

Allende, Salvador, 101, 113
American Indian Movement, 179
Amuzgo population, 27
Andrade Ibarra, José Luis, 130–31
Antequera, 11–12, 28–29
anthropology/anthropologists: colonialism imputed to, 4, 105; and dissident/radical politics, 94, 111, 117, 144, 153–54, 179; in federal agencies, 15–16; folkloric studies of, 153; and Indigenous ethnocide, 146; participation of, in development projects, 22, 26, 33–36, 41–44, 55, 58, 72, 78, 83, 89; racial typing and measurement by, 1–4, 62
anticolonialism: in educational curriculum, 20, 97–98, 161–70; global initiatives in, 94–95; IIISEO and, 101; indigeneity in relation to, 151, 153, 178–79; and linguistics research, 106; theories of, 10. *See also* decolonization
antimony, 31
antiracism, 17–19, 178–79
la aparecería (land tenure), 32. *See also* land and land tenure
Aparicio López, Servando Vérulo, 168
apertura democrática. *See* democratic opening

APPO. *See* Asamblea Popular de los Pueblos de Oaxaca
Araujo del Ángel, Refugio, 141
Argentina, 94, 100
Asamblea Popular de los Pueblos de Oaxaca (APPO), ix, 184–85
assimilationism, 11, 78–79, 105, 156, 160, 174, 179
austerity policies: development/modernization and, 24; government embrace of, 125, 128, 142–43, 147–48; multiculturalism in relation to, 17–18, 171, 176; neoliberalism and, 123; teachers' challenging of, 17, 118, 122, 130–31, 133, 140, 142–44, 171
auxiliary radio teachers, 47, 49, 58–62, 64
Ávila Camacho, Manuel, 24, 74
Aymara population, 79

Barbados Conference, 154
Barbados Declaration, 179
Bartolomé, Miguel Alberto, 154
Bartra, Armando, 168
Bartra, Roger, 143
Bautista Mariscal, Sebastián, 80
Benítez, Fernando, 22, 38, 59–60
bilingual-bicultural education, 128, 144, 146, 148, 157–61, 180
bilingualism: cultural role of, 43–44; in education, 20, 48–52, 56–58, 60, 62, 64, 157–58, 163, 175, 180; in radio schools, 19, 47–49, 60
bilingual promoters. *See* promotores
Blanco, Hugo, 112, 167
boarding schools, 30, 50, 156, 158
Bolivia, 59, 174
Bolivian Revolution, 51
Bonfil Batalla, Guillermo, 96, 146, 148, 150–51, 153–54, 170; *México profundo*, 174–75
Bracero Program, 84–86
Bravo Ahuja, Victor, 15, 102, 109, 110
Brazil, 94, 100, 125
Brena Torres, Rodolfo, 91, 102
Bufete Popular Universitario, 98
Bureau of Indian Affairs (US), 74, 78, 179

Cabañas, Lucio, 116
Cabral, Amílcar, 151
caciques, 87, 88, 109, 115, 182
Calderón, Felipe, 185, 186
campesinos: land tenure and usages of, 32, 91–92, 110; as migrant workers, 75, 85; nationalist connotations of, 10, 38, 45; political mobilization of, 13, 97, 182
Canada, 174, 179
capitalism, and social-political reform, 176
Cárdenas, Cuauhtémoc, 140
Cárdenas, Lázaro, 24, 30, 36, 50, 70, 93, 153
Carranza, Venustiano, 12, 30
Carrasco Altamirano, Diódoro, 15, 141, 170, 171, 172, 175
Carrasco Briseño, Bartolomé, 100
Casa del Estudiante Indígena, 50
Caso, Alfonso, 8–10, *9*, 14, 36, *40*, 42, 50, 59, 64, 66, *90*, 91–92, 97, 179, 182–83
castellanización (Hispanicization), 38, 103, 155–57. *See also* Spanish language
Castellanos, Rosario, 52
Catholicism: anticommunism of, 19, 48, 56, 65–68; and education, 49, 53, 55–59, 66–69; and Indigenous resurgence, 170; in Mexico, 99–100; in Mixteca, 31, 56; opposition to radio schools, 19, 48, 66–69; and politics, 17, 55–56, 67–68; Revolution critiqued by, 31. *See also* liberation theology
CCIMA. *See* Centro Coordinador Indigenista de la Mixteca Alta
Central Campesina Independiente, 67
Central Intelligence Agency (US), 153
Centro Coordinador Indigenista de la Mixteca Alta, *40*, 41
Centro Coordinador Indigenista de la Mixteca Alta (CCIMA), 39, 47, 65
Centro de Investigaciones Superiores del Instituto Nacional de Antropología e Historia, 150
Centro de Investigación para la Integración Social, 158
Centro Intercultural de Documentación, 106

Chávez Orozco, Luis, 50
Chiapas: impoverishment in, 162; Indigenous education in, 157; Indigenous resurgence in, 180–81; INI in, 35, 40, 46, 52, 56; Zapatista rebellion in, 15, 100, 123, 175, 180–81
Chile, 96, 100–101, 113, 124–25, 180
China, 78
CMPIO. *See* Coalición de Maestros y Promotores Indígenas de Oaxaca
CNTE. *See* Coordinadora Nacional de Trabajadores de la Educación
Coalición de Maestros y Promotores Indígenas de Oaxaca (CMPIO), 116, 118, 121–22, 127, 132, 135–36, 165, 167–71, 218n46
Coalición de Promotores Culturales Bilingües, 112–16
Coalición Obrera, Campesina, Estudiantil del Istmo (COCEI), 99, 113, 126, 137, 170
Coalición Obrero Campesino Estudiantil de Oaxaca (COCEO), 98, 113, 115, 126
cochineal, 28–29
coffee workers, 33, 37, 42–43
Cold War: development initiatives during, 24, 25; education during, 49; Mexico during, 16, 48, 100–101, 182; politics during, 48–49, 153; radio schools and, 48
Colegio de México, 102, 106
Colombia, 57, 67
colonialism: indigeneity in relation to, 7, 8, 10, 24, 153; indigenismo accused of, 105; INI accused of, 92; in Mixteca Alta, 28–29; multiculturalism as, 177; and Oaxaca, 11–12. *See also* anticolonialism; decolonization
colonización dirigida. *See* Mixteca Alta: relocation of people from
Comité Nacional de Comunicaciones Vecinales, 58
communism, Catholic hostility to, 19, 48, 56, 65–68
comunalidad (communality), 17, 181, 212n1
Conasupo, *97*, 124, 125, 145

Confederación Nacional de Jóvenes Indígenas (CNJI), 52, 68
Conference of Latin American Bishops, 94
Congo, 94
consciousness-raising, 108, 116, 118
Constitutionalists, 12, 30
Convention 169 (International Labour Organization), 174
Coordinadora Nacional de Trabajadores de la Educación (CNTE), 135, 140, 165
Cordera, Rolando, 168
Cornell Peru Project, 35
corporal punishment, 54
Corripio y Ahumada, Ernesto, 99–100
Costa Chica: agricultural development in, 44, 72, 74–77, 80; environment of, 27, 71–72; map of, *73*; race in, 72–73; resettlement of highland peoples in, 19, 24, 36–37, 70, 72–81, 86–92; violence in, 19, 72–73, 87, 91–92, 110
Coulthard, Glen Sean, 176–77
coyotes (intermediaries), 37
Cristero War, 31, 55
Cruz Bautista, Marcos Abraham, 145, 150, 154, 155, 171
Cruz Lorenzo, Tomás, 181
Cuba, 94, 96, 100, 147
Cuban Revolution, 48, 98
cultural pluralism. *See* multiculturalism

DAAC. *See* Departamento de Asunto Agrarios y Colonización
Dávila, José Inés, 12, 30
DDT, 22–24, 42
decolonization, 25, 96, 153, 179
de la Fuente, Julio, 33, 54
de la Madrid, Miguel, 136, 143, 148, 164
de la Peña, Moisés, 10, 26, 35–39, 41, 44–45, 76
de las Casas, Bartolomé, 105
delegados forestales (forestry officials), 32, 37
democratic opening, 95–97, 99–101, 104, 110, 114, 116, 117
Departamento de Asunto Agrarios y Colonización (DAAC), 73, 77, 80

development/modernization: and agriculture, 13, 24–25, 72, 74–78, 80; coast as site for, 36–37, 71–92; critiques of, 19–20; global programs for, 25–26; indigeneity in relation to, 13, 178; indigenismo and, 26, 35, 179–80; INI and, 26, 40, 45–46, 70, 72–81, 110; Mexican policies of, 24–26, 74, 96, 124; in Mixteca Alta, 19, 22–46; New Left politics and, 110–18; in Oaxaca, 13, 14; obstacles to, 25–26, 45; radio technology and, 49, 57, 60; relocation/resettlement as tool of, 19, 24, 36–37; rural-to-urban migration resulting from, 74; shared development policies, 96, 124; state-directed practices of, 78–79; as totalizing process, 22–23. See *also* austerity policies; underdevelopment
Dewey, John, 50
DGEI. *See* Dirección General de Educación Indígena
Díaz, Floriberto, 17
Díaz, Porfirio, 4, 8, 30
Diosa Centéotl (corn goddess), 172, 183
Dirección Federal de Seguridad, 20–21
Dirección General de Educación Extraescolar en el Medio Indígena (DGEEMI), 112–13, 138, 156
Dirección General de Educación Indígena (DGEI), 148, 150, 156–58, 163
Dirección General de Investigaciones Políticas y Sociales, 20–21
Dominican order, 11–12, 56
Durbin, Marshall, 150

Echeverría, Luis, 19–20, 88, 95–97, 100–102, 110–11, 115–17, 124–27, 179
education: access and attendance, 157, 162; anticolonialism in, 20, 97–98, 161–70; bilingualism in, 20, 48–52, 56–58, 60, 62, 64, 157–58, 163, 175, 180; Catholic involvement in, 49, 53, 55–59; Cold War influences on, 49; decentralization in, 122, 129; ethnic development model in, 145–46; experiments in Indigenous, 50–65; federal vs. local control of, 30–31; Hernández López's role in, 52–69; IIISEO and, 103; and Indigenous boarding schools, 30, 50; of Indigenous girls, 102; Indigenous language use in, 47–64, 103, 148, 157–60, 179; of Indigenous peoples, 47–70, 131, 145–71, 179–80; inequalities in, 122–23; Marxism and, 68; multiculturalism in, 156–61, 163; obstacles to effective Indigenous, 161–65; Pátzcuaro program and, 150–56; pedagogical methods in, 103, 158, 166–67, 171; primary school in Santo Tomás Ocotepec, *83*; of promotores, 107–8, 110–11, 117, 131; radio schools and, 19, 47–49, 56–69; reform of 1970s in, 96, 126–28; Spanish language and, 19, 39, 47–48, 50, 54, 58, 60, 102–3, *104*, 106, 156–59, 163, 179; of teachers, 131
Ejército Zapatista de Liberación Nacional (EZLN), 15, 100, 123, 175, 180–81
ejidal lands, 32, 77, 86, 88
elites: *gente de razón*, 48, 72, 79; of Jamiltepec, 88; mestizo, 29, 39, 72, 92; in Tlaxiaco, 25, 29, 30, 43
ENAH. *See* Escuela Nacional de Antropología e Historia
Engels, Frederick, 151
Escuela de Mejoradoras del Hogar Rural (EMHR), 102
Escuela Nacional de Agricultura at Chapingo, 111, 114
Escuela Nacional de Antropología e Historia (ENAH), 35, 36, 41, 107, 111, 148, 153
escuelas albergues, 156, 158
ethnic development (*etnodesarrollo*), 17, 144, 145–46, 149, 178
ethnocide, 105, 146
ethnolinguistics, 145–46, 148, 150–56
EZLN. *See* Ejército Zapatista de Liberación Nacional

Fanon, Franz, 98
Federación de Estudiantes Oaxaqueños, 98–99
Feria, Felipe, 107
Fernández y Fernández, Celestino, 55–56
Ferrocarril del Sur, 29

First National Congress of Indigenous
  Peoples, 153–54
Foro Construyendo la Gobernabilidad y la
  Democracia en Oaxaca, 185–86
Fox, Vicente, ix, 20, 186
Frank, Andre Gunder, 105
Freinet, Célestin, and Freinet model,
  166–67
Freire, Paulo, 94, 118, 166
Fuerzas de Liberación Nacional, 100

Gamio, Manuel, 33
García Ortega, Eleazar, 111–12, 114
Garrido Calderón, Vicente, 65
Gasca Iturribarría, Rafael, 115
gender, 150, 194–95n13, 173, 186; norms of,
  in Indigenous communities, 132. *See also*
  women and girls
gente de razón (elite), 48, 72, 79
golondrina (swallow migration), 42, 82
Gómez Sandoval, Fernando, 110
González, Martín, 1
González Casanova, Pablo, 105
González Pintos, Alberto, 107
Gordillo, Elba Esther, 141
Guatemala, 59, 67, 68, 147, 174, 180
Guelaguetza de los Lunes del Cerro, 8, 101,
  172–74, *173*, 177, 182–85
Guelaguetza Popular, 185
Guzmán, Eulalia, *9*
Guzman Böckler, Carlos, 93, 150–51

Harnecker, Marta, 111, 167
health. *See* public health
Herbert, Jean-Loup, 151
Hernández López, Ramón, 52–69, 80–81,
  88–92, 138, *149*
highland population. *See* Mixteca Alta
high modernism, 26, 36, 78, 88, 205n55
Homenaje Racial, 8
Hu Dehart, Evelyn, 150

Iglesias Meza family, 72–73, 79, 88, 92, 110
Illich, Ivan, 106
Imperialismo y descolonización (text series),
  151, *152*

import substitution industrialization (ISI),
  25
Incháustegui, Carlos, 41–42, 44, 55, 83
indigeneity: anticolonialism in relation to,
  151, 153, 178–79; colonialism in relation
  to, 7, 8, 10, 24, 153; cultural markers of,
  10; development/modernization in relation to, 13, 178; impoverishment linked
  to, 27, 45, 162; inequalities associated
  with, 10, 33–39, 44; language as marker
  of, 10, 27, 38–39, 43–45; multiculturalism and, 18, 177–78, 181; Oaxaca as
  important site for, 11, 13, 33; teachers'
  movement and, 122–23, 127
indigenismo: as Americas-wide project,
  10–11, 14; colonial attitudes imputed to,
  105; conflicts within, 93–95; critiques of,
  96–97, 104–5; defined, 7; development
  policies and, 26, 35, 179–80; double bind
  of, 7–8, 11, 27, 39, 45, 114–15, 143, 186–87;
  effects of, 7–8, 19; in global context, 153;
  Guelaguetza in relation to, 8, 172–74,
  177, 182–85; Indigenous responses to,
  4–5, 46, 91, 177, 182; international initiatives in, 93; language as criterion used by,
  10; in Mixteca Alta, 39–44; nationalist
  uses of, 8; participatory, 17, 98, 127, 146;
  Pátzcuaro program and, 150–56; PRI
  and, 15, 17; project of, 4–5; and race, 76;
  radical politics and, 97–118; relocation
  program as component of, 19, 24, 36–37,
  70, 72–81, 86–92; Rivera's *Patio del
  trabajo* and, 119–21, *120*, 143
Indigenous languages: in education, 47–64,
  103, 148, 157–60, 179; linguistic study of,
  106; monolingualism and, 38–39, 43–44,
  52–54, 82, 103, 105–7
Indigenous peoples: agriculture of, 28, 32,
  42, 80–83, 109; anthropological study
  of, 1–4; Catholic engagement with, 56;
  class distinctions among, 162; conceptions of, 4; education of, 47–70, 131,
  145–71, 179–80; and ethnocide, 105, 146;
  exploitation of, 26–27, 37, 39, 42–43, 65,
  101, 172–73; framing or characterization
  of, 7–8, 21, 38; and PRI, 16; racialization

Indigenous peoples (*continued*)
of, 81–82; radio programming by and for, 59, 69–70; regional studies of, 33–44; responses of, to indigenismo, 4–5, 46, 91, 177, 182; rights of, 97–98, 147, 167, 170–71, 174–76, 180; self-representation/self-determination of, 11, 97, 146, 148, 154–55; state in relation to, 8, 10, 16; as teachers, 131, 136, 138, 141–42. *See also* indigeneity; indigenismo; Indigenous languages; Indigenous resurgence

Indigenous resurgence: Catholicism and, 170; factors in, 18, 118, 164–65, 170; historical roots of, 10, 16, 177–82; language as crucial element in, 10, 170; New Left and, 168, 179; politics associated with, 170

inequalities: associated with indigeneity, 10, 33–39, 44; in education policy, 122–23; failures to address, 18, 45–46, 76, 176; growing, in 1980s, 147; Marxist theories of, 68; naturalization of, 27, 44–46, 76; racial basis of, 37–38; social science analysis of, 105; structural factors underlying, 45–46

Infante, Pedro, 98

INI. *See* Instituto Nacional Indigenista

Instituto de Investigación y Integración Social del Estado de Oaxaca (IIISEO), 95, 101–17, 165, 167, 168, 180, 185, 209n42

Instituto Estatal de Educación Pública de Oaxaca (IEEPO), 141, 184

Instituto Indigenista Interamericano, 93–94

Instituto Nacional Indigenista (INI), 145; and agricultural development, 72, 77, 80; Caso's leadership of, 9; Catholic opposition to, 65–69; colonial approach imputed to, 92; Conasupo store, Magdalena Peñasco, *97*; coordinating centers, 35; and development, 26, 40, 45–46, 70, 72–81, 110; and education, 49, 51–69, 156–57; indigenismo critics in leadership positions of, 96–97; indigenista practices of, 14, 17, 148; Indigenous peoples as conceptualized in, 21; in Mixteca Alta, 39; and participatory indigenismo, 147; and Pátzcuaro program, 151; PRI and, 15, 164; promotores employed by, 51–52, 69–70, 101, 108, 110–11, 132; protests against, 113–15; and race, 42, 87–88; radio school broadcasts of, 19, 47–49, 56–69; and relocation of highland population, 70, 73–81, 85–92; SEP and, 157

Instituto Politécnico Nacional, 111

Inter-American Indigenista Congress, 93, 150, 179

internados. *See* boarding schools

International Labour Organization, 18, 79, 174

International Monetary Fund, 140

Isthmus of Tehuantepec: anthropological study in, 2; as commercial and trade center, 11, 162; Indigenous resurgence in, 165; politics in, 13, 15, 29–30, 99, 126, 137, 162, 170; resettlement of highland peoples in, 73, 77, 80, 86–87; SNTE in, 130

Jamiltepec, 40, 72–73, *77*, 79, 86–88, 92
Jaramillistas, 116
Jaramillo, Ruben, 48
Jiménez, José Alfredo, 98
Jiménez Colmenares, José, 186
Jiménez Martínez, Ausencia, 129
Jiménez Ruiz, Eliseo, 126, 133, 137
Jonguitud Barrios, Carlos, 127, 130, 136, 140–41, 166
Juan Carlos I, King of Spain, 172, *173*
Juárez, Benito, 12, 175
Julián Caballero, Juan, 155, 171

King, Martin Luther, Jr., 94

labor: on coffee plantations, 33, 37, 42–43; migration driven by, 13, 14–15, 42, 74–76, 81–86, 89–90, 165. *See also* unions
Laje, Maria Inés, 163
land and land tenure: in Costa Chica, 87, 89; development policies in relation to, 36–37; dissident politics in relation to, 110, 126; distribution/redistribution of,

24, 29, 32, 36; migration driven by, 82; in Mixteca, 29–30, 32, 89; violence related to, 110. *See also* agriculture
Lang, Charles B., 2–4
language: in educational curriculum, 39, 47–64; as marker of indigeneity, 10, 27, 38–39, 43–45; in Mixteca, 43–44, 49, 62; in Oaxaca, 13, 33; preservation of, 198n71; radio as vehicle for, 47, 59, 66. *See also* bilingualism; Indigenous languages; Spanish language
La Tuza, 72–73, 86–87, 91
Left, political: and *comunalidad*, 17; Echeverría and, 101; Indigenous opposition to, 169; and liberation theology, 100; López Mateos and, 48, 77; and multiculturalism, 148–49; Pátzcuaro program critiqued by, 155; PRI and, 147–48. *See also* New Left
Lewis, Oscar, 105
liberation theology, 17, 94, 99–100, 106, 139
Línea Proletaria, 135
linguistics, 106. *See also* ethnolinguistics
Lombardo Toledano, María, *9*
Lombardo Toledano, Vicente, 68
López Alvez, José, "Canción Mixteca," *63*
López López, Alverino, 165–66, 171
López Mateos, Adolfo, 48–49, 74, 77, 80, 95
López Obrador, Andrés Manuel, 185
López Portillo, José, 121, 124–26, 128, 136, 143
Lost Decade, 124
Lukacs, George, 151

Magdalena Peñasco, 82–83, 89, *97*
Maldonado Robles, Fernando, 130–31, 134
Malinowski, Bronislaw, 33, 35
Mandel, Ernest, 111
Maoism, 100, 112, 135
Mao Zedong, 78, 151
March to the Sea, 24, 74
Marcuse, Herbert, 105
Mariátegui, José Carlos, 112, 167
Marroquín, Alejandro, 26, 35, 36–37, 41, 43, 45

Martínez Luna, Jaime, 119, 181, 212n1
Martínez Noriega, Pedro, 135
Martínez Vásquez, Victor Raúl, 139
Marx, Karl, 111, 151
Marxism, 68, 105, 111–12
Mayoral Heredia, Manuel, 15
Mayrén Rodríguez, David, 129–30, 132
Mazatec population, 35, 78
medianería (land tenure), 32
Memmi, Albert, 98
Menchú Tum, Rigoberta, 172–73, *173*, 219n2
Méndez Arceo, Sergio, 106
Mendieta y Nuñez, Lucio, 33
Mendizábal, Othón de, 50
mestizaje, 17, 174
mestizo elite, 29, 39, 72, 92
Mexican Miracle, 24–25, 96
Mexico: during Cold War, 16, 48, 100–101, 182; debt crisis (1982) in, 123–26, 136, 147; democratic opening in, 95–97, 99–101, 104, 110, 114, 116, 117; development/modernization in, 24–26, 74, 96, 124; earthquake (1985) in, 17, 123, 139; and international politics, 95–96, 100; military in, 100–101, 186; multiculturalism in, 17–18, 144, 174–75; neoliberalism in, 17, 123–26; politics of 1960s and 1970s in, 94, 101
Meza viuda de Iglesias, Francisca. *See* Pancha, Doña
migration: to the coast, 19, 24, 36–37, 72–81; government intervention in, 74–76; Guelaguetza linked to, 183–84; labor-related, 13, 14–15, 42, 74–76, 81–86, 89–90, 165; from Oaxaca, 14–15, 81–86, 125–26, 161–62, 187; rural-to-urban, 74, 82, 126; seasonal, 14–15, 33, 42, 44, 75–76, 81–86, 89; as survival strategy, 76, 85, 89–90, 125–26, 165
Mijangos Ross, Rafael, 79, 88
Milanés, Pablo, 98
Ministry of Education. *See* Secretaría de Educación Pública
Mitchell, Timothy, 71

Mixteca: Catholicism in, 31, 56; development studies of, 35–36; highland and coast compared, 36–37, 40–44, 71–72, 76, 86; impoverishment in, 82, 89; Indigenous practices likened to those of, 41–42; linguistic diversity of, 43–44, 49, 62; map of, *28*; overview of, 27–29; politics in, 29; racialization in, 29–31, 43–45; radio schools and, 56–65. *See also* Mixteca Alta

Mixteca Alta: agriculture of, 32; case study of, 19; colonialism in, 28–29; communal commitments in, 89; communal landholding in, 29–30, 32; development/modernization in, 19, 22–46; educational initiatives in, 49, 52–54, *53*, 58–64; impoverishment in, 42, 76, 165; indigenismo in, 39–44; left behind by economic development, 13; migration from, 82, 89; relocation of people from, 19, 36–37, 70, 72–81, 86–92; underdevelopment of, 25–27

Mixtec language, 21, 47–49, 57–58, 60, 62, 66, 165

Mixtec population, 27

modernization. *See* development/modernization

modern school movement, 166

Monsiváis, Carlos, 151

Monte Albán, 6–9, *7*, 183, 187

Monterrey Group, 102

Monterrubio, Donaldo, 173

Morales de Altamirano, Mariela, 102, 107

Morales Hernández, Nicolás, 71

Morris, Gerry, 106

Movimiento de Liberación Nacional, 48

Movimiento de Unificación de Lucha Triqui, 170

Movimiento Revolucionario Magisterial, 127, 130

multiculturalism: antiracism and, 17–19, 178–79; as colonialism, 177; in education, 156–61, 163; global embrace of, 144, 147, 174; and indigeneity, 18, 177–78, 181; institutionalization of, 156–61; Left's opposition to, 148–49; in Mexico, 17–18, 144, 174–75; neoliberal, 17–18, 171, 173, 176, 181; New-Left, 16, 147, 171; in Oaxaca, 18; official, 16, 17, 18, 147, 171, 177–80; PRI and, 17; in recent politics, 16–18; SNTE and, 165; Third-Worldist, 16, 147, 149, 153, 171, 178; varied attitudes toward, 149, 176–77

municipal teachers, 54

Muñoz Ledo, Porfirio, 128, 143

music, 98

Nahmad Sitton, Salomón, 148, *149*, 150, 156, 157, 164, 170

Nahuatl language, 12

nationalism: development/modernization and, 35–36; Echeverría and, 96, 100, 127; in education, 51, 127; in Mixteca, 68; Native cultures linked to, 8, 174; postrevolutionary, 8, 10, 16, 181; Quinto Centenario and, 174

Native Americans (US), 78–79

Nava Nava, Maria del Carmen, 150

neoliberalism: austerity policies and, 123; in Chile, 125; defined, 213n6; in Mexico, 17, 123–26; multiculturalism promoted by, 17–18, 171, 173, 176, 181; PRI and, 17, 125, 143, 147; privatization of industry as principle of, 140; SNTE and, 141; teachers' movement as resistance to, 123

New International Economic Order, 20, 149, 178

New Left: Indigenous opposition to, 169; and Indigenous resurgence, 167–68, 179; and multiculturalism, 16, 147, 171; promotores and, 106, 108, 114–18, 167–68; radicalized youth and, 111–18; teachers' movement and, 143

Nolasco, Margarita, 96–97, 104–8, 148

Non-Aligned Movement, 95–96

North American Free Trade Agreement (NAFTA), 123

nueva trova (music), 98

Nuevos Centros de Población Agrícolas (NCPAs), 77
Nuñez Ledezma, Salvador, 132

Oaxaca: in colonial New Spain, 28; history of, 11–13; illiteracy in, 162; impoverishment in, 14, 109, 162; indigeneity's importance in, 11, 13, 33; indigenous culture in, 10; linguistic diversity of, 13, 33; map of, *12*; markets in, 33, *34*, 35; migration from, 14–15, 81–86, 125–26, 161–62, 187; modernization in, 13, 14; multiculturalism in, 18; politics in, ix, 15, 30, 126, 182, 184–87; population of, 109; racialization of, 81–82; Revolution's effect on, 30; tourism in, 6–7, 18, 172; and trade, 11–12. *See also* Isthmus of Tehuantepec; Mixteca; Mixteca Alta; Oaxaca City; Tlaxiaco
Oaxaca City (Oaxaca de Juárez), 6, 95, 98–106, 110, 126, 133
Oaxacan Truth Commission, ix
Olivera, Mercedes, 96
Osorio Nicolás, Antolín, 60, 138–39
Osorno, Diego Enrique, 186
Ovalle Fernández, Ignacio, 150
overpopulation, 36–37, 70, 75–77, 79

Pacto de Huatulco, 186
palm production, 32, 82–83, *90*
Pan-American Highway, 25, 74
Pancha, Doña, 72, 88, 92
Papaloapan Dam, 14, 78
participatory indigenismo, 17, 98, 127, 146
Partido Acción Nacional (PAN), 67, 185–86
Partido Comunista Mexicano, 127
Partido de la Revolución Democrática (PRD), 140
Partido de los Pobres, 100
Partido Popular Socialista (PPS), 68, 130
Partido Revolucionario Institucional (PRI): campesino rhetoric of, 10; Cárdenas and, 93; Catholicism and, 67; challenges to, ix, 15–17, 99, 110, 126, 137, 139–42, 182, 186; during Cold War, 49; Echeverría and, 96, 127; and indigenismo, 15, 17; Indigenous peoples and, 16, 173; INI and, 15, 164; and the Left, 147–48; neoliberal policies of, 17, 125, 143, 147; in Oaxaca, ix, 15; SNTE and, 127, 129–31, 133, 184
Pátzcuaro and Pátzcuaro program, 93, 148, 150–56
Paz, Modesta, 73
Pérez Gasca, Alfonso, 59, 66
Perez Meza, Enrique, 67
Peru, 79, 101
Phillips, 57, *61*
Pinochet, Augusto, 113
police. See *rurales estatales* (state police)
politics: Catholicism and, 17, 55–56, 67–68; Cold War–related, 48–49; democratic opening policies, 96; dissident/radical, 94, 96–97, 103, 110–17, 126; in Isthmus of Tehuantepac, 13, 15, 29–30, 99, 126, 137, 162, 170; in Mixteca, 29; multiculturalism in, 16–18; of 1960s, 94; in Oaxaca, ix, 15, 30, 126, 182, 184–87; teachers' engagement in, 17, 68, 135–36; violence related to, 31, 48, 62, 67, 100, 126
Poole, Deborah, 4
Popoca, Héctor Manuel, 107
Popular Assembly of the Peoples of Oaxaca. *See* Asamblea Popular de los Pueblos de Oaxaca
portadores (children as bearers of culture), 103
Poulantzas, Nicos, 151
poverty: of Indigenous peoples, 27, 45, 162; in Mixteca, 82, 89; in Mixteca Alta, 42, 76, 165; in Oaxaca, 14, 109, 162; social science analysis of, 105
Prashad, Vijay, 95
presidential election (1988), 139–40
presidential election (2006), 185
Primera Asamblea de Filólogos y Lingüistas, 50
privatization of industry, 140
Programa de Licenciatura en Etnolingüística, 150

Programme to Combat Racism, 154
promotores: accomplishments of, 94–95, 141–42; conflicts among, 138; government reliance on, 180; home communities' reception of, 108–9, 139; IIISEO's employment of, 103, 105–17, 132; INI's employment of, 51–52, 69–70, 101, 108, 110–11, 132; prejudices against, 64, 131–32, 134, 142, 166–67; professional and political demands of, 101, 112–17, 121–22, 132; role of, in teachers' movement, 122–23, 134–35, 137–38, 141–44; sociopolitical activities of, 108–11, 167; tasks of, 108–9; as threat to teachers/unionists, 109, 134–37, 167; training of, 107–8, 110–11, 117, 131; union representation and power of, 134–35, 166–67; wages and working conditions of, 109, 111, 131–34; women as, 107, 115, 132
Proyecto Tarasco, 41, 51
public health, 22–24, 42, 83
Puno Tambopata project, Peru, 79

Quinto Centenario, 173–74

race: anthropological theory of, 1–4, *3*; coastal populations and, 72–73, 79; indigenismo and, 76; Indigenous Oaxacans and, 81–82; inequalities linked to, 37–38; in Mixteca, 29–31, 43–45; violence related to, 42, 72–73. *See also* Africa and African-descended peoples; antiracism
radio educational programming: bilingual education in, 19, 47–49, 60; Catholic opposition to, 19, 48, 66–69; Catholic uses of, 57, *57*, 58–59, 67; decline of, 69; and development/modernization, 49, 57, 60; and Indigenous education reform, 56–65; legacy of, 69–70; technology for, *61*, 68–69
Radio Quetzaltenango, 68
Radio Sutatenza, 57, 58
Ramírez, Rafael, 51, 179
Ramírez, Vincente, 84–85
Ramírez López, Heladio, 175, 184
Ramos Chávez, Emiliano, 73

raza cósmica, 4
RCA, 57
Rendón, Juan José, 17
resurgence. *See* Indigenous resurgence
Revolution (1910), 8, 12–13, 24, 29–30, 131, 147
Reyes, Luis, 148, 150
Reyes Bautista, Gabina, and Pauala Fería Barrios, *Manuel para la enseñanza de lecto-escritura en lengua mixteca*, *159*, *160*, 160–61
Reyes Heroles, Jesús, 126, 148, 164
rights, cultural, 97–98, 147, 167, 170–71, 174–76, 180
Rivera, Diego, *Patio del trabajo*, 119–21, *120*, 143
Rodríguez, Nemesio, 151, 163
Rodríguez, Silvio, 98
Roque, Maribel, 172
Ruiz, Eva, 106, 115, 132, 180
Ruiz, Samuel, 100
Ruiz Cortines, Adolfo, 24, 74, 77
Ruiz de Bravo Ahuja, Gloria, 102–3, 106, 117
Ruiz Ortiz, Ulises, ix, 184–86
rurales estatales (state police), 39, 43

Sac and Fox Tribe, 59
Salazar, Santiago, 106–7, 111, 114, 121, 136, 180
Salcedo Guarin, José Joaquin, 57
Salinas de Gotari, Carlos, 140, 142, 172–73, *173*, 219n2
San Andrés Chicahuaxtla, 1–4
Sánchez Cano, Edmundo, 15
Sánchez García, José, 64
Sánchez López, Isaías, 47, 68, 137, 142, 180
San Juan, Rufino, 145
Santiago Méndez, Pedro "El Chino," 114
Santiago Pérez, Ignacio, 134, 139
Santo Tomás Ocotepec, 22–24, *83*
Scott, James, 22
Sección 22, 16, 20, 122, 129–38, 140–42, 161, 165–67, 171, 184–85, 187. *See also* Sindicato Nacional de Trabajadores de la Educación
Secretaria de Educación Publica (SEP): during Cold War, 49; indigenista practices

of, 14, 17, 119–20; and Indigenous education, 50–51, 54–55, 59, 64, 69, 156, 175; INI and, 157; and participatory indigenismo, 147; and Pátzcuaro program, 151; PRI and, 15; and promotores, 112–16, 121–22; and radio schools, 58; and SIL, 153; SNTE and, 122, 128–29; teachers' occupation of, 120–21, *121*, 143
Servicio Nacional de Promotores Culturales y Maestros Bilingües, 69
SIL. *See* Summer Institute of Linguistics
Sindicato de Trabajadores Petroleros de la República Mexicana, 140
Sindicato Nacional de Trabajadores de la Educación (SNTE): dissident movements within, 16, 122, 127, 130, 132–44, 161; and multiculturalism, 165; neoliberal sympathies of, 141; power struggles in, 17, 20, 123, 127–42, 161, 166; PRI and, 127, 129–31, 133, 184; promotores and, 121–22; public opinion about, 185; SEP and, 122, 128–29; strikes by, ix, 30, 184–85; violence used by, 127, 136–37, 161, 165. *See also* teachers' movement
Soberanes, Fernando, 114, 139, 168
Sophia, Queen of Spain, 172
Souraski, Elías, 103
sovereignty movement, 12–13, 30
Soviet Union, 78
Spanish language: in education, 19, 39, 47–48, 50, 54, 58, 60, 102–3, *104*, 106, 156–59, 163, 179; as national language, 26; sociocultural role of, 26, 38, 43, 45, 48, 51, 58. *See also* castellanización
squatters, 110, 126
Starr, Frederick, 1–4, 62
Stavenhagen, Rodolfo, 105, 150
Summer Institute of Linguistics (SIL), 51, 106, 148, 153–54, 164
Swadesh, Morris, 41, 51, 158

Taibo, Paco Ignacio, II, 115–16, 168
Taylor, Charles, 174
teachers: employment prospects of, 15, 20; Indigenous, 131, 136, 138, 141–42; and Indigenous education reform, 52; payment troubles affecting, 128, 129; political engagement of, 17, 68, 135–36; in rural school, 54; training of, 131, 157; women as, 134. *See also* auxiliary radio teachers; promotores; Sindicato Nacional de Trabajadores de la Educación; teachers' movement
teachers' movement: bilingual teachers' role in, 122–23, 134–35, 137–38, 141–44; conflicts within, 138; governance of, 135, 141; and indigeneity, 122–23, 127; protest against SEP, 120–21; public support for, 139, 162; as resistance to neoliberal reform, 123; rise of, 133–39; violence employed against, 127, 136–37
teachers' union. *See* Sección 22; Sindicato Nacional de Trabajadores de la Educación
Teatro Petul, 52
textbooks, 49, 66
Third Worldism: and anticolonialism, 94–95; conceptions of, 150; development approach of, 97; Mexico and, 95–96, 100, 113, 117, 127; and multiculturalism, 16, 147, 149, 153, 171, 178; teachers' movement and, 143
Tlaxiaco: Catholicism in, 31; as commercial and trade center, 25, 29, 31–32; elites in, 25, 29, 30, 43; indigenismo in, 26–27; INI in, 39–40; market in, 26, 31–32, *34*, 35–37; as migration departure point, 84; politics in, 30–31; and resettle project, 79
Torres, Rafael, 22–24, *23*
Torres Bodet, Jaime, 49, 66
tourism, 6–7, 18, 72, 172
Triqui language, 57, 62
Triqui population, 1–3, *2*, 27, 43–45, 62–63, 170
Trotskyism, 112
Trouyet, Carlos, 103
Tutu sa'an ñuu savi (textbook), 158–60

UABJO. *See* Universidad Autónoma Benito Juárez de Oaxaca
UNAM. *See* Universidad Nacional Autónoma de México

underdevelopment, 13, 19, 25–27, 29, 37, 45, 49, 69, 194n10
Unión del Pueblo, 100
unions: neoliberal attack on, 140; PRI and, 16, 118; radical politics and, 98, 115. *See also* Sindicato Nacional de Trabajadores de la Educación
United Nations, 96, 147
United Nations Educational, Scientific and Cultural Organization (UNESCO), 6, 56, 57, 103
United Nations Security Council, 96
United States: migration to, 13, 15, 75, 84–86; Native American activism in, 179; Native American relocation initiatives in, 74, 78
Universidad Autónoma Benito Juárez de Oaxaca (UABJO), 15, 98, 110, 185
Universidad Autónoma Metropolitana, Mexico City, 96
Universidad Nacional Autónoma de México (UNAM), 36, 98, 111, 168
Universidad Pedagógica Nacional, 166
University of Texas at Austin, 106
Urban Relocation Program (US), 78–79
usos y costumbres (customary law), 12, 15, 81, 89, 108, 175, 182

Vallejo, Demetrio, 48
vallistas (people of the central valleys), 13
Vanguardia Revolucionaria, 127–28, 130, 132, 135–38, 140–42, 148, 161, 165
Varese, Stefano, 154
Vargas Llosa, Mario, 49
Vasconcelos, José, 4, 119–20
Vásquez, Genaro Vicente, 15, 30, 116
Ve'e Tu'un Savi, 155–56
Velasco Alvarado, Juan, 101
Velásquez Gallardo, Pablo, 22–24, 26–27, 41–45

Velázquez Vázquez, René, 129
Venezuela, 125
Veracruz, 14, 42, 81, 86–87, 109
Villalana Castillejos, Roberto, 137
Villaverde Hernández, Héctor, 65
violence: of Calderón presidency, 186; in Costa Chica, 19, 72–73, 87, 91–92, 110; highland-coastal conflicts as source of, 19, 72–73, 87, 91–92; imputed to Indigenous peoples, 21, 62; labor-related, 43; land conflict as source of, 110; in Oaxaca strike (2006), ix, 186; political conflicts as source of, 31, 48, 62, 67, 100, 126; promotores as targets of, 114–15; racialized, 42, 72–73; SNTE's use of, 127, 136–37, 161, 165; state-sponsored, 100

Walcott, Derek, 6
Warisata School, Bolivia, 51
women and girls, 1–4, 86, 150, 173, 186, 189n1, 190–91n7; education of, 102; as promotores, 59, 107–9, 115, 132; rights of, 118; as teachers, 134, 150
World Bank, 140
World Council of Churches, 154
Worsley, Peter, 150

XEINI (radio station), 49, 68
XFX (radio station), 50

Zafra, Isauro, 43
Zapatista rebellion. *See* Ejército Zapatista de Liberación Nacional
Zapotec language, 13, 162, 165, 170
Zapotec population, 29, 99, 170
Zárate Aquino, Manuel, 15, 98, 110, 113, 115, 126, 130